Beginning R

An Introduction to Statistical Programming

Second Edition

Dr. Joshua F. Wiley
Larry A. Pace

Apress®

ISBN-13 (pbk): 978-1-4842-0374-3

ISBN-13 (electronic): 978-1-4842-0373-6

Managing Director: Welmoed Spahr
Lead Editor: Steve Anglin
Technical Reviewer: Sarah Stowell
Editorial Board: Steve Anglin, Louise Corrigan, Jonathan Gennick, Robert Hutchinson,
    Michelle Lowman, James Markham, Susan McDermott, Matthew Moodie, Jeffrey Pepper,
    Douglas Pundick, Ben Renow-Clarke, Gwenan Spearing, Steve Weiss
Coordinating Editor: Mark Powers
Copy Editor: Lori Jacobs
Compositor: SPi Global
Indexer: SPi Global
Artist: SPi Global

Distributed to the book trade worldwide by Springer Science+Business Media New York, 233 Spring Street, 6th Floor, New York, NY 10013. Phone 1-800-SPRINGER, fax (201) 348-4505, e-mail orders-ny@springer-sbm.com, or visit www.springer.com. Apress Media, LLC is a California LLC and the sole member (owner) is Springer Science + Business Media Finance Inc (SSBM Finance Inc). SSBM Finance Inc is a Delaware corporation.

For information on translations, please e-mail rights@apress.com, or visit www.apress.com.

Apress and friends of ED books may be purchased in bulk for academic, corporate, or promotional use. eBook versions and licenses are also available for most titles. For more information, reference our Special Bulk Sales–eBook Licensing web page at www.apress.com/bulk-sales.

Any source code or other supplementary material referenced by the author in this text is available to readers at www.apress.com/9781484203743. For detailed information about how to locate your book's source code, go to www.apress.com/source-code/. Readers can also access source code at SpringerLink in the Supplementary Material section for each chapter.

To Family.

Contents at a Glance

Contents

About the Author

Joshua Wiley is a research fellow at the Mary MacKillop Institute for Health Research at the Australian Catholic University and a senior partner at Elkhart Group Limited, a statistical consultancy. He earned his Ph.D. from the University of California, Los Angeles. His research focuses on using advanced quantitative methods to understand the complex interplays of psychological, social, and physiological processes in relation to psychological and physical health. In statistics and data science, Joshua focuses on biostatistics and is interested in reproducible research and graphical displays of data and statistical models. Through consulting at Elkhart Group Limited and his former work at the UCLA Statistical Consulting Group, Joshua has supported a wide array of clients ranging from graduate students to experienced researchers and biotechnology companies. He also develops or co-develops a number of R packages including varian, a package to conduct Bayesian scale-location structural equation models, and MplusAutomation, a popular package that links R to the commercial Mplus software.

In Memoriam

Larry Pace was a statistics author, educator, and consultant. He lived in the upstate area of South Carolina in the town of Anderson. He earned his Ph.D. from the University of Georgia in psychometrics (applied statistics) with a content major in industrial-organizational psychology. He wrote more than 100 publications including books, articles, chapters, and book and test reviews. In addition to a 35-year academic career, Larry worked in private industry as a personnel psychologist and organization effectiveness manager for Xerox Corporation, and as an organization development consultant for a private consulting firm. He programmed in a variety of languages and scripting languages including FORTRAN-IV, BASIC, APL, C++, JavaScript, Visual Basic, PHP, and ASP. Larry won numerous awards for teaching, research, and service. When he passed, he was a Graduate Research Professor at Keiser University, where he taught doctoral courses in statistics and research. He also taught adjunct classes for Clemson University. Larry and his wife, Shirley, were volunteers with Meals on Wheels and avid pet lovers—six cats and one dog, all rescued.

Larry wrote the first edition of *Beginning R*, as well as the beginning chapters of this second edition. He passed away on April 8, 2015.

Larry was married to Shirley Pace. He also leaves four grown children and two grandsons.

About the Technical Reviewer

Sarah Stowell is a contract statistician based in the UK. Previously, she has worked with Mitsubishi Pharma Europe, MDSL International, and GlaxoSmithKline. She holds a master of science degree in statistics.

Acknowledgments

I would like to acknowledge my coauthor, Larry Pace. This book would never have been without him, and my heart goes out to his family and friends.

I would also like to thank my brother, Matt, who spent many hours reading drafts and discussing how best to convey the ideas. When I needed an opinion about how to phrase something, he unflinchingly brought several ideas to the table (sometimes too many).

Introduction

This book is about the R programming language. Maybe more important, this book is for you.

These days, R is an impressively robust language for solving problems that lend themselves to statistical programming methods. There is a large community of users and developers of this language, and together we are able to accomplish things that were not possible before we virtually met.

Of course, to leverage this collective knowledge, we have to start somewhere. Chapters 1 through 5 focus on gaining familiarity with the R language itself. If you have prior experience in programming, these chapters will be very easy for you. If you have no prior programming experience, that is perfectly fine. We build from the ground up, and let us suggest you spend some thoughtful time here. Thinking like a programmer has some very great advantages. It is a skill we would want you to have, and this book is, after all, for you.

Chapters 6 through 10 focus on what might be termed *elementary statistical methods* in R. We did not have the space to introduce those methods in their entirety—we are supposing some knowledge of statistics. An introductory or elementary course for nonmajors would be more than enough. If you are already familiar with programming and statistics, we suggest you travel through these chapters only briefly.

With Chapter 11, we break into the last part of the book. For someone with both a fair grasp of traditional statistics and some programming experience, this may well be a good place to start. For our readers who read through from the first pages, this is where it starts to get very exciting. From bootstrapping to logistic regression to data visualization to high-performance computing, these last chapters have hands-on examples that work through some much applied and very interesting examples.

One final note: While we wrote this text from Chapter 1 to Chapter 19 in order, the chapters are fairly independent of each other. Don't be shy about skipping to the chapter you're most interested in learning. We show all our code, and you may well be able to modify what we have to work with what you have.

Happy reading!

CHAPTER 1

■ ■ ■

Getting Started

There are compelling reasons to use R. Enthusiastic users, programmers, and contributors support R and its development. A dedicated core team of R experts maintains the language. R is accurate, produces excellent graphics, has a variety of built-in functions, and is both a functional language and an object-oriented one. There are (literally) thousands of contributed packages available to R users for specialized data analyses.

Developing from a `novice` into a more competent `user` of R may take as little as three months by only using R on a part-time basis (disclaimer: n = 1). Realistically, depending on background, your development may take days, weeks, months, or even a few years, depending on how often you use R and how quickly you can learn its many intricacies. R `users` often develop into R `programmers` who write R functions, and R `programmers` sometimes want to develop into R `contributors`, who write packages that help others with their data analysis needs. You can stop anywhere on that journey you like, but if you finish this book and follow good advice, you will be a competent R `user` who is ready to develop into a serious R `programmer` if you want to do it. We wish you the best of luck!

1.1 What is R, Anyway?

R is an open-source implementation of the S language created and developed at Bell Labs. S is also the basis of the commercial statistics program S-PLUS, but R has eclipsed S-PLUS in popularity. If you do not already have R on your system, the quickest way to get it is to visit the CRAN (Comprehensive R Network Archive) website and download and install the precompiled binary files for your operating system. R works on Windows, Mac OS, and Linux systems. If you use Linux, you may already have R with your Linux distribution. Open your terminal and type $ `R --version`. If you do not already have R, the CRAN website is located at the following URL:

`http://cran.r-project.org/`

Download and install the R binaries for your operating system, accepting all the defaults. At this writing, the current version of R is 3.2.0, and in this book, you will see screenshots of R working in both Windows 7 and Windows 8.1. Your authors run on 64-bit operating systems, so you will see that information displayed in the screen captures in this book. Because not everything R does in Unix-based systems can be done in Windows, I often switch to Ubuntu to do those things, but we will discuss only the Windows applications here, and leave you to experiment with Ubuntu or other flavors of Unix. One author runs Ubuntu on the Amazon Cloud, but that is way beyond our current needs.

Go ahead and download Rstudio (current version as of this writing is 0.98.1103) now too, again, accepting all defaults from the following URL:

`http://www.rstudio.com/products/rstudio/download/`

Rstudio is a very forgiving environment for the novice user, and code written in here will work just as well in R itself.

Launch Rstudio and examine the resulting interface. Make sure that you can identify the following parts of the R interface shown in Figure 1-1: the menu bar, the script editing area, the R console, and the R command prompt, which is >.

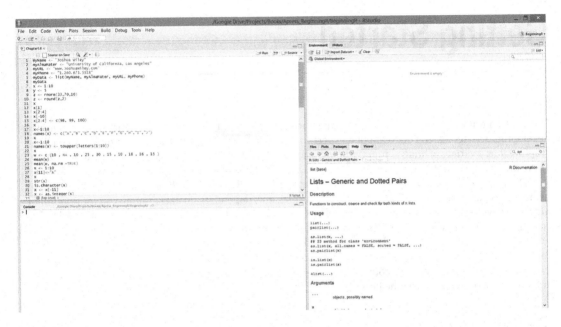

Figure 1-1. *The R console running in Rstudio*

Before we continue our first R session, let's have a brief discussion of how R works. R is a high-level vectorized computer language and statistical computing environment. You can write your own R code, use R code written by others, and use R packages you write and those written by you or by others. You can use R in batch mode, terminal mode, in the R graphical user interface (RGui), or in Rstudio, which is what we will do in this book. As you learn more about R and how to use it effectively, you will find that you can integrate R with other languages such as Python or C++, and even with other statistical programs such as SPSS.

In some computer languages, for instance, C++, you have to declare a data type before you assign a value to a new variable, but that is not true in R. In R, you simply assign a value to the object, and you can change the value or the data type by assigning a new one. There are two basic assignment operators in R. The first is < –, a left-pointing assignment operator produced by a less than sign followed by a "minus" sign, which is really a hyphen. You can also use an equals sign = for assignments in R. I prefer the < – assignment operator, and will use it throughout this book.

You must use the = sign to assign the parameters in R functions, as you will learn. R is not sensitive to white space the way some languages are, and the readability of R code is benefited from extra spacing and indentation, although these are not mandatory. R is, however, case-sensitive, so to R, the variables x and X are two different things. There are some reserved names in R, which I will tell you about in Chapter 5.

The best way to learn R is to use R, and there are many books, web-based tutorials, R blog sites, and videos to help you with virtually any question you might have. We will begin with the basics in this book but will quickly progress to the point that you are ready to become a purposeful R programmer, as mentioned earlier.

Let us complete a five-minute session in R, and then delve into more detail about what we did, and what R was doing behind the scenes. The most basic use of R is as a command-line interpreted language. You type a command or statement after the R prompt and then press <Enter>, and R attempts to implement the command. If R can do what you are asking, it will do it and return the result in the R console. If R cannot do what you are asking, it will return an error message. Sometimes R will do something but give you warnings, which are messages concerning what you have done and what the impact might be, but that are sometimes warnings that what you did was not what you probably wanted to do. Always remember that R, like any other computer language, cannot think for you.

1.2 A First R Session

Okay, let's get started. In the R console, type <Ctrl> + L to clear the console in order to have a little more working room. Then type the following, pressing the <Enter> key at the end of each command you type. When you get to the personal information, substitute your own data for mine:

```
> 1 + 1
[1] 2
> 1 ^ 1
[1] 1
> 1 * 1
[1] 1
> 1 - 1
 [1] 0
> 1 : 10
[1]   1   2   3   4   5   6   7   8   9  10
> ( 1 : 10 ) ^ 2
[1]   1   4   9  16  25  36  49  64  81 100
> myName <- "Joshua Wiley"
> myAlmaMater <- "University of California, Los Angeles"
> myURL <- "www.JoshuaWiley.com"
> myPhone <- "1.260.673.5518"
> myData <- list(myName, myAlmaMater, myURL, myPhone)
> myData
[[1]]
[1] "Joshua Wiley"

[[2]]
[1] "University of California, Los Angeles"

[[3]]
[1] "www.JoshuaWiley.com"

[[4]]
[1] "1.260.673.5518"
```

We began with the use of R as a basic calculator. We can create sequences of integers by using the colon operator. Using the exponentiation operator (1:10) ^2 gives us the squares of all the numbers in the vector 1 to 10. Observe that when you type a command and press the <Enter> key, R will return the result on the next line, prefaced by an index, such as [1]. You can assign values to variables without declaring the variable type, as we discussed, so you can just type myName   < – "Joshua Wiley" to give the variable a value.

3

This might have seemed a strange way to start, but it shows you some of the things you can enter into your R workspace simply by assigning them. Character strings must be enclosed in quotation marks, and you can use either single or double quotes. Numbers can be assigned as they were with the myPhone variable. With the name and address, we created a list, with is one of the basic data structures in R. Unlike vectors, lists can contain multiple data types. We also see square brackets [and], which are R's way to index the elements of a data object, in this case our list. We can also create vectors, matrices, and data frames in R. Let's see how to save a vector of the numbers from 1 to 10. We will call the vector x. We will also create a "constant" called y:

```
> x <- 1 : 1 0
> x
[ 1 ]    1    2    3    4    5    6    7    8    9 1 0
> y <- 5
> y
[ 1 ] 5
```

See that R starts its listing of both x and y with an index [1]. This is because R does not recognize a scalar value. To R, even a single number is a vector. The object y is a vector with one element. The [1] in front of x means that the first element of the vector appears at the beginning of the line. Let's make another vector, z, containing a sequence of 33 randomly generated numbers from a normal distribution with a mean of 70 and a standard deviation of 10. Because the numbers are random, your z vector will not be the same as mine, though if we wanted to, we could set the seed number in R so that we would both get the same vector:

```
> z <- r n o r m ( 3 3 , 70 , 1 0 )
> z <- r o u n d ( z , 2 )
> z
[ 1 ] 81 . 56  70 . 85  77 . 48  64 . 02  68 . 94  80 . 24  60 . 84
70 . 93  75 . 21  75 . 05  52 . 17  52 . 29
[ 13 ] 70 . 20  79 . 29  84 . 75  64 . 88  73 . 74  71 . 19  61 . 01
63 . 43  55 . 74  71 . 54  69 . 71  82 . 52
[ 25 ] 73 . 40  75 . 39  79 . 28  80 . 36  65 . 79  73 . 15  75 . 41
69 . 56  85 . 87
```

When R must wrap to a new line in the console to print additional output, it shows the index of the first element of each line.

To see a list of all the objects in your R session, type the command ls():

```
> ls()
[1] "myAlmaMater" "myData"      "myName"      "myPhone"     "myURL"      "x"      "y"      "z"
```

To see the current working directory, type the command getwd(). You can change the working directory by typing setwd(), but I usually find it easier to use the File menu. Just select File > Change dir... and navigate to the directory you want to become the new working directory. As you can see from the code listing here, the authors prefer working in the cloud. This allows us to gain access to our files from any Internet-connected computer, tablet, or smartphone. Similarly, our R session is saved to the cloud, allowing access from any of several computers at home or office computers.

```
> getwd()
[1] "C:/Users/Joshua Wiley/Google Drive/Projects/Books/Apress_BeginningR/BeginningR"
```

In addition to ls(), another helpful function is dir( ), which will give you a list of the files in your current working directory.

To quit your R session, simply type q( ) at the command prompt, or if you like to use the mouse, select File > Exit or simply close Rstudio by clicking on the X in the upper right corner. In any of these cases, you will be prompted to save your R workspace.

Go ahead and quit the current R session, and save your workspace when prompted. We will come back to the same session in a few minutes. What was going on in the background while we played with R was that R was recording everything you typed in the console and everything it wrote back to the console. This is saved in an R history file. When you save your R session in an RData file, it contains this particular workspace. When you find that file and open it, your previous workspace will be restored. This will keep you from having to reenter your variables, data, and functions.

Before we go back to our R session, let's see how to use R for some mathematical operators and functions (see Table 1-1). These operators are vectorized, so they will apply to either single numbers or vectors with more than one number, as we will discuss in more detail later in this chapter. According to the R documentation, these are "unary and binary generic functions" that operate on numeric and complex vectors, or vectors that can be coerced to numbers. For example, logical vectors of TRUE and FALSE are coerced to integer vectors, with TRUE = 1 and FALSE = 0.

Table 1-1. *R's mathematical operators and functions*

Operator/Function	R Expression	Code Example
Addition	+	2 + 2
Subtraction	−	3 - 2
Multiplication	*	2 * 5
Division	/	4 / 2
Exponent	^	3 ^ 2
Square Root	sqrt()	sqrt(81)
Natural Logarithm	log()	log(10)
Modulus	% %	x % % y
Absolute Value	abs()	abs(-3)

Table 1-2 shows R's comparison operators. Each of these evaluates to a logical result of TRUE or FALSE. We can abbreviate TRUE and FALSE as T and F, so it would be unwise to name a variable T or F, although R will let you do that. Note that the equality operator == is different from the = used as an assignment operator. As with the mathematical operators and the logical operators (see Chapter 4), these are also vectorized.

Table 1-2. *Comparison operators in R*

Operator	R Expression	Code Example
Equality	==	x == 3
Inequality	!=	x != 4
Greater than	>	5 > 3
Less than	<	3 < 5
Greater than or equal to	>=	3 >= 1
Less than or equal to	<=	3 <= 3

R has six "atomic" vector types (meaning that they cannot be broken down any further), including `logical`, `integer`, `real`, `complex`, `string` (or character), and `raw`. Vectors must contain only one type of data, but lists can contain any combination of data types. A `data frame` is a special kind of list and the most common data object for statistical analysis. Like any list, a data frame can contain both numerical and character information. Some character information can be used for `factors`. Working with factors can be a bit tricky because they are "like" vectors to some extent, but they are not exactly vectors.

My friends who are programmers who dabble in statistics think factors are evil, while statisticians like me who dabble in programming love the fact that character strings can be used as factors in R, because such factors communicate group membership directly rather than indirectly. It makes more sense to have a column in a data frame labeled `sex` with two entries, `male` and `female`, than it does to have a column labeled `sex` with 0s and 1s in the data frame. If you like using 1s and 0s for factors, then use a scheme such as labeling the column `female` and entering a 1 for a woman and 0 for a man. That way the 1 conveys meaning, as does the 0. Note that some statistical software programs such as SPSS do not uniformly support the use of strings as factors, whereas others, for example, Minitab, do.

In addition to vectors, lists, and data frames, R has language objects including `calls`, `expressions`, and `names`. There are `symbol` objects and `function` objects, as well as `expression` objects. There is also a special object called `NULL`, which is used to indicate that an object is absent. Missing data in R are indicated by `NA`, which is also a valid logical object.

1.3 Your Second R Session

Reopen your saved R session by navigating to the saved workspace and launching it in R. We will put R through some more paces now that you have a better understanding of its data types and its operators, functions, and "constants." If you did not save the session previously, you can just start over and type in the missing information again. You will not need the list with your name and data, but you will need the x, y, and z variables we created earlier.

As you have learned, R treats a single number as a vector of length 1. If you create a vector of two or more objects, the vector must contain only a single data type. If you try to make a vector with multiple data types, R will coerce the vector into a single type.

1.3.1 Working with Indexes

R's indexing is quite flexible. We can use it to add elements to a vector, to substitute new values for old ones, and to delete elements of the vector. We can also subset a vector by using a range of indexes. As an example, let's return to our x vector and make some adjustments:

```
> x
[1]    1    2    3    4    5    6    7    8    9   10
> x[1]
[1] 1
> x[2:4]
[1] 2 3 4
> x[-10]
[1] 1 2 3 4 5 6 7 8 9
> x
[1]    1    2    3    4    5    6    7    8    9   10
> x[2:4] <- c(98,99,100)
> x
[1]    1   98   99  100    5    6    7    8    9   10
```

Note that if you simply ask for subsets, the x vector is not changed, but if you reassign the subset or modified vector, the changes are saved. Observe that the negative index removes the selected element or elements from the vector but only changes the vector if you reassign the new vector to x. We can, if we choose, give names to the elements of a vector, as this example shows:

```
> x <- 1:10
> x
[1]    1    2    3    4    5    6    7    8    9   10
> names(x) <- c("A","B","C","D","E","F","G","H","I","J")
> x
 A  B  C  D  E  F  G  H  I  J
 1  2  3  4  5  6  7  8  9 10
```

This showcases the difference between thinking as a user versus thinking as a programmer! R has a variety of built-in functions that automate even the simplest kind of operations. You just saw me waste our time by typing in the letters A through J. R already knows the alphabet, and all you have to do is tell R you want the first 10 letters. The more you know about R, the easier it is to work with, because it keeps you from having to do a great deal of repetition in your programming. Take a look at what happens when we ask R for the letters of the alphabet and use the power of built-in character manipulation functions to make something a reproducible snippet of code. Everyone starts as an R user and (ideally) becomes an R programmer, as discussed in the introduction:

```
> x
[1]    1    2    3    4    5    6    7    8    9   10
> names(x) <- toupper(letters[1:10])
> x
 A  B  C  D  E  F  G  H  I  J
 1  2  3  4  5  6  7  8  9 10
```

The toupper function coerces the letters to uppercase, and the letters[1:10] subset gives us A through J. Always think like a programmer rather than a user. If you wonder if something is possible, someone else has probably thought the same thing. Over two million people are using R right now, and many of those people write R functions and code that automates the things that we use on such a regular basis that we usually don't even have to wonder whether but simply need to ask where they are and how to use them. You can find many examples of efficient R code on the web, and the discussions on StackExchange are very helpful.

If you are trying to figure something out that you don't know how to do, don't waste much time experimenting. Use a web search engine, and you are very likely to find that someone else has already found the solution, and has posted a helpful example you can use or modify for your own problem. The R manual is also helpful, but only if you already have a strong programming background. Otherwise, it reads pretty much like a technical manual on your new toaster written in a foreign language.

It is better to develop good habits in the beginning than it is to develop bad habits and then having to break them first before you can learn good ones. This is what Dr. Lynda McCalman calls a BFO. That means a blinding flash of the obvious. I have had many of those in my experience with R.

1.3.2 Representing Missing Data in R

Now let's see how R handles missing data. Create a simple vector using the c() function (some people say it means combine, while others say it means concatenate). I prefer combine because there is also a cat() function for concatenating output. For now, just type in the following and observe the results. The built-in function for the mean returns NA because of the missing data value. The na.rm = TRUE argument does not remove the missing value but simply omits it from the calculations. Not every built-in function includes the na.rm option, but it is something you can program into your own functions if you like. We will discuss functional programming in Chapter 5, in which I will show you how to create your own custom function to handle missing data. We will add a missing value by entering NA as an element of our vector. NA is a legitimate logical character, so R will allow you to add it to a numeric vector:

```
> w   <- c ( 1 0 , NA , 10 , 25 , 30 , 15 , 10 , 18 , 16 , 1 5 )
> w
[ 1 ] 1 0  NA   1 0  25  30  15  10  18  16  15
> mean ( w ) [ 1 ] N A
> mean ( w , na . r m   = T R U E ) [ 1 ] 16 . 5 5 5 5 6
```

Observe that the mean is calculated when you omit the missing value, but unless you were to use the command w   <- w[-2], the vector will not change.

1.3.3 Vectors and Vectorization in R

Remember vectors must contain data elements of the same type. To demonstrate this, let us make a vector of 10 numbers, and then add a character element to the vector. R coerces the data to a character vector because we added a character object to it. I used the index [11] to add the character element to the vector. But the vector now contains characters and you cannot do math on it. You can use a negative index, [-11], to remove the character and the R function as.integer() to coerce the vector back to integers.

To determine the structure of a data object in R, you can use the str() function. You can also check to see if our modified vector is integer again, which it is:

```
> x  <- 1 : 1 0
> x [ 1 1 ] <- " A "
> x
[ 1 ] " 1 "    " 2 "    " 3 "    " 4 "    " 5 "    " 6 "    " 7 "    " 8 "    " 9 "    " 1 0
" " A "
> s t r ( x )
c h r [ 1 : 1 1 ] " 1 " " 2 " " 3 " " 4 " " 5 " " 6 " " 7 " " 8 " " 9 " " 1 0 " . . .
> is . c h a r a c t e r ( x )
 [ 1 ] T R U E
> x  <- x [ - 1 1 ]
> x  <- as . i n t e g e r ( x )
> is . i n t e g e r ( x )
[ 1 ] T R U E
```

Add y to x as follows. See that R recycles y for each value of x, so that the addition operation results in a new vector. No explicit looping was required:

```
> x + y
[ 1 ]   6    7    8    9  10  11  12  13  14  1 5
```

The way vectorization works when you use operations with two vectors of unequal length is that the shorter vector is recycled. If the larger vector's length is a multiple of the length of the shorter vector, this will produce the expected result. When the length of the longer vector is not an exact multiple of the shorter vector's length, the shorter vector is recycled until R reaches the end of the longer vector. This can produce unusual results. For example, divide z by x. Remember that z has 33 elements and x has 10:

```
> z
 [1] 81.56 70.85 77.48 64.02 68.94 80.24 60.84
70.93 75.21 75.05 52.17 52.29 [13] 70.20 79.29
84.75 64.88 73.74 71.19 61.01 63.43 55.74 71.54
69.71 82.52 [25] 73.40 75.39 79.28 80.36 65.79
73.15 75.41 69.56 85.87
> x
 [1]  1  2  3  4  5  6  7  8  9 10
> round(z/x,2)
 [1] 81.56 35.42 25.83 16.00 13.79 13.37  8.69
8.87  8.36  7.50 52.17 26.14 [13] 23.40 19.82 16.95
10.81 10.53  8.90  6.78  6.34 55.74 35.77 23.24
20.63 [25] 14.68 12.56 11.33 10.04  7.31  7.32
75.41 34.78 28.62
Warning message:
In z/x : longer object length is not a multiple of sho
rter object length
```

R recycled the x vector three times, and then divided the last three elements of z by 1, 2, and 3, respectively. Although R gave us a warning, it still performed the requested operation.

1.3.4 A Brief Introduction to Matrices

Matrices are vectors with dimensions. We can build matrices from vectors by using the cbind() or rbind() functions. Matrices have rows and columns, so we have two indexes for each cell of the matrix. Let's discuss matrices briefly before we create our first matrix and do some matrix manipulations with it.

A matrix is an m × n (row by column) rectangle of numbers. When n = m, the matrix is said to be "square." Square matrices can be symmetric or asymmetric. The diagonal of a square matrix is the set of elements going from the upper left corner to the lower right corner of the matrix. If the off-diagonal elements of a square matrix are the same above and below the diagonal, as in a correlation matrix, the square matrix is symmetric.

A vector (or array) is a 1-by-n or an n-by-1 matrix, but not so in R, as you will soon see. In statistics, we most often work with symmetric square matrices such as correlation and variance-covariance matrices. An entire matrix is represented by a boldface letter, such as A:

$$A_{m,n} = \begin{bmatrix} a_{1,1} & a_{1,2} & \cdots & a_{1,n} \\ a_{2,1} & a_{2,2} & \cdots & a_{2,n} \\ \cdot & \cdot & \ddots & \cdot \\ a_{m,1} & a_{m,2} & \cdots & a_{m,n} \end{bmatrix}$$

Matrix manipulations are quite easy in R. If you have studied matrix algebra, the following examples will make more sense to you, but if you have not, you can learn enough from these examples and your own self-study to get up to speed quickly should your work require matrices.

Some of the most common matrix manipulations are transposition, addition and subtraction, and multiplication. Matrix multiplication is the most important operation for statistics. We can also find the determinant of a square matrix, and the inverse of a square matrix with a nonzero determinant.

You may have noticed that I did not mention division. In matrix algebra, we write the following, where B^{-1} is the inverse of B. This is the matrix algebraic analog of division (if you talk to a mathematician, s/he would tell you this is how regular 'division' works as well. My best advice, much like giving a mouse a cookie, is don't):

$$AB = C$$
$$A = B^{-1}C$$

(1, 1)

We define the inverse of a square matrix as follows. Given two square matrices, A and B, if AB = I, the identity matrix with 1s on the diagonals and 0s on the off-diagonals, then B is the right-inverse of A, and can be represented as A^{-1}. With this background behind us, let's go ahead and use some of R's matrix operators. A difficulty in the real world is that some matrices cannot be inverted. For example, a so-called singular matrix has no inverse. Let's start with a simple correlation matrix:

$$A = \begin{bmatrix} 1.00 & 0.14 & .. & 0.35 \\ 0.14 & 1.00 & .. & 0.09 \\ & & & \\ 0.35 & 0.98 & .. & 1.00 \end{bmatrix}$$

In R, we can create the matrix first as a vector, and then give the vector the dimensions 3 × 3, thus turning it into a matrix. Note the way we do this to avoid duplicating A; for very large data, this may be more compute efficient. The is.matrix(X) function will return TRUE if X has these attributes, and FALSE otherwise. You can coerce a data frame to a matrix by using the as.matrix function, but be aware that this method will produce a character matrix if there are any nonnumeric columns. We will never use anything but numbers in matrices in this book. When we have character data, we will use lists and data frames:

```
> A <- c(1.00, 0.14, 0.35, 0.14, 1.00, 0.09, 0.35, 0.09, 1.00)
> dim(A)<-c(3,3)
>  A
      [,1] [,2] [,3]
[1,] 1.00 0.14 0.35
[2,] 0.14 1.00 0.09
[3,] 0.35 0.09 1.00
>  d i m ( A )
[ 1 ] 3  3
```

Some useful matrix operators in R are displayed in Table 1-3.

Table 1-3. *Matrix operators in R*

Operator	Operator	Code Example
Transposition	t	t(A)
Matrix Multiplication	%*%	A %*% B
Inversion	solve()	solve(A)

Because the correlation matrix is square and symmetric, its transpose is the same as A. The inverse multiplied by the original matrix should give us the identity matrix. The matrix inversion algorithm accumulates some degree of rounding error, but not very much at all, and the matrix product of A^{-1} and A is the identity matrix, which rounding makes apparent:

```
> Ainv <- solve(A)
> matProd <- Ainv %*% A
> round(matProd)
     [,1] [,2] [,3]
[1,]    1    0    0
[2,]    0    1    0
[3,]    0    0    1
```

If A has an inverse, you can either premultiply or postmultiply A by A^{-1} and you will get an identity matrix in either case.

1.3.5 More on Lists

Recall our first R session in which you created a list with your name and alma mater. Lists are unusual in a couple of ways, and are very helpful when we have "ragged" data arrays in which the variables have unequal numbers of observations. For example, assume that my coauthor, Dr Pace, taught three sections of the same statistics course, each of which had a different number of students. The final grades might look like the following:

```
> section1 <- c(57.3, 70.6, 73.9, 61.4, 63.0, 66.6, 74.8, 71.8, 63.2, 72.3, 61.9, 70.0)
> section2 <- c(74.6, 74.5, 75.9, 77.4, 79.6, 70.2, 67.5, 75.5, 68.2, 81.0, 69.6, 75.6,
69.5, 72.4, 77.1)
> section3 <- c(80.5, 79.2, 83.6, 74.9, 81.9, 80.3, 79.5, 77.3, 92.7, 76.4, 82.0, 68.9,
77.6, 74.6)
> allSections <- list(section1,section2,section3)
> allSections
[[1]]
 [1] 57.3 70.6 73.9 61.4 63.0 66.6 74.8 71.8 63.2 72.3 61.9 70.0

[[2]]
 [1] 74.6 74.5 75.9 77.4 79.6 70.2 67.5 75.5 68.2 81.0 69.6 75.6 69.5 72.4 77.1

[[3]]
 [1] 80.5 79.2 83.6 74.9 81.9 80.3 79.5 77.3 92.7 76.4 82.0 68.9 77.6 74.6

> section_means <- sapply(allSections, mean)
> round(section_means, 2)
[1] 67.23 73.91 79.24
> section_sdev <- sapply(allSections, sd)
> round(section_sdev,2)
[1] 5.74 4.17 5.40
```

We combined the three classes into a list and then used the `sapply` function to find the means and standard deviations for the three classes. As with the name and address data, the list uses two square brackets for indexing. The [[1]] indicates the first element of the list, which is a number contained in another list. The `sapply` function produces a simplified view of the means and standard deviations. Note that the `lapply` function works here as well, as the calculation of the variances for the separate sections shows, but produces a different kind of output from that of `sapply`, making it clear that the output is yet another list:

```
> lapply(allSections,var)
[[1]]
[1] 32.99515

[[2]]
[1] 17.3521

[[3]]
[1] 29.18879
```

1.3.6 A Quick Introduction to Data Frames

As I mentioned earlier, the most common data structure for statistics is the data frame. A data frame is a list, but rectangular like a matrix. Every column represents a variable or a factor in the dataset. Every row in the data frame represents a *case*, either an object or an individual about whom data have been collected, so that, ideally, each case will have a score for every variable and a level for every factor. Of course, as we will discuss in more detail in Chapter 2, real data are far from ideal.

Here is the roster of the 2014-2015 Clemson University mens' basketball team, which I downloaded from the university's website. I saved the roster as a comma-separated value (CSV) file and then read it into R using the `read.csv` function. Please note that in this case, the file 'roster.csv' was saved in our working directory. Recall that earlier we discussed both `getwd()` and `setwd()`, these can be quite helpful. As you can see, when you create data using this method, the file will automatically become a data frame in R:

```
> roster<-read.csv("roster.csv")
> roster
```

	Jersey	Name	Position	Inches	Pounds	Class
1	0	Rooks,Patrick	G	74	190	freshman
2	1	Ajukwa,Austin	G	78	205	sophomore
3	3	Holmes,Avry	G	74	205	junior
4	5	Blossomgame,Jaron	F	79	215	sophomore
5	10	DeVoe,Gabe	G	75	200	freshman
6	12	Hall,Rod	G	73	205	senior
7	15	Grantham,Donte	F	80	205	freshman
8	20	Roper,Jordan	G	72	165	junior
9	21	Harrison,Damarcus	G	76	205	senior

(*continued*)

	Jersey	Name	Position	Inches	Pounds	Class
10	33	Smith,Josh	F	80	245	junior
11	35	Nnoko,Landry	C	82	255	junior
12	44	McGillan,Riley	G	72	175	junior
13	50	Djitte,Sidy	C	82	240	sophomore

```
> str(roster)
'data.frame':	13 obs. of  6 variables:
$ Jersey  : int  0 1 3 5 10 12 15 20 21 33 ...
$ Name    : Factor w/ 13 levels "Ajukwa,Austin",..: 1
1 1 8 2 3 6 5 12 7 13 ...
$ Position: Factor w/ 3 levels "C","F","G": 3 3 3 2 3
3 2 3 3 2 ...
$ Inches  : int  74 78 74 79 75 73 80 72 76 80 ...
$ Pounds  : int  190 205 205 215 200 205 205 165 20
5 245 ...
$ Class   : Factor w/ 4 levels "freshman","junior",
..: 1 4 2 4 1 3 1 2 3 2 ...
```

To view your data without editing them, you can use the View command (see Figure 1-2).

	Jersey	Name	Position	Inches	Pounds	Class
1	0	Rooks, Patrick	G	74	190	freshman
2	1	Ajukwa, Austin	G	78	205	sophomore
3	3	Holmes, Avry	G	74	205	junior
4	5	Blossomgame, Jaron	F	79	215	sophomore
5	10	DeVoe, Gabe	G	75	200	freshman
6	12	Hall, Rod	G	73	205	senior
7	15	Grantham, Donte	F	80	205	freshman
8	20	Roper, Jordan	G	72	165	junior
9	21	Harrison, Damarcus	G	76	205	senior
10	33	Smith, Josh	F	80	245	junior
11	35	Nnoko, Landry	C	82	255	junior
12	44	McGillan, Riley	G	72	175	junior
13	50	Djitte, Sidy	C	82	240	sophomore

Figure 1-2. *Data frame in the viewer window*

CHAPTER 2

■ ■ ■

Dealing with Dates, Strings, and Data Frames

The world of data and data analytics is changing rapidly. Data analysts are facing major issues related to the use of larger datasets, including cloud computing and the creation of so-called data lakes, which are enterprise-wide data management platforms consisting of vast amounts of data in their original format stored in an single unmanaged and unstructured location available to the entire organization. This flies in the face of the carefully structured and highly managed data most of us have come to know and love.

Data lakes solve the problem of independently managed information silos (an old problem in information technology), and the newer problem of dealing with Big Data projects, which typically require large amounts of highly varied data. If you are particularly interested in using R for cloud computing, I recommend Ajay Ohri's book R for Cloud Computing: An Approach for Data Scientists. We will touch lightly on the issues of dealing with R in the cloud and with big (or at least bigger) data in subsequent chapters.

You learned about various data types in Chapter 1. To lay the foundation for discussing some ways of dealing with real-world data effectively, we first discuss working with dates and times and then discuss working with data frames in more depth. In later chapters, you will learn about data tables, a package that provides a more efficient way to work with large datasets in R.

2.1 Working with Dates and Times

Dates and times are handled differently by R than other data. Dates are represented as the number of days since January 1, 1970, with negative numbers representing earlier dates. You can return the current date and time by using the date() function and the current day by using the Sys.Date() function:

```
> date ()
[1] "Fri Dec 26 07:00:28 2014 "
> Sys . Date ()
[1] " 2014 -12 -26 "
```

By adding symbols and using the format() command, you can change how dates are shown. These symbols are as follows:

- %d The day as a number

- %a Abbreviated week day

- %A Unabbreviated week day

- %b Abbreviated month

- %B Unabbreviated month

- %y Two-digit year

- %Y Four-digit year

See the following example run by the author on 1 January 2015. Notice the use of cat() to concatenate and output the desired objects:

```
> today <- Sys . Date ()
> cat ( format (today , format = "%A, %B %d, %Y")," Happy New Year !", "\n")
Thursday , January 01, 2015 Happy New Year !
```

2.2 Working with Strings

You have already seen character data, but let's spend some time getting familiar with how to manipulate strings in R. This is a good precursor to our more detailed discussion of text mining later on. We will look at how to get string data into R, how to manipulate such data, and how to format string data to maximum advantage. Let's start with a quote from a famous statistician, R. A. Fisher:

> *The null hypothesis is never proved or established, but is possibly disproved, in the course of experimentation. Every experiment may be said to exist only to give the facts a chance of disproving the null hypothesis." R. A. Fisher*

Although it would be possible to type this quote into R directly using the console or the R Editor, that would be a bit clumsy and error-prone. Instead, we can save the quote in a plain text file. There are many good text editors, and I am using Notepad++. Let's call the file "fishersays.txt" and save it in the current working directory:

```
> dir ()
[1] " fishersays . txt " " mouse _ weights _ clean . txt"
[3] " mouseSample . csv " " mouseWts . rda "
[5] " zScores . R"
```

You can read the entire text file into R using either readLines() or scan(). Although scan() is more flexible, in this case a text file consisting of a single line of text with a "carriage return" at the end is very easy to read into R using the readLines() function:

```
> fisherSays <- readLines ("fishersays.txt")
> fisherSays
[1] "The null hypothesis is never proved or established , but is possibly disproved ,
    in the course of experimentation . Every experiment may be said to exist only to
    give the facts a chance of disproving the null hypothesis . R. A. Fisher "
>
```

Note that I haven't had to type the quote at all. I found the quote on a statistics quotes web page, copied it, saved it into a text file, and then read it into R.

As a statistical aside, Fisher's formulation did not (ever) require an alternative hypothesis. Fisher was a staunch advocate of declaring a null hypothesis that stated a certain population state of affairs, and then determining the probability of obtaining the sample results (what he called facts), assuming that the null hypothesis was true. Thus, in Fisher's formulation, the absence of an alternative hypothesis meant that Type II errors were simply ignored, whereas Type I errors were controlled by establishing a reasonable significance level for rejecting the null hypothesis. We will have much more to discuss about the current state and likely future state of null hypothesis significance testing (NHST), but for now, let's get back to strings.

A regular expression is a specific pattern in a string or a set of strings. R uses three types of such expressions:

- Regular expressions

- Extended regular expressions

- Perl-like regular expressions

The functions that use regular expressions in R are as follows (see Table 2-1). You can also use the glob2rx() function to create specific patterns for use in regular expressions. In addition to these functions, there are many extended regular expressions, too many to list here. We can search for specific characters, digits, letters, and words. We can also use functions on character strings as we do with numbers, including counting the number of characters, and indexing them as we do with numbers. We will continue to work with our quotation, perhaps making Fisher turn over in his grave by our alterations.

Table 2-1. *R Functions that use regular expressions*

Purpose	Function	Explanation
Substitution	sub()	Both sub() and gsub() are used to make substitutions in a string
Extraction	grep()	Extract some value from a string
Detection	grepl()	Detect the presence of a pattern

The simplest form of a regular expression are ones that match a single character. Most characters, including letters and digits, are also regular expressions. These expressions match themselves. R also includes special reserved characters called metacharacters in the extended regular expressions. These have a special status, and to use them, you must use a double backslash \\to escape these when you need to use them as literal characters. The reserved characters are ., \, |, (,), [, {, $, *, +, and ?.

Let us pretend that Jerzy Neyman actually made the quotation we attributed to Fisher. This is certainly not true, because Neyman and Egon Pearson formulated both a null and an alternative hypothesis and computed two probabilities rather than one, determining which hypothesis had the higher probability of having generated the sample data. Nonetheless, let's make the substitution. Before we do, however, look at how you can count the characters in a string vector. As always, a vector with one element has an index of [1], but we can count the actual characters using the nchar() function:

```
> length ( fisherSays )
[1] 1
> nchar ( fisherSays )
[1] 230
sub ("R. A. Fisher", "Jerzy Neyman", fisherSays )
[1] "The null hypothesis is never proved or established, but is possibly disproved, in the
course of experimentation. Every experiment may be said to exist only to give the facts a
chance of disproving the null hypothesis." Jerzy Neyman"
```

2.3 Working with Data Frames in the Real World

Data frames are the workhorse data structure for statistical analyses. If you have used other statistical packages, a data frame will remind you of the data view in SPSS or of a spreadsheet. Customarily, we use columns for variables and rows for units of analysis (people, animals, or objects). Sometimes we need to change the structure of the data frame to accommodate certain situations, and you will learn how to stack and unstack data frames as well as how to recode data when you need to.

There are many ways to create data frames, but for now, let's work through a couple of data frames built into R. The data frame comes from the 1974 *Motor Trend* US Magazine, and contains miles per gallon, number of cylinders, displacement, gross horsepower, rear axle ratio, weight, quarter mile time in seconds, 'V' or Straight engine, transmission, number of forward gears, and number of carburetors.

The complete dataset has 32 cars and 10 variables for each car. We will also learn how to find specific rows of data:

```
> str(mtcars)
'data.frame': 32 obs. of  11 variables:
 $ mpg : num  21 21 22.8 21.4 18.7 18.1 14.3 24.4 22.8 19.2 ...
 $ cyl : num  6 6 4 6 8 6 8 4 4 6 ...
 $ disp: num  160 160 108 258 360 ...
 $ hp  : num  110 110 93 110 175 105 245 62 95 123 ...
 $ drat: num  3.9 3.9 3.85 3.08 3.15 2.76 3.21 3.69 3.92 3.92 ...
 $ wt  : num  2.62 2.88 2.32 3.21 3.44 ...
 $ qsec: num  16.5 17 18.6 19.4 17 ...
 $ vs  : num  0 0 1 1 0 1 0 1 1 1 ...
 $ am  : num  1 1 1 0 0 0 0 0 0 0 ...
 $ gear: num  4 4 4 3 3 3 3 4 4 4 ...
 $ carb: num  4 4 1 1 2 1 4 2 2 4 ...

> summary(mtcars $ mpg)
   Min. 1st Qu.  Median    Mean 3rd Qu.    Max.
  10.40   15.42   19.20   20.09   22.80   33.90

> summary(mtcars $ wt)
   Min. 1st Qu.  Median    Mean 3rd Qu.    Max.
  1.513   2.581   3.325   3.217   3.610   5.424
```

To refer to a given column in a data fame, you can use either indexing or the $ operator with the data frame name followed by the variable name. Because data frames have both rows and columns, you must use indexes for both the row and the column. To refer to an entire row or an entire column, you can use a comma, as you can with a matrix. To illustrate, the rear axle ratio variable is the fifth column in the data frame. We can refer to this column in two ways. We can use the dataset$variable notation mtcars $ drat, or we can equivalently use matrix-type indexing, as in [, 5] using the column number. The head() function returns the first part or parts of a vector, matrix, data frame, or function, and is useful for a quick "sneak preview":

```
> head( mtcars $ drat)
[1] 3.90 3.90 3.85 3.08 3.15 2.76

> head( mtcars [,5] )
[1] 3.90 3.90 3.85 3.08 3.15 2.76
```

2.3.1 Finding and Subsetting Data

Sometimes, it is helpful to locate in which row a particular set of data may be. We can find the row containing a particular value very easily using the which() function:

```
> which ( mtcars $ hp >= 300)
[1] 31
> mtcars [31 ,]
             mpg cyl disp  hp drat   wt qsec vs am gear carb
Maserati Bora 15   8  301 335 3.54 3.57 14.6  0  1    5    8
```

Suppose the Maserati's horsepower need to be recoded to NA because it turns out there was an error in recording the data (note: this occurs on occasion in real world data), just do the following:

```
mtcars $ hp [ mtcars $ hp >= 300] <- NA
> mtcars [31 ,]
             mpg cyl disp hp drat   wt qsec vs am gear carb
Maserati Bora 15   8  301 NA 3.54 3.57 14.6  0  1    5    8
```

With the one observation recoded to missing, a histogram of the horsepower data is shown (see Figure 2-1):

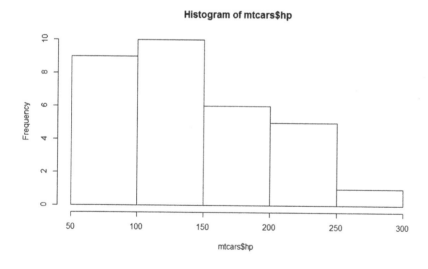

Figure 2-1. *Car horsepower (with Maserati removed) vs frequency*

The data frame indexing using square brackets is similar to that of a matrix. As with vectors, we can use the colon separator to refer to ranges of columns or rows. For example, say that we are interested in reviewing the car data for vehicles with manual transmission. Here is how to subset the data in R. Attaching the data frame makes it possible to refer to the variable names directly, and thus makes the subsetting operation a little easier. As you can see, the resulting new data frame contains only the manual transmission vehicles:

```
> attach ( mtcars )
> mpgMan <- subset ( mtcars , am == 1, select = mpg : disp )
> summary ( mpgMan $ mpg)
   Min. 1st Qu.  Median    Mean 3rd Qu.    Max.
  15.00   21.00   22.80   24.39   30.40   33.90
```

You can remove a column in a data frame by assigning it the special value NULL. For this illustration, let us use a small sample of the data. We will remove the displacement variable. First, recall the data frame:

```
> mpgMan
                mpg cyl  disp
Mazda RX4      21.0   6 160.0
Mazda RX4 Wag  21.0   6 160.0
Datsun 710     22.8   4 108.0
Fiat 128       32.4   4  78.7
Honda Civic    30.4   4  75.7
Toyota Corolla 33.9   4  71.1
Fiat X1-9      27.3   4  79.0
Porsche 914-2  26.0   4 120.3
Lotus Europa   30.4   4  95.1
Ford Pantera L 15.8   8 351.0
Ferrari Dino   19.7   6 145.0
Maserati Bora  15.0   8 301.0
Volvo 142E     21.4   4 121.0
```

Now, simply type the following to remove the variable, and note that the disp variable is no longer part of the data frame. Also, don't try this at home unless you make a backup copy of your important data first.

```
> mpgMan $ disp <- NULL
> mpgMan
                mpg cyl
Mazda RX4      21.0   6
Mazda RX4 Wag  21.0   6
Datsun 710     22.8   4
Fiat 128       32.4   4
Honda Civic    30.4   4
Toyota Corolla 33.9   4
Fiat X1-9      27.3   4
Porsche 914-2  26.0   4
Lotus Europa   30.4   4
Ford Pantera L 15.8   8
Ferrari Dino   19.7   6
Maserati Bora  15.0   8
Volvo 142E     21.4   4
```

We can add a new variable to a data frame simply by creating it, or by using the cbind() function. Here's a little trick to make up some data quickly. I used the rep() function (for replicate) to generate 15 "observations" of the color of the vehicle. First, I created a character vector with three color names, then I replicated the vector five times to fabricate my new variable. By defining it as mpgMan$colors, I was able to create it and add it to the data frame at the same time. Notice I only used the first 13 entries of colors as mpgMan only has 13 manual vehicles:

```
colors <- c(" black ", " white ", " gray ")
> colors <- rep (colors, 5)
> mpgMan $ colors <- colors[1:13]
> mpgMan
                 mpg cyl  colors
Mazda RX4        21.0   6   black
Mazda RX4 Wag    21.0   6   white
Datsun 710       22.8   4    gray
Fiat 128         32.4   4   black
Honda Civic      30.4   4   white
Toyota Corolla   33.9   4    gray
Fiat X1-9        27.3   4   black
Porsche 914-2    26.0   4   white
Lotus Europa     30.4   4    gray
Ford Pantera L   15.8   8   black
Ferrari Dino     19.7   6   white
Maserati Bora    15.0   8    gray
Volvo 142E       21.4   4   black
```

2.4 Manipulating Data Structures

Depending on the required data analysis, we sometimes need to restructure data by changing narrow format data to wide-format data, and vice versa. Let's take a look at some ways data can be manipulated in R. Wide and narrow data are often referred to as unstacked and stacked, respectively. Both can be used to display tabular data, with wide data presenting each data value for an observation in a separate column. Narrow data, by contrast, present a single column containing all the values, and another column listing the "context" of each value. Recall our roster data from Chapter 1.

It is easier to show this than it is to explain it. Examine the following code listing to see how this works. We will start with a narrow or stacked representation of our data, and then we will unstack the data into the more familiar wide format:

```
> roster <- read.csv("roster.csv")
> sportsExample <- c("Jersey", "Class")
> stackedData <- roster [ sportsExample ]
> stackedData
   Jersey     Class
1       0  freshman
2       1 sophomore
3       3    junior
4       5 sophomore
5      10  freshman
6      12    senior
7      15  freshman
```

```
8       20    junior
9       21    senior
10      33    junior
11      35    junior
12      44    junior
13      50 sophomore
> unstack(stackedData)
$freshman
[1]   0 10 15

$junior
[1]   3 20 33 35 44

$senior
[1] 12 21

$sophomore
[1]   1  5 50
```

2.5 The Hard Work of Working with Larger Datasets

As I have found throughout my career, real-world data present many challenges. Datasets often have missing values and outliers. Real data distributions are rarely normally distributed. The majority of the time I have spent with data analysis has been in preparation of the data for subsequent analyses, rather than the analysis itself. Data cleaning and data munging are rarely included as a subject in statistics classes, and included datasets are generally either fabricated or scrubbed squeaky clean.

The General Social Survey (GSS) has been administered almost annually since 1972. One commentator calls the GSS "America's mood ring." The data for 2012 contain the responses to a 10-word vocabulary test. Each correct and incorrect responses are labeled as such, with missing data coded as NA. The GSS data are available in SPSS and STATA format, but not in R format. I downloaded the data in SPSS format and then use the R library foreign to read that into R as follows. As you learned earlier, the View function allows you to see the data in a spreadsheet-like layout (see Figure 2-2):

```
> library(foreign)
> gss2012 <- read.spss("GSS2012merged_R5.sav", to.data.frame = TRUE)
> View(gss2012)
```

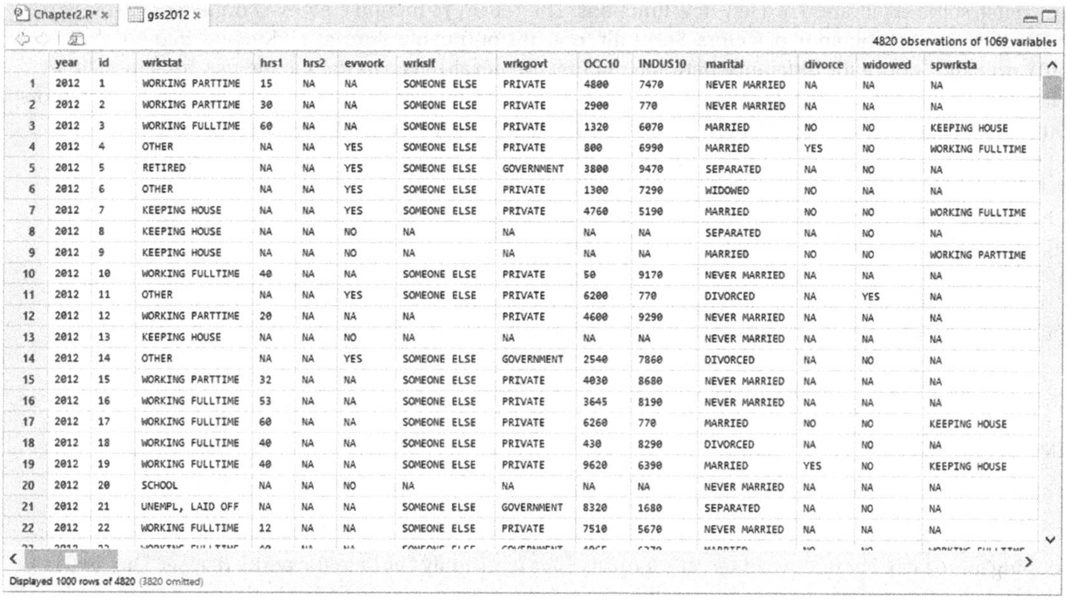
Chapter2.R* × gss2012 ×

4820 observations of 1069 variables

	year	id	wrkstat	hrs1	hrs2	evwork	wrkslf	wrkgovt	OCC10	INDUS10	marital	divorce	widowed	spwrksta
1	2012	1	WORKING PARTTIME	15	NA	NA	SOMEONE ELSE	PRIVATE	4800	7470	NEVER MARRIED	NA	NA	NA
2	2012	2	WORKING PARTTIME	30	NA	NA	SOMEONE ELSE	PRIVATE	2900	770	NEVER MARRIED	NA	NA	NA
3	2012	3	WORKING FULLTIME	60	NA	NA	SOMEONE ELSE	PRIVATE	1320	6070	MARRIED	NO	NO	KEEPING HOUSE
4	2012	4	OTHER	NA	NA	YES	SOMEONE ELSE	PRIVATE	800	6990	MARRIED	YES	NO	WORKING FULLTIME
5	2012	5	RETIRED	NA	NA	YES	SOMEONE ELSE	GOVERNMENT	3800	9470	SEPARATED	NA	NO	NA
6	2012	6	OTHER	NA	NA	YES	SOMEONE ELSE	PRIVATE	1300	7290	WIDOWED	NO	NA	NA
7	2012	7	KEEPING HOUSE	NA	NA	YES	SOMEONE ELSE	PRIVATE	4760	5190	MARRIED	NO	NO	WORKING FULLTIME
8	2012	8	KEEPING HOUSE	NA	NA	NO	NA	NA	NA	NA	SEPARATED	NA	NO	NA
9	2012	9	KEEPING HOUSE	NA	NA	NO	NA	NA	NA	NA	MARRIED	NO	NO	WORKING PARTTIME
10	2012	10	WORKING FULLTIME	40	NA	NA	SOMEONE ELSE	PRIVATE	50	9170	NEVER MARRIED	NA	NA	NA
11	2012	11	OTHER	NA	NA	YES	SOMEONE ELSE	PRIVATE	6200	770	DIVORCED	NA	YES	NA
12	2012	12	WORKING PARTTIME	20	NA	NA	NA	PRIVATE	4600	9290	NEVER MARRIED	NA	NA	NA
13	2012	13	KEEPING HOUSE	NA	NA	NO	NA	NA	NA	NA	NEVER MARRIED	NA	NA	NA
14	2012	14	OTHER	NA	NA	YES	SOMEONE ELSE	GOVERNMENT	2540	7860	DIVORCED	NA	NO	NA
15	2012	15	WORKING PARTTIME	32	NA	NA	SOMEONE ELSE	PRIVATE	4030	8680	NEVER MARRIED	NA	NA	NA
16	2012	16	WORKING FULLTIME	53	NA	NA	SOMEONE ELSE	PRIVATE	3645	8190	NEVER MARRIED	NA	NA	NA
17	2012	17	WORKING FULLTIME	60	NA	NA	SOMEONE ELSE	PRIVATE	6260	770	MARRIED	NO	NO	KEEPING HOUSE
18	2012	18	WORKING FULLTIME	40	NA	NA	SOMEONE ELSE	PRIVATE	430	8290	DIVORCED	NA	NO	NA
19	2012	19	WORKING FULLTIME	40	NA	NA	SOMEONE ELSE	PRIVATE	9620	6390	MARRIED	YES	NO	KEEPING HOUSE
20	2012	20	SCHOOL	NA	NA	NO	NA	NA	NA	NA	NEVER MARRIED	NA	NA	NA
21	2012	21	UNEMPL, LAID OFF	NA	NA	NA	SOMEONE ELSE	GOVERNMENT	8320	1680	SEPARATED	NA	NO	NA
22	2012	22	WORKING FULLTIME	12	NA	NA	SOMEONE ELSE	PRIVATE	7510	5670	NEVER MARRIED	NA	NA	NA

Displayed 1000 rows of 4820 (3820 omitted)

Figure 2-2. *Viewing the GSS dataset*

Here's a neat trick: The words are in columns labeled "worda", "wordb", . . . , "wordj". I want to subset the data, as we discussed earlier, to keep from having to work with the entire set of 1069 variables and 4820 observations. I can use R to make my list of variable names without having to type as much as you might suspect. Here's how I used the `paste0` function and the built-in `letters` function to make it easy. There is an acronym among computer scientists called DRY that was created by Andrew Hunt and David Thomas: "Don't repeat yourself." According to Hunt and Thomas, pragmatic programmers are early adopters, fast adapters, inquisitive, critical thinkers, realistic, and jacks of all trades:

```
> myWords <- paste0 ("word", letters [1:10])
> myWords
 [1] "worda" "wordb" "wordc" "wordd" "worde" "wordf" "wordg" "wordh" "wordi" "wordj"
> vocabTest <- gss2012 [ myWords ]
> head ( vocabTest )
    worda   wordb     wordc   wordd   worde   wordf     wordg     wordh   wordi     wordj
1 CORRECT CORRECT INCORRECT CORRECT CORRECT CORRECT INCORRECT INCORRECT CORRECT   CORRECT
2    <NA>    <NA>      <NA>    <NA>    <NA>    <NA>      <NA>      <NA>    <NA>      <NA>
3    <NA>    <NA>      <NA>    <NA>    <NA>    <NA>      <NA>      <NA>    <NA>      <NA>
4 CORRECT CORRECT   CORRECT CORRECT CORRECT CORRECT   CORRECT   CORRECT CORRECT INCORRECT
5 CORRECT CORRECT INCORRECT CORRECT CORRECT CORRECT INCORRECT      <NA> CORRECT INCORRECT
6 CORRECT CORRECT   CORRECT CORRECT CORRECT CORRECT   CORRECT      <NA> CORRECT INCORRECT
```

We will also apply the DRY principle to our analysis of our subset data. For each of the words, it would be interesting to see how many respondents were correct versus incorrect. This is additionally interesting because we have text rather than numerical data (a frequent enough phenomena in survey data). There are many ways perhaps to create the proportions we seek, but let us explore one such path. Of note here is that we definitely recommend using the top left Rscript area of Rstudio to type in these functions, then selecting that code and hitting `<Ctrl>` + R to run it all in the console.

First, some exploration of a few new functions. The `table()` function creates a contingency table with a count of each combination of factors. Secondly, note the output of `myWords[1]`. Keeping in mind the DRY principle, notice the difference between our first use of `table` versus the second use. It seems a little changed, no? And yet, if we wanted to get counts for each of our words a through j, the second is much more powerful if we could simply find a way to increase that counter by 1 each time we ran the code.

```
> myWords[1]
[1] "worda"

> table(vocabTest[, "worda"], useNA = "ifany")

INCORRECT    CORRECT        <NA>
      515       2619        1686
> table(vocabTest[, myWords[1]], useNA = "ifany")

INCORRECT    CORRECT        <NA>
      515       2619        1686
```

Thinking of increasing a counter by 1 and repeating several times is called *looping*, and we will explore looping more later. For now, we'll secretly loop via `lapply` to apply `table` to the entire dataset. Our goal is to count all corrects/incorrects at once, rather than doing it piecemeal by typing in the same commands repeatedly and just changing variable names. Also, while headcounts are nice enough, we generally see such data summarized via proportions. Let's work our way backward. At the end, we use `do.call` to use the `rbind` function on the percents of each word correct vs incorrect; `do.call` simply runs `rbind` on *each* percents value in sequence – more looping! The `rbind` function is used to simply make it all look pretty (consider typing in `percents` into your Rstudio console *after* running the below code to see why `rbind` is so helpful). Before we could do that, we needed to build up `percents`, which we did by running a proportion table to create those percents. Since we want a proportion table for *each* word, we use `lapply` on our dataset. Of course, the above tables we had created for just `worda` were not enough, so we had to create each `table`, take a `prop.table` of their data, store all proportion data into `percents`, and finally make it all look good as we've done on the next page:

```
> proportion.table <- function(x) {
+     prop.table( table( x ) )
+ }
>
> percents <- lapply(vocabTest, proportion.table)
>
> do.call(rbind, percents)
        INCORRECT    CORRECT
worda 0.16432674 0.8356733
wordb 0.06868752 0.9313125
wordc 0.76188761 0.2381124
wordd 0.04441624 0.9555838
worde 0.17356173 0.8264383
wordf 0.18032787 0.8196721
wordg 0.65165877 0.3483412
wordh 0.63088235 0.3691176
wordi 0.23732057 0.7626794
wordj 0.71540984 0.2845902
```

The GSS dataset also has a variable for the total score on the vocabulary test, which is simply the sum of the number of words defined correctly. We have added that to the data frame using the cbind function. I won't show all the steps here, but will show you after all the recoding of missing data that the distribution of scores on the vocabulary test is negatively skewed but pretty "normal-looking" by the eyeball test (see Figure 2-3).

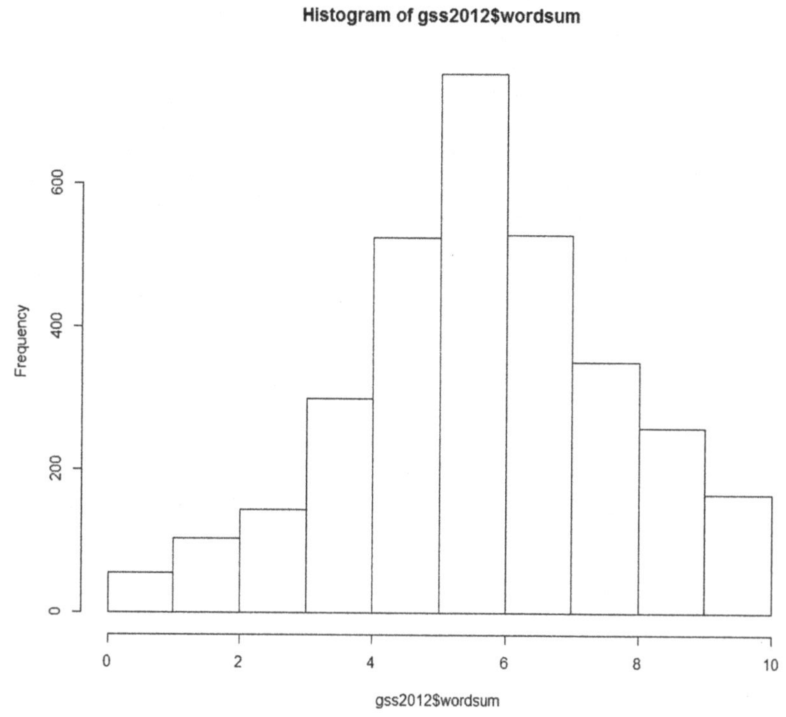

Figure 2-3. *Histogram of scores on the 10-word vocabulary test*

CHAPTER 3

███ ███ ███

Input and Output

As a scripting language, R is perhaps not as flexible as Python or other languages, but as a statistical language, R provides all of the basic input and output capabilities that an average user is likely to need. In Chapter 3, you will learn how to get data into R and how to get output from R in the form and format you desire.

To prepare for our discussion of input and output, let me first remind you of some functions we have discussed and tell you about a few that we haven't yet discussed. This will help greatly with your file management for both input and output.

Remember the functions getwd() and setwd() are used to identify and change the working directory. If the file is in the current directory, you can access it using only the file name. If you need a file in a different directory, you must give the path to the file as well as the name. If you want to know the information about a particular file, you can use the file.info() function. Sometimes, you might forget whether or not you saved a file to your working directory. You can find out whether you did by using the file.exists() function. As you have already seen, we can use ls() to get a list of all of the objects in the workspace and dir() to get a list of all of the files in the working directory. To get a complete list of all of the functions related to files and directories, just type ?files at the command prompt. Knowing these functions will make your life easier. Until you have memorized them, you may want to make a cheat sheet and keep it close at hand when you are programming.

3.1 R Input

You have already used the R console extensively to type in data and commands. When the demands of data input exceed the capacity of the console, you can access the R Editor for typing scripts (R code) and import worksheets to input data.

You also learned in Chapter 2 how to read in string data from a text file. In the example of the statistics quote, we made a simple replacement of one name with another. There are many more things you can do with strings, and we will discuss those in Chapter 15.

We can use the scan() function to read in data instead of typing the data in by using the c() function. For example, say we want to create a vector with 10 numbers. People are usually better at entering data in columns than rows. Here's how to use scan() to build a vector:

```
> newVector <- scan ()
1: 11
2: 23
3: 44
4: 15
5: 67
```

```
6: 15
7: 12
8: 8
9: 9
10:
Read 9 items
> newVector
[1] 11 23 44 15 67 15 12 8 9
```

You simply type the numbers in one at a time and hit < Enter> when you are finished. It is also possible to read a vector into your workspace by using the scan function. Say you have a text file called "yvector.txt," and have separated the numbers by spaces. Read it into the workspace as follows:

```
> yvector <- scan (" yvector . txt ", sep = " ")
Read 12 items
> yvector
[1] 11 22 18 32 39 42 73 27 34 32 19 15
```

In a similar way, we can get keyboard input using the readline() function. Examine the following code fragment so see how this works:

```
> myName <- readline (" What shall I call you ? ")
What shall I call you ? Larry
> myName
[1] " Larry "
```

3.1.1 The R Editor

Rstudio has some very convenient features in its graphical user interface. The Rstudio Editor is shown in Figure 3-1. You open this window by selecting from the menu bar the commands File ➤ New File ➤ R script.

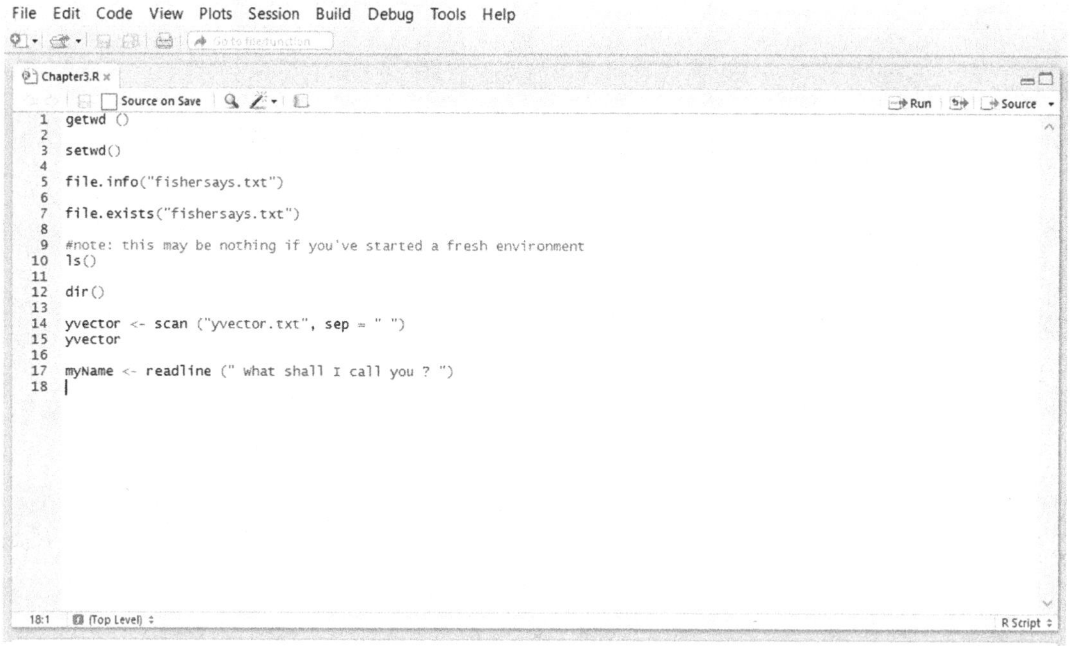

Figure 3-1. *The Rstudio editor open*

This is similar to a text processor; and many R programmers prefer to use different text editors. I find the Rstudio editor useful for writing lines of code and editing them before executing them. RStudio's editor also includes a built-in debugger, which is very helpful in code development.

3.1.2 The R Data Editor

As you saw at the end of Chapter 1, the R Data Editor is a spreadsheet-like window into which you can type and edit data. To open the Data Editor, you must either already have a data frame, or you must create one. Although the Data Editor is not suitable for creating larger datasets, it is very good for quick changes to an existing dataset, as we discussed in Chapter 2. For example, suppose with our sports roster we needed to change Josh Smith's Inches to 81. We might use the fix() function, which will allow us to click inside the variables replace '80' with '81'. When you fix the labels, or make any other changes to the data frame, just close the R Data Editor to save the changes (see Figure 3-2).

```
> roster <- read.csv("roster.csv")
> fix(roster)
```

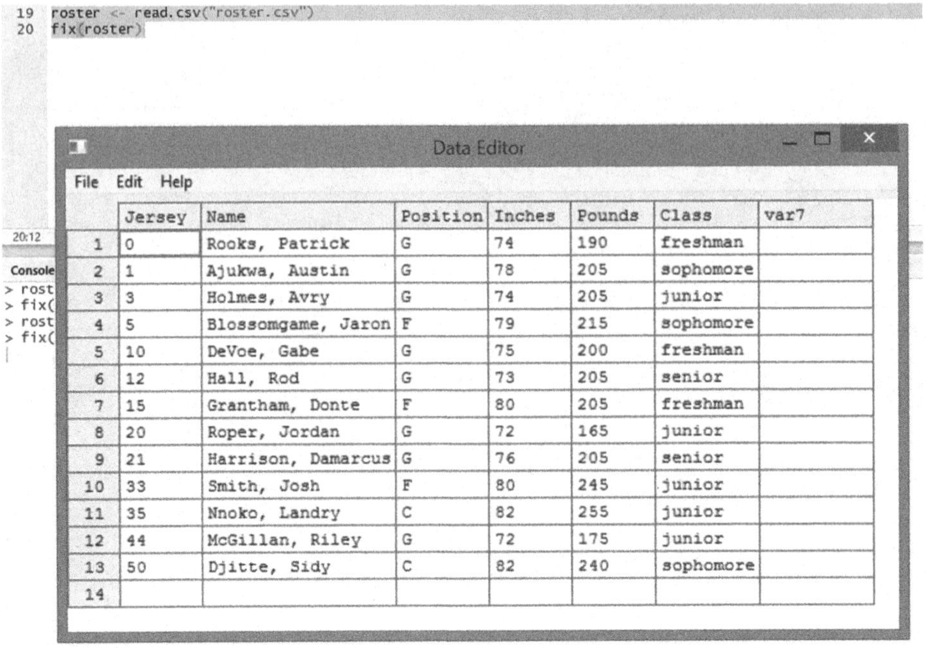

```
19  roster <- read.csv("roster.csv")
20  fix(roster)
```

	Jersey	Name	Position	Inches	Pounds	Class	var7
1	0	Rooks, Patrick	G	74	190	freshman	
2	1	Ajukwa, Austin	G	78	205	sophomore	
3	3	Holmes, Avry	G	74	205	junior	
4	5	Blossomgame, Jaron	F	79	215	sophomore	
5	10	DeVoe, Gabe	G	75	200	freshman	
6	12	Hall, Rod	G	73	205	senior	
7	15	Grantham, Donte	F	80	205	freshman	
8	20	Roper, Jordan	G	72	165	junior	
9	21	Harrison, Damarcus	G	76	205	senior	
10	33	Smith, Josh	F	80	245	junior	
11	35	Nnoko, Landry	C	82	255	junior	
12	44	McGillan, Riley	G	72	175	junior	
13	50	Djitte, Sidy	C	82	240	sophomore	
14							

Figure 3-2. *The Rstudio Data Editor open*

3.1.3 Other Ways to Get Data Into R

We can read data into R from different kinds of files, including comma-separated value (CSV) files, text files, R data files, and others. The scan() function and the readline() function can be used as well.

You can also request user input via the console. Let's examine these various approaches. We will discuss functional programming in more depth in Chapter 5, but as a teaser, see the following code to create a function that requests user input to calculate one's body mass index (BMI):

```
BMI <- function () {
  cat (" Please enter your height in inches and weight in pounds :","\n")
  height <- as.numeric ( readline (" height = "))
  weight <- as.numeric ( readline (" weight = "))
  bmi <- weight/(height^2)*703
  cat (" Your body mass index is:",bmi ,"\n")
  if ( bmi < 18.5) risk = " Underweight "
  else if ( bmi >= 18.5 & bmi <= 24.9) risk = "Normal"
  else if ( bmi >= 25 & bmi <= 29.9) risk = "Overweight"
  else risk = "Obese"
  cat (" According to the National Heart, Lung, and Blood Institute,","\n")
  cat (" your BMI is in the",risk ,"category.","\n")
}
```

Open the R Editor and type the code just as you see it. Omit the R command prompts when typing code in the Editor window. To read the function into your R session, press <Ctrl> + A to select all the lines, and then press <Ctrl> + R to run the code. You should see the code in the R console now. When the function is executed, it will prompt the user for his or her height and weight. After the user enters these, the function then calculates and evaluates the person's BMI. Because we provide the input from the keyboard, the function has no arguments, and we simply type BMI() and then press <Enter> to execute it. For example:

```
> BMI ()
Please enter your height in inches and weight in pounds :
height = 67
weight = 148
Your body mass index is: 23.17755
According to the National Heart, Lung, and Blood Institute,
your BMI is in the Normal category.
```

3.1.4 Reading Data from a File

The foreign and the Hmisc packages can read files produced by SPSS and many other programs (we've already met foreign). The basic operation in R to read in a data file is read.table. For text files, you must tell R if the first row of the dataset contains column headers that will be used as variable names. You must also tell read.table what your separator between variables is, that is, whether it is a tab, a space, or something else. If you use the read.csv function, it will assume that your data have a header row. You can control whether R converts strings to factors when it reads in the data by setting stringsAsFactors to TRUE or FALSE. The default behavior is TRUE. I usually set it to FALSE, because I do not necessarily want all strings to become factors. We will discuss factors in much more detail later.

Let's see how these various input operations work in R. I've typed a brief history (from memory) of my recent cell phone purchases). We will read in the entire cellphone dataset from a tab-delimited text file called "cellphonetab.txt". Remember that when the data are in text format, you must specify header = TRUE if you want to use the row of column headings in the first line. In this case, I want the strings to be recognized as factors, so I accept the default in this case by omitting stringsAsFactors = FALSE:

```
> cellPhones <- read.table ("cellphonetab.txt ", sep = "\t", header = TRUE )
> str ( cellPhones )
'data.frame':    5 obs. of  2 variables:
 $ CellPhone: Factor w/ 5 levels "iPhone 4","iPhone 5",..: 4 5 1 2 3
 $ Year     : int  2006 2008 2010 2012 2014
```

3.1.5 Getting Data from the Web

It is also quite easy to download data from the web. For example, the Institute for Digital Research and Education at the University of California in Los Angeles has a series of tutorials on R with many example datasets (see Figure 3-3). Let's download one of those lessons and work with it briefly.

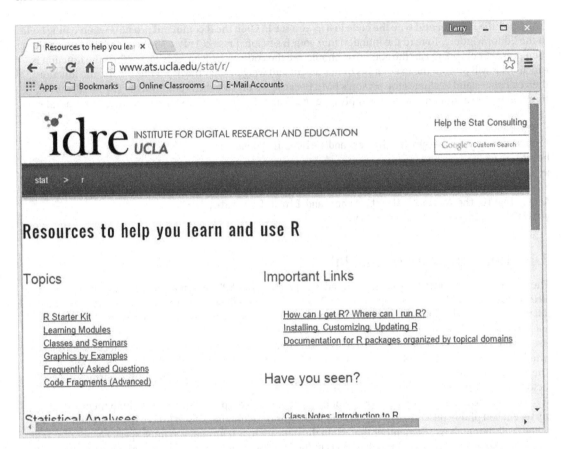

Figure 3-3. *The UCLA Institute for Digital Research and Education website*

Although we have already discussed subsetting data, let's go ahead and download the IDRE lesson and work with it briefly. See how easy it is to get the information from the website. We simply use the read.csv function with the URL to the data on the web as our source. Examine the following code snippet to see how the small dataset from IDRE can be used to help you learn subsetting:

```
> hsb2.small <- read.csv ("http://www.ats.ucla.edu/stat/data/hsb2_small.csv")
> names(hsb2.small)
[1] "id" "female" "race" "ses" "schtyp" "prog" "read" "write" "math" "science" "socst"
> (hsb3 <- hsb2.small [, c(1, 7, 8) ])
   id read write
1  70  57    52
2 121  68    59
3  86  44    33
4 141  63    44
5 172  47    52
6 113  44    52
##this data continues through 25 lines.
```

For example, you can learn how to subset the data by using comparison operators, such as selecting only the individuals with reading scores above or below a certain number. You can also combine the comparison operators so that you could select on multiple conditions. Here are all the variables, which makes it more obvious what the code above did. I learned the trick of enclosing a command in parentheses to print the result of the command from the IDRE lessons. The one command (hsb3 <- hsb2.small[, c(1, 7, 8)]) creates and prints the data frame hsb3, which contains the first, the seventh, and the eighth columns of hsb2.small, and prints the new data frame all in one statement. That's efficiency at work:

```
> head (hsb2.small)
   id female race ses schtyp prog read write math science socst
1  70      0    4   1      1    1   57    52   41      47    57
2 121      1    4   2      1    3   68    59   53      63    61
3  86      0    4   3      1    1   44    33   54      58    31
4 141      0    4   3      1    3   63    44   47      53    56
5 172      0    4   2      1    2   47    52   57      53    61
6 113      0    4   2      1    2   44    52   51      63    61
```

3.2 R Output

R results appear by default in the R console or in the R graphics device, which we will examine in more detail in Chapter 10. We can also save output in different ways, for example, by writing data objects to files or saving graphics objects.

As you saw earlier with the example of the BMI function, You can use the cat() function, short for concatenate, to string together output to the console a line at a time. This is a very helpful way to print a combination of text and values. Note that you must use quotes and a backslash \"n" to "escape" the new line character. If you want to enter a tab instead of a new line, use \"t".

3.2.1 Saving Output to a File

The output analog of reading a file is writing it. In R, the basic operation is write.table. You can also use write.csv. When the data are to be saved in R format, you use the save command. Here is how to save the UCLA file data to a native R data file, which uses the extension .rda. You see that the new R data file is saved in the working directory. To read the file into R, instead of using read, you use load instead:

```
> save (hsb3, file = "hsb3save.rda")
> dir ()
 [1] "BeginningR.Rproj"                          "Chapter1.R"
 [3] "Chapter2.R"                                "Chapter3.R"
 [5] "desktop.ini"                               "fishersays.txt"
 [7] "GSS2012.sav"                               "GSS2012merged_R5.sav"
 [9] "hsb3.RDS"                                  "hsb3save.rda"
[11] "Release Notes for the GSS 2012 Merged R5.pdf" "roster.csv"
[13] "stack.txt"                                 "yvector.txt"
> load ("hsb3save.rda")
> head (hsb3, 3)
   id read write
1  70   57    52
2 121   68    59
3  86   44    33
```

Let's also save this data to a CSV file for practice. The following does the trick. We will also check to make sure the new file is in the working directory:

```
> write.csv( hsb3, file = "hsb3.csv")
> file.exists ("hsb3.csv")
[1] TRUE
```

Finally, we shall subject our poor hsb3 data to one last save, using a rather helpful set of commands saveRDS( ) and readRDS( ). Notice we take the object, save it as a file (it will show up in our working directory) and then we can read that file back in as a data object – notice we may even give it a new name as we read it back!

```
> saveRDS(hsb3, "hsb3.RDS")
> hsb3Copy <- readRDS("hsb3.RDS")
```

CHAPTER 4

■ ■ ■

Control Structures

In Chapter 3, you saw an example of a simple function for calculating a person's body mass index (BMI). The function used logic to determine the person's risk category. The use of logic, conditional statements, and loops are all inherent in controlling the flow of a program. Although there are many different ways to write conditional statements, and loops, too, for that matter, they all boil down to testing to see if some condition is true or false and then behaving accordingly. A program is nothing more or less than a series of instructions telling a computer what to do. As I have mentioned, R is both functional and objected-oriented, so every R program consists of function calls that operate on objects.

4.1 Using Logic

We have spoken frequently about the use of logic. R provides several different ways to select which statement or statements to perform based on the result of a logical test.

You saw the comparison operators in R in Table 1-2. There are also binary logical operators for Boolean expressions in R (see Table 4-1).

Table 4-1. *Binary Operators in R*

Operator	R Expression	Explanation
NOT	!	Logical negation
Boolean AND	&	Element-wise
Boolean AND	&&	First element only
Boolean OR	|	Element-wise
Boolean OR	||	First element only

As you can see, the shorter form acts in a fashion similar to the arithmetic operators, proceeding element-wise along the vector. The longer form evaluates left to right, and examines only the first element of each vector. Examples make these easier to understand. See that the shorter form of OR evaluates the truth of either the elements of x being less than the elements of y OR of the elements of x being less than 10. All of these conditions are true. But when we use the longer form, it evaluates only the first element in each vector.

Similarly, the shorter version of AND function evaluates to FALSE because on the last comparison, x < y AND x < 10 are not both true:

```
> x <- 1:10
> y <- 11:15
> x < y | x < 10
[1] TRUE TRUE TRUE TRUE TRUE TRUE TRUE TRUE TRUE TRUE
> x < y || x < 10
[1] TRUE
> x < y & x < 10
[1]  TRUE  TRUE  TRUE  TRUE  TRUE  TRUE  TRUE  TRUE  TRUE FALSE
> x < 6 && x < 10
[1] TRUE
```

4.2 Flow Control

The programmer must control the flow from one part of the program to another. Flow control involves the use of loops, conditional statements and branching, and conditions that cause the program to stop doing something and do something else or to quit entirely. Virtually all computer programming languages implement these capabilities, but often in very different ways. We will discuss these concepts in the abstract briefly, but then will illustrate them with very specific examples. As you will see, with R, as with most other languages, there is often more than one way to accomplish the same purpose. Some of these ways are more efficient and effective than others, whereas others are not as efficient or effective. Our goal will be to learn how to program in such a way that we can write efficient, reproducible code. We will cover looping and conditional statements and branching before we move into a more general discussion of programming in R.

4.2.1 Explicit Looping

R provides three types of *explicit* loops. You can use one type of looping to accomplish the same purpose as the other types, but the most commonly used loop in R is the for loop. We also have while loops and repeat loops. Although most R coders will typically use for loops, we will also illustrate while and repeat loops, which could work better for some given purpose, especially when iteration through a data structure is not the primary objective.

Let's start with a very simple example. We want to multiply 1 through 5 by 10 and print the results to the R console. Although this is a rather uninteresting example, it shows the syntax of a for loop, which is for(names in values) expression. Here's our code and result:

```
> x <- 1:5
> for (i in x) print (i * 10)
[1] 10
[1] 20
[1] 30
[1] 40
[1] 50
```

We defined x as the integers from 1 to 5, and wrote the for statement in such a way that the names attribute i iterated through the values in x one at a time, while the expression print(i * 10) printed the result of multiplying each successive value in the x vector by 10. Not very fancy, but it worked. Of course, the loop we just wrote was also totally unnecessary, as we could simply ask R to print the results as follows, using implicit looping (vectorization) rather than explicit looping:

```
> x <- 1:5
> x * 10
[1] 10 20 30 40 50
```

We can also use for loops with lists and vectors. For example, we may have a character vector such as the following, and want to loop through it:

```
> shoppingBasket <- c("apples", "bananas", "butter", "bread", "milk", "cheese")
> for(item in shoppingBasket) {
+ print(item)
+ }
[1] " apples "
[1] " bananas "
[1] " butter "
[1] " bread "
[1] " milk "
[1] " cheese "
```

Once again, while possible, this loop is also unnecessary, as we can simply print the shopping list without the need for looping. As users who come to R from languages that are not vectorized learn about vectorization and especially about a family of implicit looping functions called apply, such users learn that implicit looping can be accomplished across not just vectors or lists but also with matrices and even entire data frames.

The while loop will continue to execute until a stopping condition is met. For example, we can write a loop such as the following, which will accomplish the same results as our for loop. The while loop required a few more lines of code. Thus, it is less efficient than the for loop. We specified a counter and iterated the counter by 1 until the stopping condition in the while statement was met. Some languages begin vector indexing with 0 rather than 1, while R begins with 1. This is the reason for setting the counter to 0 initially. As you will see in Chapter 5, there are some situations in which while loops have potential advantages over for loops:

```
> count <- 0
> end <- 5
> while (count < end ) {
+    count <- count + 1
+    print(count * 10)
+ }
[1] 10
[1] 20
[1] 30
[1] 40
[1] 50
```

The repeat loop is similar to the while loop. Just as with a while loop, the statement or statements after the repeat are executed until a stopping constraint is met. However, the only way to exit a repeat loop is with a break statement. For this reason, it is quite possible (voice of experience speaking here) to write repeat loops that keep repeating infinitely if one is not careful. Here is a simple example of a repeat loop:

```
> total <- 0
> repeat {
+    total <- total + 1
+    print (total*10)
+    if (total == 5)
+      break
+ }
[1] 10
[1] 20
[1] 30
[1] 40
[1] 50
```

4.2.2 Implicit Looping

The apply function family in R provides users implicit looping capabilities. You should be aware that the apply function, contrary to the beliefs of many, does not result in speed advantages over explicit loops. In fact, if you simply type apply and press <Enter> to see the actual apply function, you will observe loops in that function definition itself. The primary advantage of such "higher-order" functions as the apply family is the improvement of the clarity or the objective(s) of one's code. Let's examine several of the most commonly used apply functions—there are additional ones that we will not cover in this basic text. The basic apply function applies a function over the margins of an array. The "margins" in this context are either the rows (1), the columns (2), or both (1:2). Let's delve deeper

The apply function can be used to calculate the marginal (row or column) means or sums, as shown here, but the newer rowMeans, colMeans, rowSums, and colSums functions are designed for speed. Recall the ten-word vocabulary test from the GSS we used in Chapter 2. Because the test was not administered every year, there were many missing cases. What if for some reason we wanted to do an analysis on the individual participants' scores, which are simply the total of the numbers of words the respondent defined correctly? We could use the apply function for this purpose. However, just to get rid of those annoying NAs, let's choose only the complete cases, that is, those in which there are no NAs (missing values). We can use the complete.cases function as follows:

```
> library(foreign)
> gss2012 <- read.spss("GSS2012merged_R5.sav", to.data.frame = TRUE)
> myWords <- paste0 ("word", letters [1:10])
> vocabTest <- gss2012 [ myWords ]

> vocab <- vocabTest[complete.cases(vocabTest) ,]

> #Our download of GSS2012 has CORRECT & INCORRECT.  We convert those to 1 and 0 respectively.
> wordsToNum<-function(x) {
+ as.integer(x=="CORRECT")
+ }
>
> vocab<-apply(vocab,2,wordsToNum)
```

```
#apply gives back a matrix, we can turn this back into a data frame > vocab
<- as.data.frame(vocab)
> head(vocab, 3)
  worda wordb wordc wordd worde wordf wordg wordh wordi wordj
1   1     1     0     1     1     1     0     0     1     1
2   1     1     1     1     1     1     1     1     1     0
3   0     1     0     1     1     0     0     0     0     0
```

From the entire GSS dataset, there are 2,494 individuals who responded to the vocabulary words. Let's compare the apply function with the colSums function by using the rbenchmark package, which is a convenient wrapper around system.time. By default, it will perform 100 replications of the expression being tested, which should be sufficient for our purposes of comparing the speed of the two functions. The difference in elapsed times is impressive, with the colSums function producing almost a fivefold improvement. Sometimes a significant speed improvement is as simple as using a newer function designed for speed. There are also other ways to achieve speed increases, as we will discuss later:

```
> install.packages("rbenchmark")
> library(rbenchmark)
> benchmark(apply(vocab, 2, sum))
                   test replications elapsed relative user.self sys.self user.child sys.child
1 apply(vocab, 2, sum)          100    0.43        1      0.42        0         NA        NA
> benchmark(colSums(vocab))
                   test replications elapsed relative user.self sys.self user.child sys.child
1       colSums(vocab)          100    0.09        1       0.1        0         NA        NA
```

The sapply function applies a function to the elements in a list but returns the results in a vector, matrix, or a list. If the argument simplify = FALSE, sapply will return its results in a list, just as does the lapply function. If simplify = TRUE (which is the default), then sapply will return a simplified form of the results if that is possible. If the results are all single values, sapply will return a vector. If the results are all of the same length, sapply will return a matrix with a column for each element in the list to which the function was applied. Let's illustrate these two functions again, each of which avoids explicit looping. We will use an example similar to our previous one, in which we have three numeric vectors of different lengths combined into a list and then use the sapply and lapply functions to find the means for all three vectors:

```
> x1
[1] 55 47 51 54 53 47 45 44 46 50
> x2
[1] 56 57 63 69 60 57 68 57 58 56 67 56
> x3
[1] 68 63 60 71 76 67 67 78 69 69 66 63 78 72
> tests <- list (x1 , x2 , x3)
> tests
[[1]]
[1] 55 47 51 54 53 47 45 44 46 50

[[2]]
[1] 56 57 63 69 60 57 68 57 58 56 67 56

[[3]]
[1] 68 63 60 71 76 67 67 78 69 69 66 63 78 72
```

```
> sapply (tests , mean )
[1] 49.20000 60.33333 69.07143
> lapply (tests , mean )
[[1]]
[1] 49.2

[[2]]
[1] 60.33333

[[3]]
[1] 69.07143
```

Another very useful function is the tapply function, which applies a function to each cell of a ragged array. To demonstrate this function, assume that we have 20 students who have each studied either alone or in a study group, and each of whom was taught a different study method. The scores for the 20 students on a quiz may look like the following, with the factors as shown:

```
> QuizScores
   score approach group
1     80  method1 alone
2     80  method2 alone
3     76  method1 alone
4     79  method2 alone
5     80  method1 alone
6     81  method2 alone
7     83  method1 alone
8     72  method2 alone
9     83  method1 alone
10    77  method2 alone
11    73  method1 group
12    69  method2 group
13    66  method1 group
14    67  method2 group
15    70  method1 group
16    72  method2 group
17    76  method1 group
18    71  method2 group
19    71  method1 group
20    72  method2 group
```

We can use the tapply function to summarize the scores by the method used and by whether the student studied alone or in a group. We can also combine the two factors and find the means for each of the cells of a two-way table. To make our code a little easier to understand, let's attach the QuizScores data frame so that we can refer to the scores and the two factors directly. Without doing any statistical analyses, it appears that studying alone using method 1 may be a good strategy for maximizing one's quiz score:

```
> attach(QuizScores)
> tapply(score, approach, mean)
method1 method2
   75.8    74.0
```

```
> tapply(score, group, mean)
alone group
 79.1  70.7
> tapply (score, list(approach, group), mean)
        alone group
method1   80.4  71.2
method2   77.8  70.2
```

It's worth mentioning here that the aggregate function can be used to apply a function such as the mean to a combination of factors as well. For the quiz data, we can get a convenient summary by using aggregate as follows. We supply a "formula"—in this case, the score by the two factors—identify the data frame, and then identify the function. We get a slightly differently formatted result from that of tapply, although the results are identical:

```
> aggregate ( score ~ approach + group, data = QuizScores, mean)
  approach group score
1  method1 alone  80.4
2  method2 alone  77.8
3  method1 group  71.2
4  method2 group  70.2
```

4.3 If, If-Else, and ifelse() Statements

In addition to looping, we can use various forms of if statements to control the flow of our programs. The if statement is the simplest. If evaluates simply as:

```
if (condition) expression
```

The expression may be a single line of code, or it may be multiple statements (what the R documentation refers to as a compound statement) enclosed in braces. If the condition evaluates to TRUE, the expression is performed, and if the conditions evaluates to FALSE, the expression is not performed.

We can also use an if-else statement, which evaluates as follows. Expression1 is performed if the condition is TRUE, and expression2 is performed if the condition is FALSE:

```
if (condition) expression1 else expression2
```

There is also an ifelse function, which takes the form ifelse(test, yes, no). The test is the logical condition, "yes" is what is returned if the logical condition is TRUE and "no" is what is returned when the logical condition is false. As usual, examples make the use of these statements clearer.

An if statement leads to the evaluation of the expression if the condition is TRUE. Otherwise, the expression is not evaluated. For example, say we are conducting a hypothesis test with an alpha level of .05. We will reject the null hypothesis if the p-value is equal to or lower than .05, and will not reject the null hypothesis if the p-value is greater than .05. We can use an if statement to specify rejection of the null hypothesis, Note that in the second case, the condition is false because .051 is greater than .05, so nothing happens. We can make our function a little more flexible by specifying a default alpha level, which we can then change as necessary:

```
> rejectNull <- function(pValue, alpha = .05) {
+ if (pValue <= alpha) print("Reject Null")
+ }
```

```
> rejectNull(.05)
[1] "Reject Null"
> rejectNull (.051)
>
```

Adding an else condition covers both bases:

```
> rejectNull <- function(pValue, alpha = .05) {
+    if (pValue <= alpha) print("Reject Null")
+    else print ("Do not Reject")
+ }
> rejectNull (.07)
[1] "Do not Reject"
> rejectNull(.05)
[1] "Reject Null"
> rejectNull(.05, .01)
[1] "Do not Reject"
```

The ifelse function is quite interesting. For if and else statements, the condition must result in a single logical condition being TRUE or FALSE. If you supply a vector, only the first element will be evaluated. But the ifelse function works on vectors. Say we create a sequence of integers from –5 to + 5 and then attempt to take the square roots of the elements of the vector. This will return NaNs for all the negative numbers and will give us a warning. We can avoid the warning, extract the square roots of the non-negative numbers, and define the square roots of the negative numbers as NA all at once by using ifelse:

```
> x <- -5:5
> x
 [1] -5 -4 -3 -2 -1  0  1  2  3  4  5
> sqrt (x)
 [1]      NaN      NaN      NaN      NaN      NaN 0.000000 1.000000 1.414214
 [9] 1.732051 2.000000 2.236068
Warning message:
In sqrt(x) : NaNs produced

> sqrt(ifelse(x >= 0, x, NA))
 [1]       NA       NA       NA       NA       NA 0.000000 1.000000 1.414214
 [9] 1.732051 2.000000 2.236068
```

CHAPTER 5

■ ■ ■

Functional Programming

The longer one programs, the easier it becomes to think like a programmer. You learn that the best way to solve a problem is to solve it once in such a way that the adjustments you need to make when the problem changes slightly are very small ones. It is better to use variables and even other functions in your code so that you can change a single value once rather than many times. This is the essence of the pragmatic programmer who writes with purpose. Programmers who come to R from other languages such as C++ or Python tend to think in loops. You are probably convinced by now that R's vectorization allows us to avoid loops in many situations. As you saw in Chapter 4, looping is possible when it is needed. Efficient code allows us to automate as many tasks as we can so that we don't repeat ourselves, and to avoid looping as much as possible.

Soon after I started using R, I quickly decided I needed to be more systematic in my learning, and I bought a couple of books on R. The R documentation itself is adequate, but was often confusing and difficult to read on a computer screen. What I soon found was that R functions are also objects in their own right. As a general rule, we can say that every function has three components. These are the body of the function (the code inside the function), the formals (or arguments) that control how the function is called, and the environment, which you might think of as the location indicator of the function's variables.

One of the nicest things about R is its transparency. You can literally view any function simply by typing its name without any arguments. Here is the mad() function from the base version of R. You see that its environment is the stats package that is part of the base R implementation. When no environment is printed, this means the function was created in the global environment, that is, the current R session:

```
> mad
function (x, center = median (x), constant = 1.4826 , na.rm = FALSE ,
low = FALSE , high = FALSE )
{
if (na.rm)
x <- x[!is.na(x)]
n <- length (x)
constant * if (( low || high ) && n%%2 == 0) {
if ( low && high )
stop ("'low ' and 'high ' cannot be both TRUE ")
n2 <- n%/%2 + as. integer ( high )
sort ( abs (x - center ), partial = n2)[n2]
}
else median ( abs (x - center ))
}
<bytecode : 0 x00000000077b8458 >
< environment : namespace :stats >
```

Functions usually have names, but we can also use anonymous, or unnamed functions. We might use an anonymous function when there's no advantage to giving the function a name. For example, we could define a function to calculate the coefficient of variation, which is the ratio of the standard deviation to the mean. Say that we have no particular recurring use for this statistic but needed it for the displacement, gross horsepower, and rear axle ratio of the cars in our mtcars data. We could write an anonymous function as follows:

```
> sapply (mtcars [, 3:5], function (x) sd(x)/ mean (x))
      disp        hp       drat
0.5371779 0.4674077 0.1486638
```

Just as all R functions do, an anonymous function has formals, a body, and an environment:

```
> formals(function(x) sd(x)/mean(x))
$x
> body(function(x) sd(x)/mean(x))
sd(x)/mean (x)
> environment (function(x) sd(x)/mean(x))
< environment: R_GlobalEnv>
```

5.1 Scoping Rules

In R, scoping describes how R "looks up" the value of a symbol. If an "unknown" name is not defined in a function, R will look one level up, and keep doing so all the way up to the global environment. The same is true of functions. R will keep looking up from the current level until it gets to the global environment, and then begin looking in any packages loaded in the current workspace until it reaches the empty environment. Once the empty environment is reached, if R cannot find the value for a given symbol, an error is produced. This kind of scoping is one of the ways in which R is different from the original S language. R uses what is known as static or lexical scoping. A free variable is not a formal argument or a local variable, that is, assigned within the function body. Lexical scoping means that the values of a free variable are searched for within the environment in which the function was defined and then in the parent environment.

When we try to bind a value to a symbol in R, R searches through the series of environments, as described earlier. The search list can be found by use of the search function. The global environment (that is, the user's workspace) is always the first element of the search list (although a different environment may be first when the searching is done within a function within a package, rather than by the user). The base packages is always the last element of the search list, as shown below. The order of the packages in the search list is important because users are able to configure which packages are loaded at startup. When you load a new package with the library() or require() functions, that package is placed in the second position in the search list, and everything else moves down the list:

```
> search()
[1] ".GlobalEnv"        "tools:rstudio"     "package:stats"     "package:graphics"  "
    package:grDevices"  "package:utils "
[7] "package:datasets"  "package : methods " "Autoloads"        "package:base"
> library(swirl)
> search ()
```

```
[1] " GlobalEnv"        "package:swirl"   "tools:rstudio"    "package:stats"    "
    package:graphics"   "package:grDevices"
[7] "package:utils"     "package:datasets"  "package:methods"  "Autoloads"        "
    package:base"
```

Typically, we define functions within the global environment, so the values of free variables are located in the user's workspace. But in R, it is also possible to define a function within the body of another function, and to create functions that themselves create additional functions. The lexical scoping provided by R makes statistical computing easier. We call functions written by other functions "closures." If you will, they enclose, or encapsulate the environment of the parent function and can access its variables. This gives us the ability to have a parent level controlling operation, and a child function in which the actual work is done. Here, for example, is a function called take.root that defines another function, root. By assigning different values to n, we can take different roots, such as a square root or a cube root:

```
> take.root <- function(n) {
+   root <- function(x) {
+     x ^(1/n)
+   }
+   root
+ }
> square.root <- take.root(2)
> cube.root <- take.root(3)
> square.root(81)
[1] 9
> cube.root(27)
[1] 3
> ls(environment(square.root))
[1] "n"    "root"
> get ("n", environment(square.root))
[1] 2
> ls(environment(cube.root))
[1] "n"    "root"
> get("n", environment(cube.root))
[1] 3
```

5.2 Reserved Names and Syntactically Correct Names

The following words are reserved in R: if, else, repeat, while, function, for, in, next, break, TRUE, FALSE, NULL, Inf, NaN, NA, NA_integer_, NA_real_, NA_complex_, and NA_character_. In R, syntactically valid names consist of letters, numbers, and the dot or underline characters. Names must start with a letter or with a dot, which cannot be followed immediately by a number. The use of dots in function names could be for several different purposes. For example, visual separation can be accomplished by the use of dots or underscores, as in data.frame or is.na. Underlines can be used for the same purpose. Another use of the dot is to identify underlying functions of generic methods. Finally, we can "hide" internal functions or objects by beginning the name with a dot. This is only a partial obscurity, because we can ask for all names to be shown, as the following code shows. See that our object .y as well as the .getSymbols and .Random.seed functions are also "in" the R workspace but visible only when we ask to see everything:

```
> x <- 10
> .y <- 20
> ls ()
[1] "x"
> ls(all.names = TRUE)
[1] ".getSymbols"  ".Random.seed"  ".y"                "x"
```

5.3 Functions and Arguments

We create functions and store them as R objects. We must tell R we are creating a function by using the function() directive. In R, a function is a "first class object," meaning that it can be passed as an argument to another function, and functions can be nested (defined inside another function, as discussed earlier). Functions have arguments (also called parameters), and these can potentially have default values. Some functions do not have arguments at all, as in the BMI function we used in Chapter 3.

R matches the arguments in functions either by position, or by name. In particular, function arguments are matched in the following order:

1. check for an exact match for a named argument

2. check for a partial match

3. check for a positional match

R also uses "lazy" evaluation, which means that an argument is evaluated only when it is needed. For example, we can create a function with two arguments, one of which is not used, because the first argument is matched positionally. The following example illustrates. No error is produced, because the 10 matched x positionally. Note that supplying a value for y makes no difference, either, as it is not needed by the function. Our function does not set a default for x, so there can be some damaged ways to call the function. Note that in the last call to our function, we explicitly name x in the 'wrong' position. These examples, of course, are not meant to encourage bad programming practice but simply to illustrate the way R works. We will hope to produce effective and efficient functions rather than ones that capitalize on R's quirks:

```
> myFun <- function (x,y) {
+    print (x ^2)
+ }
> myFun (10)
[1] 100
> myFun (10 ,20)
[1] 100
> myFun(,10)
Error in print(x^2) : argument "x" is missing, with no default
> myFun(20,x=10)
[1] 100
```

5.4 Some Example Functions

In the following sections, I will show you a couple of examples of functions that I have written just for fun. The first is a function like the BMI function that we used earlier that queries for user input using the readline function, making the function interactive. As with the BMI function, it does not require arguments. The second is one that requires arguments, and we will examine in more detail how the arguments are evaluated.

5.4.1 Guess the Number

Here's a problem similar to one used in many programming classes and books. The computer "thinks" of a number, and the user guesses until he or she either gets the number right, or runs out of tries. Although R may not be the best language for writing such a function, it is possible, and we can see at work in the function many of the things we have talked about. We will use the uniform distribution to pick a number between 1 and 100, and then let the user determine how many guesses he or she wants. The function has no arguments, instead querying the user for a new guess if the number is either too high or too low. If the person guess the number, R reports that fact and tells the user how many tries it took. If the person does not guess the number, R tells the user he or she is out of tries and then reveals the number it was "thinking" about. We use the while loop rather than the for loop, because in this case we are not iterating through a vector, per se. It would of course be possible to rewrite this with a for loop based on the number of attempts. Note that the break statements halt the execution of the while loop when the person either guesses the number correctly or runs out of turns:

```
guessIt <- function(){
cat ("I am thinking of a number between 1 and 100","\n")
computerPicks <- as.integer(round(runif(1,1,100),0))
attempts <- as.integer(readline("How many guesses do you want? "))
count = 0
while (count < attempts){
count <- count + 1
  userGuess <- as.integer(readline("Enter your guess: "))
  if (count == attempts && userGuess != computerPicks) {
    cat("Sorry, out of tries. My number was ",computerPicks,"\n")
    break
    }
  if (userGuess == computerPicks) {
    cat("You got it in ", count, "tries.","\n")
   break
   }
  if (userGuess < computerPicks ) {
    cat("Your guess is too low.","\n")
    }
  if (userGuess > computerPicks){
    cat ("Your guess is too high.","\n")
    }
  }
}
```

Here's one of my attempts at guessing the correct number. I used the "splitting the difference" strategy, but there's a bit of luck involved as well. You can adjust the function in various ways to make it more interesting, for example by letting the user pick the lower and upper bounds. I set the counter to zero initially so that when R increments it, I get the correct number for the number of tries:

```
> guessIt ()
I am thinking of a number between 1 and 100
How many guesses do you want? 7
Enter your guess: 50
Your guess is too high.
Enter your guess: 25
Your guess is too high.
Enter your guess: 13
Your guess is too low.
Enter your guess: 17
Your guess is too low.
Enter your guess: 22
You got it in 5 tries.
```

5.4.2 A Function with Arguments

Many students learn the general quadratic formula in their algebra classes. Compared to other approaches to solving quadratic equations, the general formula has the advantage that it always works. As a reminder, here is the general quadratic formula:

$$x = \frac{-b - \sqrt{b^2 - 4ac}}{2a} \qquad (5.1)$$

The discriminant of a quadratic equation is the expression under the radical. If the discriminant is positive, the equation will have two real roots. If the discriminant is zero, the equation will have one (repeated) real root, and if the discriminant is negative, the equation will have two complex roots. Assume that we are interested only in real roots. Let's write a function to find the real root(s) of a quadratic equation. We will then test the function with different coefficients for a, b, and c to make sure that it works correctly:

```
> # function for finding the real root(s) of a quadratic equation
> quadratic <- function (a, b, c) {
+    discrim <- b^2 - 4*a*c
+    cat("The discriminant is: ", discrim, "\n")
+    if(discrim < 0){
+      cat("There are no real roots. ","\n")}else {
+    root1 <- (-b+ sqrt ( discrim )) / (2*a)
+    root2 <- (-b- sqrt ( discrim )) / (2*a)
+    cat("root1: ",  root1,   "\n")
+    cat("root2: ",  root2,   "\n")
+      }
+ }
```

```
> quadratic (2, -1, -8)
The discriminant is: 65
root1:  2.265564
root2:  -1.765564
> quadratic (1, -2, 1)
The discriminant is: 0
root1:  1
root2:  1
> quadratic (3, 2, 1)
The discriminant is: -8There are no real roots.
```

5.5 Classes and Methods

R supports various classes and methods. In particular, there are now three object-oriented systems that work in R: the S3 class, the S4 class, and the newer Reference Classes, called refclasses (previously talked about as R5 and also R6, an R package that implements simplified reference classes), which do not depend on S4 classes and the methods package. In this book, we will focus on some examples of S3 classes and methods. S4 classes and refclasses are more formal and typically only make sense in the context of larger programming projects, such as when developing an R package.

5.5.1 S3 Class and Method Example

To create an S3 class, we first form a list, and then we set the class attribute by using the class() or the attr() function. Say we are building a list of the donors to one of our favorite charities. Our list will include the person's name, gender, and the amount last donated.

First, our S3 class is as shown. We create the list, set the class attribute, and show the results by typing the object name:

```
> info <- list(name = "Jon", gender = "male", donation = 100)
> class(info) <- "member"
> attributes(info)
$ names
[1]  "name"     "gender"     "donation"

$ class
[1]  "member"

> print ( info )
$name
[1] "Jon"

$gender
[1] "male"

$donation
[1] 100

attr(,"class")
[1] "member"
```

When we have R print the object, it shows each the elements, data, and also reports the attributes, here the class we defined. It is not very pretty, because R does not have any special methods defined for the print() function to deal with an object of class member. However, using S3 classes and methods, it is easy to create a specific method for a generic function like print(). The generic way to define a method for a function in S3 classes is function.class(). In this case, our function is print() and our class is member, so we call the function, print.member() and define that. This gives us prettier results than before.

```
> print.member <- function(person) {
+   cat("Name: ", person $name , "\n")
+   cat("Gender: ", person $ gender, "\n")
+   cat("Donation: ", person $ donation, "\n")
+ }
> print ( info )
Name:    Jon
Gender:    male
Donation:    100
```

5.5.2 S3 Methods for Existing Classes

We can also write new S3 methods for existing classes. For example, again using the built in mtcars data, suppose we conducted an independent samples t-test comparing the miles per gallon for cars with manual versus automatic transmissions. We'll do more with t-tests later, for now, focus on the creation of the new method below:

```
> results <- t.test(mpg ~ am, data = mtcars)

> results

        Welch Two Sample t-test

data:  mpg by am
t = -3.7671, df = 18.332, p-value = 0.001374
alternative hypothesis: true difference in means is not equal to 0
95 percent confidence interval:
 -11.280194  -3.209684
sample estimates:
mean in group 0 mean in group 1
       17.14737        24.39231
```

R gives us nice text output, but what if we wanted to plot the results? Calling plot() on the t-test object does not give useful results.

```
> plot( results )
Error in xy.coords(x, y, xlabel, ylabel, log) :
  'x' is a list, but does not have components 'x' and 'y'
```

plot() does not work because there are no specific methods defined. To know this, first check the class of the t-test output, and then we can see if any plot() methods are defined for that class using the methods() function.

```
> class ( results )
[1] "htest"
> methods( plot )
 [1] plot.acf*              plot.correspondence*  plot.data.frame*
 [4] plot.decomposed.ts*    plot.default          plot.dendrogram*
 [7] plot.density*          plot.ecdf             plot.factor*
[10] plot.formula*          plot.function         plot.ggplot*
[13] plot.gtable*           plot.hclust*          plot.histogram*
[16] plot.HoltWinters*      plot.isoreg*          plot.lda*
[19] plot.lm*               plot.mca*             plot.medpolish*
[22] plot.mlm*              plot.ppr*             plot.prcomp*
[25] plot.princomp*         plot.profile*         plot.profile.nls*
[28] plot.ridgelm*          plot.spec*            plot.stepfun
[31] plot.stl*              plot.table*           plot.ts
[34] plot.tskernel*         plot.TukeyHSD*

Non-visible functions are asterisked
```

Since there is no plot.htest() function, no method is defined. Let's define a simple plot method for a t-test now. The plot method is designed to take an object, the results from a t-test, and has a second argument to control how many digits the p-value should be rounded to. We set a default value of 4, so that it will be rounded to four decimals if another value is not explicitly specified. Now we can again call plot()on our t-test results object, and this time we get a nice figure. Notice that even though we called our function plot.htest() we only have to call plot(), methods dispatching means that R looks for a specific version of plot that matches the class of the first argument, in our case, class htest with output shown in Figure 5-1. Using methods can be an easy way to write functions that help extend the functionality already available in R and from the numerous R packages available to fit your individual needs and workflow.

```
> plot.htest <- function(object, digits.to.round = 4) {
+
+    rounded.pvalue <- round(object$p.value, digits.to.round)
+
+    barplot(object$estimate,
+            ylim = c(0, max(object$estimate) * 1.1),
+            main = paste(object$method, "of", object$data.name),
+            sub = paste("p =", rounded.pvalue))
+ }
>
> plot( results )
```

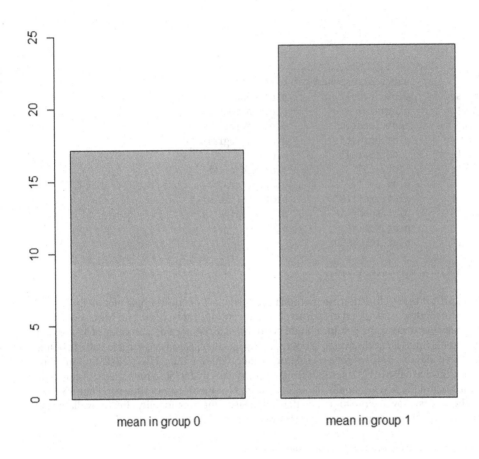

Figure 5-1. *S3 method plot rewrite graph*

■ ■ ■

Probability Distributions

In Chapter 6, you will learn how to use R for several important probability distributions. We cover the binomial distribution, the Poisson distribution, the normal distribution, the t distribution, the F distribution, and the chi-square distribution. R uses a standardized method for naming the functions associated with each of these, so that it is easy to remember them. We use the letters d (for density), p (for probability), q (for quantile), and r (for random) to preface the function, so for the normal distribution, dnorm returns the density, pnorm returns the probability associated with an area under the curve, qnorm returns the score associated with a given probability, and rnorm produces the desired number of randomly generated scores from a normal distribution with a given mean and standard deviation.

Probability distributions may be *discrete*, as in the case of the binomial and Poisson distributions, or they may be *continuous*, as in the case of the normal, t, F, and chi-square distributions. We will consider discrete probability distributions first.

6.1 Discrete Probability Distributions

Probability can be defined in different ways. For example, we can define the probability of receiving a heads on the flip of a fair coin as 1/2 or .50. This is the theoretical probability, because the sample space has two possible outcomes, and there is only one outcome resulting in heads. We could also wait until we have tossed the coin a number of times to determine how many heads we got as a proportion of the total number of tosses. This is an empirical probability. Specifically, the probability of an event, E, is the relative proportion of the number of times E occurs as a proportion of the total number of observed occurrences.

There are any number of discrete probability distributions. A discrete random variable can take on only clearly separated values, such as heads or tails, or the number of spots on a six-sided die. The categories must be mutually exclusive and exhaustive. Every event belongs to one and only one category, and the sum of the probabilities is 1. We can in general calculate the mean and variance of a discrete probability distribution as follows, though as you will see, we can often simplify the calculations for certain distributions. First, the mean of any discrete probability distribution can be computed by the following:

$$\mu = \sum \left[xP(x) \right] \tag{6.1}$$

The variance for a discrete probability distribution is calculated as follows:

$$\sigma^2 = \sum \left[(x - \mu)^2 P(x) \right] \tag{6.2}$$

6.2 The Binomial Distribution

Statisticians rely on the law of large numbers, which tells us that when we perform the same experiment a large number of times, the average of the results obtained from repeated trials (the empirical value) should be close to the expected (theoretical) value. The law of large numbers was first derived by Swiss mathematician Jacob Bernoulli, for whom the Bernoulli process is also named. A Bernoulli process is a finite or infinite sequence of independent random variables $X_1, X_2, X_3, \ldots$ such that for each i, the value of X_i is either 0 or 1. An obvious, if perhaps unimaginative, form of a Bernoulli process is a coin-flipping experiment. The extension of the Bernoulli process to more than two possible outcomes is known as the Bernoulli scheme (e.g., the possible outcomes of throwing a six-sided die).

The discrete binomial distribution is very useful for modeling processes in which the binary outcome can be either a success (1) or a failure (0). The random variable X is the number of successes in N independent trials, for each of which the probability of success, p, is the same. The number of successes can range from 0 to N. The expected value of k is $N p$, the number of trials times the probability of success on a given trial, and the variance of the binomial distribution is $N pq$, where $q = 1 - p$. We calculate the binomial probability as follows:

$$p(X = k \mid p, N) = \binom{N}{k} p^k (1-p)^{N-k} \qquad (6.3)$$

The binomial coefficient $\binom{N}{k}$ is not related to the fraction $\dfrac{N}{k}$, and it is often written $_nC_k$, read "N choose k." The binomial coefficient can be calculated as follows:

$$\binom{N}{k} = \frac{N!}{k!(N-k)!} \qquad (6.4)$$

We can use the choose() function in R to find a binomial coefficient, for example, the number of ways you can select six individual objects from a total of 10. Simply type choose(N, k), substituting the desired values:

```
> choose (10, 6)
[1] 210
```

We use the binomial distribution in many ways. In each case, the number of "successes" is counted, and we determine the probability of either an exact number of successes given n and p or the probability of a range of numbers of successes. As it materializes, the binomial distribution also gives us a good approximation of the normal distribution as the number of trials increases, and as the probability of success is close to .50. Here is a binomial distribution for the number of successes (heads) in 10 tosses of a fair coin, in which the probability of success for each independent trial is .50. We establish a vector of the number of successes (heads), which can range from 0 to 10, with 5 being the most likely value. The dbinom function produces a vector of values, but to make ours easier to read in a more customary tabular format, we use cbind again to create a matrix instead, changing the row names from the standard 1 to 11 to the more sensible 0 to 10 by using the rownames function.

```
> x <- 0:10
> x
 [1]  0  1  2  3  4  5  6  7  8  9  10
> binomCoinToss <- cbind(dbinom(x,  10, .50))
> rownames(binomCoinToss) <- x
> binomCoinToss
            [ ,1]
 0  0.0009765625
 1  0.0097656250
 2  0.0439453125
 3  0.1171875000
 4  0.2050781250
 5  0.2460937500
 6  0.2050781250
 7  0.1171875000
 8  0.0439453125
 9  0.0097656250
10  0.0009765625

> class(binomCoinToss)
[1] "matrix"
```

Careful examination reveals that the distribution is symmetrical, and a plot of the distribution against the values of x makes this clearer. The shape of the distribution is close to "normal looking," even though the binomial distribution is discrete, as shown in the probability mass function (PMF) in Figure 6-1. Here's how I plotted the PMF and added the points and the horizontal line for the x axis. Somewhat confusingly, the type = "h" plots *vertical* lines on the graph. According to the R documentation, the h is for "histogram like" or "high-density" vertical lines.

```
> binomDist <- dbinom (x, 10, 0.50)
> plot (x, binomDist, type = "h")
> points (x, binomDist)
> abline (h = 0)
> lines (x, binomDist)
```

The addition of lines to "connect the dots" makes it more obvious that the distribution is "normal" in appearance. We find that the binomial distribution serves as a good approximation of the normal distribution as the probability of success gets closer to .50 and as the number of trials increases.

Traditionally, statistics books provided tables of various quantiles of the binomial probability distribution. Modern texts depend on some form of tech (such as the built-in functions in R) to render the tables unnecessary. For example, if we want to know the probability of any exact number of successes, we can use the dbinom function, and if we are interested in finding the probability of a range of successes, we can use the pbinom function. For example, what is the probability of throwing 5 or fewer heads in our 10 tosses of a fair coin? We could calculate the individual probabilities for 0, 1, 2, 3, 4, and 5 and then add them up, and that would produce the correct answer, but it would be wasteful, as we can use pbinom for the same answer as follows. Note that when we change the default lower.tail = TRUE argument to lower.tail = FALSE, we are getting a right-tailed probability. It is important to note that for the pbinom function, the boundary value is included in the lower-tailed probability interval but excluded from the upper-tailed interval, as the following code illustrates. Adding the last two probabilities should produce 1, as 5 cannot "be" in both intervals.

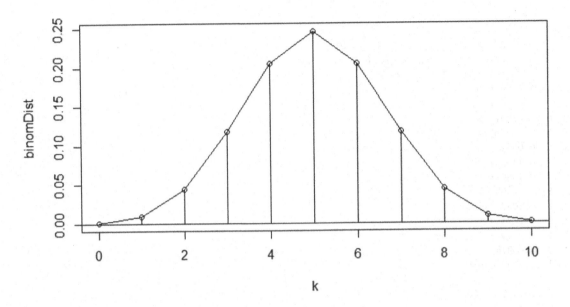

Figure 6-1. *Binomial distribution of the number of heads in 10 coin tosses*

```
> sum (dbinom(0:5, 10, .50))
[1] 0.6230469
> # calculate the probability k <= 5
> pbinom(5, 10, .50)
[1] 0.6230469
> # calculate the probability k > 5
> pbinom(5, 10, .50, lower.tail = FALSE)
[1] 0.3769531
```

The problem of whether to include the endpoint or not is important only with discrete probability distributions, because with continuous distributions, the probability of an exact point on the probability density curve is essentially zero.

Let us perform a simulation using the rbinom function to see how it works. We will also get an idea of whether the law of large numbers mentioned earlier can be demonstrated effectively. We will simulate the tossing of a fair coin 1,000 times, recording whether the coin is heads (1) or tails (0) for each coin toss. We will also plot the running average of the number of heads against the trial number. We can use the cumsum() function to keep track of the number of heads, as heads are 1s and tails are 0s, and then we can calculate the running averages as follows. We can then plot the proportion of heads over the series of trials and add a horizontal reference line at $p = .50$ (see Figure 6-2)

```
> tosses <- rbinom(1000, 1, .5)
> heads <- cumsum(tosses)/1:1000
> plot(heads, type = "l", main = "Proportion of Heads")
> abline (h = .5)
```

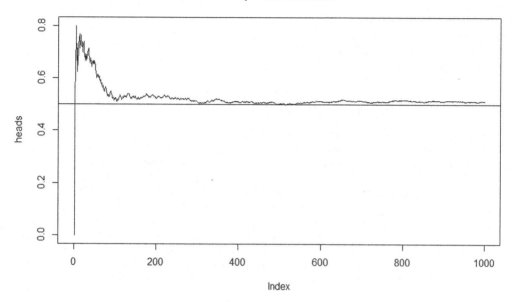

Figure 6-2. *Proportion of heads in 1,000 simulated coin tosses*

6.2.1 The Poisson Distribution

The Poisson distribution is a special case of the binomial distribution. We define success and failure in the usual way as 1 and 0, respectively, and as with the binomial distribution, the distinction is often arbitrary. For example, it makes little sense to talk about a hurricane or a work-related death as a "success." For that reason, we will change the word "success" to occurrence. The Poisson distribution, unlike the binomial distribution, has no theoretical upper bound on the number of occurrences that can happen within a given interval. We assume the number of occurrences in each interval is independent of the number of occurrences in any other interval. We also assume the probability that an occurrence will happen is the same for every interval. As the interval size decreases, we assume the probability of an occurrence in the interval becomes smaller. In the Poisson distribution, the count of the number of occurrences, X, can take on whole numbers 0, 1, 2, 3, ... The mean number of successes per unit of measure is the value μ. If k is any whole number 0 or greater, then

$$P(X=k)=\frac{e^{-\mu}\mu^{k}}{k!} \tag{6.5}$$

The variance of the Poisson distribution is also μ, and the standard deviation is therefore $\sqrt{\mu}$. As with the binomial distribution, we have the dpois, the ppois, the qpois, and the rpois functions.

As an example, the U.S. Bureau of Labor Statistics reported that in 2012, a year for which complete data are available, the number of work-related deaths per day averaged 12.7. Assuming the count of work-related deaths follows a Poisson distribution, what is the probability of exactly 10 deaths on a given day? What is the probability of 10 or fewer deaths in one day? What is the probability of more than 10 deaths in a day? Just as with the binomial distribution, the discrete Poisson distribution includes the boundary value in the lower-tailed probability and excludes it from the upper-tailed probability.

```
> dpois(10, 12.7)
[1] 0.09177708
> ppois(10, 12.7)
[1] 0.2783314
> ppois(10, 12.7, lower.tail = FALSE)
[1] 0.7216686
```

6.2.2 Some Other Discrete Distributions

In addition to the binomial and the Poisson distributions, there are other useful discrete probability distributions. The negative binomial distribution is one of these. Instead of determining the distribution of successes over a fixed number of trials, as we do in the binomial distribution, we determine the number of failures that are likely to occur before a target number of successes occur. The negative binomial distribution is built into R as well. A special case of the negative binomial distribution is the geometric distribution, which is the distribution of the number of failures that occur before the first success. As you would suspect, this distribution is built into R, too. The nice thing about the discrete probability distributions as well as the continuous probability distributions in R is that in a sense once you have learned one, you have learned them all, as the standardized function naming makes it easy to understand how to look up probabilities, how to find areas, and how to do reverse-lookups, that is, how to find the value associated with a given probability.

6.3 Continuous Probability Distributions

Continuous variables can take on any value within some specified range. Thus continuous probability functions plot a probability density function (PDF) instead of a discrete probability mass function (PMF). In contrast to discrete probability distributions, the probability of a single point on the curve is essentially zero, and we rarely examine such probabilities, rather focusing on areas under the curve. In statistics, the four most commonly used continuous probability distributions are the normal distribution and three other distributions theoretically related to the normal distribution, namely, the t distribution, the F distribution, and the chi-square distribution.

6.3.1 The Normal Distribution

The normal distribution serves as the backbone of modern statistics. As the distribution is continuous, we are usually interested in finding areas under the normal curve. In particular, we are often interested in left-tailed probabilities, right-tailed probabilities, and the area between two given scores on the normal distribution. There are any number of normal distributions, each for any non-zero value of σ, the population standard deviation, so we often find it convenient to work with the unit or standard normal distribution. The unit normal distribution has a mean of 0 (not to be confused in any way with a zero indicating the absence of a quantity), and a standard deviation of 1. The normal distribution is symmetrical and mound shaped, and its mean, mode, and median are all equal to 0. For any normal distribution, we can convert the distribution to the standard normal distribution as follows:

$$z = \frac{(x - \mu_x)}{\sigma_x} \tag{6.6}$$

which is often called z-scoring or standardizing. The empirical rule tells us that for mound-shaped symmetrical distributions like the standard normal distribution, about 68% of the observations will lie between plus and minus 1 standard deviation from the mean. Approximately 95% of the observations will lie within plus or minus 2 standard deviations, and about 99.7% of observations will lie within plus or minus 3 standard deviations. We can use the built-in functions for the normal distribution to see how accurately this empirical rule describes the normal distribution. We find the rule is quite accurate.

```
> pnorm(3) - pnorm(-3)
[1] 0.9973002
> pnorm(2) - pnorm(-2)
[1] 0.9544997
> pnorm(1) - pnorm(-1)
[1] 0.6826895
```

By subtracting the area to the left of the lower z score from the area to the left of the higher z score, we retain the area between the two scores. The qnorm function can be used to locate precise z scores that correspond to a given probability. For example, in statistics we commonly accept .05 or .01 as our standard for statistical significance. To find the critical values of z that will put half of the alpha level in the upper tail and half in the lower tail, we find the z score associated with a probability of $1 - \alpha/2$. Let's start with an alpha level of .05, and then find the critical values for .01 and .10 as well:

```
> qnorm(1 - .05/2)
[1] 1.959964
> qnorm(1 - .01/2)
[1] 2.575829
> qnorm(1 - .10/2)
[1] 1.644854
```

Of course, it is more direct just to type qnorm(.975), but the listing makes it obvious to the reader what we are really doing. These are standard critical values of z that can be found in any table of the standard normal distribution, but the advantage of R is that it makes such tables unnecessary, as we can find critical values more quickly and more accurately with technology than by reading printed tables. To prove the point, let's determine the area between z scores of +1.96 and -1.96 using our previous subtraction strategy. Indeed the area is almost exactly .95 or 95%.

```
> pnorm(1.96) - pnorm(-1.96)
[1] 0.9500042
```

If we are doing a one-tailed test, we place the entire alpha level in one tail of the standard normal distribution. Conducting a one-tailed test has the simultaneous effect of making the statistical test more powerful given that the results are in the hypothesized direction and making it technically inappropriate to talk about findings that are not in the hypothesized direction. The default for most statistical software is to perform a two-tailed test, but it is possible also to specify a left-tailed or a right-tailed test as well.

One of the most important applications of the normal distribution is its ability to describe the distributions of the means of samples from a population. The central limit theorem tells us that as the sample size increases, the distribution of sample means becomes more and more normal, regardless of the shape of the parent distribution. This is the statistical justification for using the normal distribution and theoretically related distributions such as the t, F, and chi-square distribution, for tests on means, proportions, and deviations from expectation.

The faithful dataset supplied in the base version of R shows the distributions of the duration of the eruptions of the Old Faithful geyser and the waiting times between eruptions (Figure 6-3). Both measurements are in minutes.

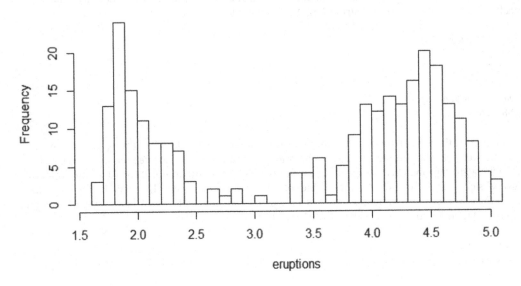

Figure 6-3. *Duration of eruptions of Old Faithful geyser*

Let us illustrate the central limit theorem (CLT) using this unusual dataset. We will first take samples of size 5 and calculate their means, and then we'll repeat the process with samples of size 20 for the sake of comparison. If the CLT is correct, the shape of the sampling distribution of means should approach a normal distribution as the sample size increases, even though the parent distribution is far from normal.

We take $N = 999$ samples of size 5 from the eruption data, calculating the mean for each sample, and saving the means using the `replicate()` function. The `replicate()` function runs R code (an expression) N times and is as if we typed and re-ran the code manually N times. We can then repeat the process with a sample size of 20. Using the `par()` function allows us to control the graphics output so that we can show the histograms with the sampling distributions of means for the two sample sizes in side-by-side comparison (see Figure 6-4).

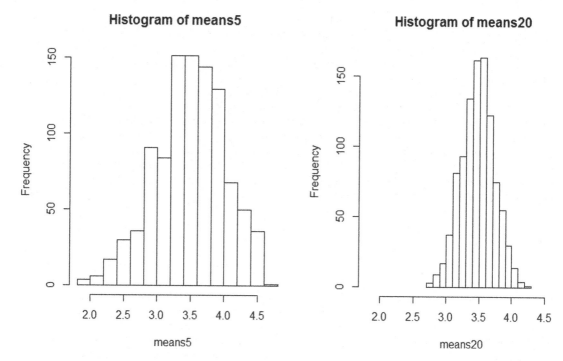

Figure 6-4. *Sample distributions of means for samples of size 5 and 20*

Observation of the histograms reveals two important things. First, the spread of the sample means is larger with small sample sizes. Second, as promised by the CLT, we see that as the sample size increases, the shape of the sampling distribution becomes more normal looking. This gives us the reassurance we need to rely on the normal distribution as a descriptor of the shape of sampling distributions of means, even from uniform distributions, skewed distributions, or even bimodal distributions like that of the eruption data.

```
> attach(faithful)

> sampsize5 <- 5
> means5 <- replicate(999, mean(sample(eruptions, sampsize5, replace = TRUE)))

> sampsize20 <- 20
> means20 <- replicate(999, mean(sample(eruptions, sampsize20, replace = TRUE)))
> par (mfrow=c(1,2))

> hist (means5, breaks = 15, xlim = c(1.8, 4.7))
> hist (means20, breaks = 15, xlim = c(1.8, 4.7))

> detach(faithful)
```

6.3.2 The *t* Distribution

Although the mathematical function for the PDF of the *t* distribution is quite different from that for the normal distribution, the *t* distribution approaches the normal distribution as the degrees of freedom increase. The degrees of freedom parameter is based on the sample size. The *t* distribution was developed as a way to examine the sampling distribution of means for small samples, and it works more effectively for that purpose than does the normal distribution.

Most statistical software programs, including R and SPSS, use the *t* distribution for calculating confidence intervals for means. As the examination of the listing reveals, the *t* distribution is definitely needed for small sample sizes, and it works adequately for large sample sizes. The normal distribution, on the other hand, is appropriate only for situations in which the population standard deviation is known or where the sample size is large.

If we were to develop a 95% confidence interval for the mean using the standard normal distribution, we would find that the critical values of ±1.96 would apply in all cases. With the *t* distribution, the critical values would vary with the degrees of freedom. Critical values of *t* for various one- and two-tailed hypothesis tests were once located in the backs of most statistics texts, but as with the other probability distributions, the tables are not necessary when one has access to R. The built-in functions for the *t* distribution work in the same way as those for the other probability distributions. We can determine the exact two-tailed probability or one-tailed probability for a given value of *t*, or the critical value for any one- or two-tailed hypothesis test. The critical values of *t* for a 95% confidence interval with 18 degrees of freedom are found as follows:

```
> qt(0.975, 18)
[1] 2.100922
```

To find a critical value for *t*, we must use the same strategy we use for the normal distribution. However, we must supply the degrees of freedom parameter as well. As with the normal distribution, we use the strategy of placing half of alpha in each tail of the *t* distribution for a two-tailed test or a confidence interval. With one-tailed tests, we place all of alpha in the upper or lower tail. For example, with a right-tailed test and 18 degrees of freedom, we find the critical value placing all of alpha in the right tail. Because the *y* axis never touches the *x* axis, there are no theoretical upper or lower bounds to the *t* or *z* distributions. In most programs or calculators one can substitute an arbitrarily large number such as ±999 for the lower or upper bound, as the *z* scores or *t* values at such extremes are essentially zero. R, however, provides the Inf and -Inf objects to represent positive and negative infinity. We see that indeed the value of 1.734 cuts off the upper 5% of the *t* distribution for 18 degrees of freedom from the lower 95%.

```
> qt (0.95, 18)
[1] 1.734064
> pt (1.734064, 18) - pt(-Inf, 18)
[1] 0.95
```

As mentioned earlier, the *t* distribution converges on the standard normal distribution as the degrees of freedom become larger, making the differences between the two smaller and smaller. Let us plot the standard normal distribution and then overlay the *t* distributions for 1, 4, and 9 degrees of freedom. We see that even with a sample size of 10, the *t* distribution becomes "normal looking" very quickly (see Figure 6-5).

```
xaxis <- seq(-4, 4, .05)
y <- dnorm(xaxis)
y1 <- dt(xaxis, 1)
y4 <- dt(xaxis, 4)
y9 <- dt(xaxis, 9)
plot(xaxis, y, type = "l")
lines(xaxis, y1, col = "purple")
lines(xaxis, y4, col = "red")
lines(xaxis, y9, col = "blue")
```

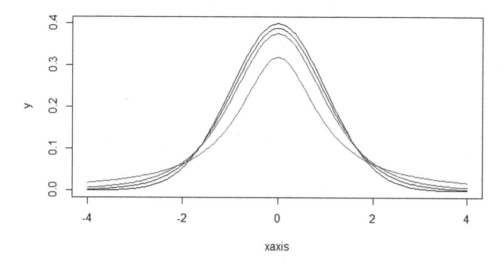

Figure 6-5. *Comparison of the standard normal and t distributions*

6.3.3 The *F* distribution

The *F* distribution, like the *t* distribution, has degrees of freedom, but in this case, because *F* is the ratio of two variances or variance estimates, there are degrees of freedom for both the numerator term and the denominator term. Again, traditionally, statistics textbooks included tables of critical values of *F* for varying combinations of degrees of freedom, but as before, these are found to be unnecessary when R or other technology is available and those tables are more and more likely to be found absent.

The *F* distribution is positively skewed, and for most purposes, we place the critical values in the upper tail by following the expedient of dividing the larger variance estimate by the smaller variance estimate, though it is entirely possible to have a left-tailed critical value of *F*. As the degrees of freedom increase, the *F* distribution become asymptotically normal. Let's produce *F* distributions for several combinations of degrees of freedom, using the ylim argument to specify the limits of the *y* axis:

```
> xaxis <- seq(0, 8, .05)
> y1 <- df(xaxis, 3, 5)
> y2 <- df(xaxis, 6, 10)
> y3 <- df(xaxis, 9, 20)
> y4 <- df(xaxis, 49, 49)
> plot(xaxis, y1, type = "l", xlab = "Value of F", main = "PDF of F Dist.",
  ylim = c(0, 1.5), col = "green")
> lines (xaxis, y2, col = "red")
> lines (xaxis, y3, col = "blue")
> lines (xaxis, y4, col = "purple")
```

The plot shows that as the degrees of freedom increase, the *F* distribution becomes more symmetrical and clusters around a value of 1 (see Figure 6-6). This is because when the null hypothesis is true that the variances being compared are equal, the value of the *F* ratio would be 1.

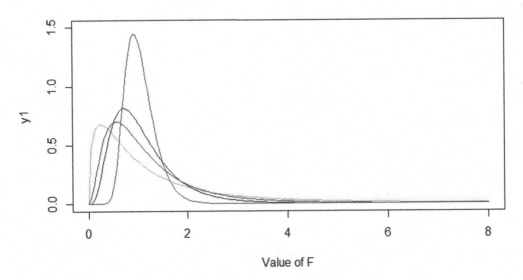

Figure 6-6. *The F distribution becomes more symmetrical as the degrees of freedom increase*

6.3.4 The Chi-Square Distribution

The chi-square distribution has one parameter, the degrees of freedom. We use the chi-square distribution for tests of frequency counts and cross- tabulations. The chi-square distribution is also very useful for tests involving model fit. Like the *F* distribution, the chi-square distribution is positively skewed. Figure 6-7 shows the chi-square distributions for varying degrees of freedom. We will discuss it in more detail in our chapters on graphics (Chapter 9) and data visualization (Chapter 17), but here I introduce the addition of text to a plot by use of the text function. I used the built-in locator() function to determine the (x, y) coordinates where I wanted the labels to be placed. The default is to center the label at the coordinate pair, but the adj = c(0,0) argument begins the label at the coordinate pair.

```
> xaxis <- seq(0, 20, .05)
> y1 <- dchisq(xaxis, 4)
> y2 <- dchisq(xaxis, 6)
> y3 <- dchisq(xaxis, 10)
> plot(xaxis, y1, type = "l", xlab = "Chi - square Value")
> lines(xaxis, y2, col = "blue")
> lines(xaxis, y3, col = "red")
> xcoords <- c(3.4, 5.75, 10.6)
> ycoords <- c(0.17, 0.13, 0.09)
> labels <- c("df = 4", "df = 6", "df = 10")
> text(xcoords, ycoords, labels, adj = c(0,0))
```

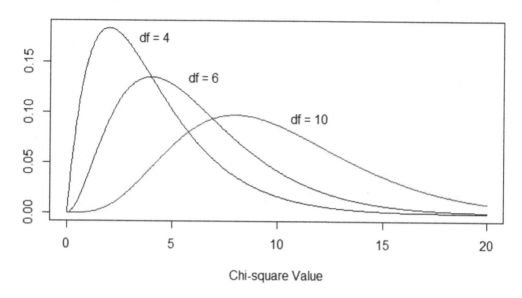

Figure 6-7. *The chi-square distribution also becomes more symmetrical as the degrees of freedom increase*

As with the *F* distribution, the chi-square distribution shifts rightward and becomes more mound shaped as the degrees of freedom increase. The mean of any chi-square distribution is equal to its degrees of freedom, and the mode is equal to the degrees of freedom minus 2.

The chi-square distribution is usually attributed to Karl Pearson in his development of tests of goodness of fit. In truth, Pearson independently rediscovered a distribution identified by German statistician Friedrich Robert Helmert a quarter-century earlier. Helmert described the chi-square distribution in relation to the distribution of the sample variance. Thus, the chi-square distribution can also be used in hypothesis tests and confidence intervals for the variance and standard deviation. With the assumption that a sample is drawn from a normal population, we can test the hypothesis that the population variance is equal to some specified value, σ^2, by calculating the following chi-square statistic:

$$\chi^2 = \frac{(n-1)s^2}{\sigma^2} \tag{6.7}$$

With a firm grasp on the most common discrete and continuous probability distributions, we are now ready to discuss the analysis of tables, including chi-square tests of both goodness of fit and independence, in Chapter 7.

■ **Note** In this chapter, we mentioned critical value(s) which may be equivalently used in null hypothesis testing in place of *p* value. Most modern introductory statistical textbooks have deemphasized critical value in favor of *p* value. There are even modern practitioners who choose not to use either as all-or-nothing rules to accept or reject the null hypothesis. In this text, we will limit ourselves to simply describing both critical and *p*-value R coding.

References

1. J. T. Roscoe, *Fundamental Research Statistics for the Behavioural Sciences*, 2nd ed. (New York: Holt, Rinehart & Winston, 1975).

CHAPTER 7

■ ■ ■

Working with Tables

Tables are very useful for summarizing data. We can use tables for all kinds of data, ranging from nominal to ratio. In Chapter 7, you will learn how to use tables to create frequency distributions and cross-tabulations as well as how to conduct chi-square tests to determine whether the frequencies are distributed according to some null hypothesis.

The table() function in R returns a contingency table, which is an object of class table, an array of integer values indicating the frequency of observations in each cell of the table. For a single vector, this will produce a simple frequency distribution. For two or more variables, we can have rows and columns, the most common of which will be a two-way contingency table. We can also have higher-order tables. For example, the HairEyeColor data included with R are in the form of a three-way table, as we see in the following code:

```
> data(HairEyeColor)
> HairEyeColor
, , Sex = Male
       Eye
Hair   Brown Blue Hazel Green
Black     32   11    10     3
Brown     53   50    25    15
Red       10   10     7     7
Blond      3   30     5     8
, , Sex = Female

       Eye
Hair   Brown Blue Hazel Green
Black     36    9     5     2
Brown     66   34    29    14
Red       16    7     7     7
Blond      4   64     5     8

> class(HairEyeColor)
[1] "table"
```

7.1 Working with One-Way Tables

For those who are not familiar with the terminology of a "one-way" table, it is a listing of the possible values for the variable being summarized and an adjacent list of the frequency of occurrence for each of the values. A table can summarize the counts for anything that can be considered or interpreted as a factor, and we can build tables from both raw data and summary data. For example, in an analysis we might perform on the hsb data we met in Chapter 3, I created categories for the math variable so they could be used as an ordinal factor. Figure 7-1 shows the original data.

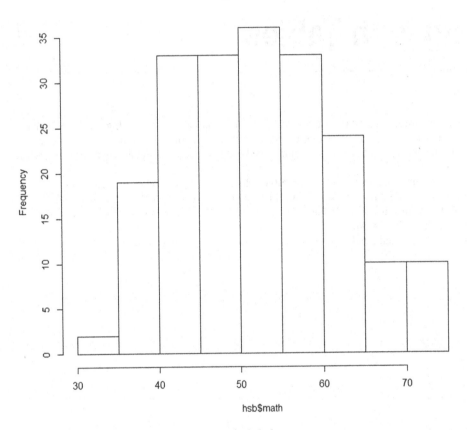

Figure 7-1. *Histogram of math scores from the hsb data*

The cut2 function in the Hmisc package makes it easy to create the new variable, and the table function shows that the groups are indeed roughly equal in size. Through a bit of experimentation, I found that a good choice was five math groups (I rather thought of the five American letter grades of ABCDF). I assigned an integer to represent each group by adding the as.numeric function. The g argument specifies the number of groups. Note that if you do not use a convenient label for the group membership, the cut2 function will provide the interval limits as labels.

```
> hsb <- read.csv ("http://www.ats.ucla.edu/stat/data/hsb.csv")
> install.packages("Hmisc")
> library(Hmisc)

> hsb$mathGp <- as.numeric(cut2(hsb$math, g = 5))
> head(hsb)
     id female race ses schtyp prog read write math science socst mathGp
```

1	70	0	4	1	1	1	57	52	41	47	57	1
2	121	1	4	2	1	3	68	59	53	63	61	3
3	86	0	4	3	1	1	44	33	54	58	31	3
4	141	0	4	3	1	3	63	44	47	53	56	2
5	172	0	4	2	1	2	47	52	57	53	61	4
6	113	0	4	2	1	2	44	52	51	63	61	3

```
> table(hsb$math)
```

```
33 35 37 38 39 40 41 42 43 44 45 46 47 48 49 50 51 52 53 54 55 56 57 58 59 60 61 62
 1  1  1  2  6 10  7  7  7  4  8  8  3  5 10  7  8  6  7 10  5  7 13  6  2  5  7  4
63 64 65 66 67 68 69 70 71 72 73 75
 5  5  3  4  2  1  2  1  4  3  1  2
```

```
> hsb$mathGp2 <- cut2(hsb$math, g = 5)
> head(hsb)
   id female race ses schtyp prog read write math science socst mathGp mathGp2
1  70      0    4   1      1    1   57    52   41      47    57      1 [33,44)
2 121      1    4   2      1    3   68    59   53      63    61      3 [50,56)
3  86      0    4   3      1    1   44    33   54      58    31      3 [50,56)
4 141      0    4   3      1    3   63    44   47      53    56      2 [44,50)
5 172      0    4   2      1    2   47    52   57      53    61      4 [56,62)
6 113      0    4   2      1    2   44    52   51      63    61      3 [50,56)
```

```
> table(hsb$mathGp2)
```

```
[33,44) [44,50) [50,56) [56,62) [62,75]
     42      38      43      40      37
```

Let's examine a table of the frequencies of the three different SES (socioeconomic status) levels in the hsb data. These vary substantially from level to level.

```
> table(hsb$ses)
```

```
 1  2  3
47 95 58
```

When we have observed frequencies in two or more categories, as in this example, we can perform a chi-square test of goodness of fit comparing the observed frequencies with the expected frequencies if each category had an equal number of observations. We can also test to see if an observed frequency distribution matches a theoretical one when the expected frequencies are not equal. With a total of k categories, the value of chi square is calculated as:

$$\chi^2 = \sum_{i=1}^{k} \frac{(O_i - E_i)^2}{E_i} \tag{7.1}$$

where O is the observed frequency in each cell and E is the expected frequency for that cell under the null hypothesis that the observed and expected frequencies are equal. As the deviations between the observed and expected frequencies become larger in absolute value, the value of chi square increases, and if the p value is lower than our specified alpha level, we reject the null hypothesis. Let's test to see if the SES levels are evenly distributed, adopting an alpha level of .01.

```
> chisq.test(table(hsb$ses))

        Chi-squared test for given probabilities

data:  table(hsb$ses)
X-squared = 18.97, df = 2, p-value = 7.598e-05
```

We reject the null hypothesis. Clearly, SES is distributed unequally. Note the degrees of freedom are the number of categories minus one. As indicated earlier, there is no particular reason the expected cell frequencies must be uniformly distributed. Chi-square tests of goodness of fit can be used to determine whether an observed frequency distribution departs significantly from a given theoretical distribution. The theoretical distribution could be uniform, but it might also be normal or some other shape.

We can use summary data in addition to tables for chi-square tests. For example, suppose we find that in a sample of 32 automobiles, there are 11 four-cylinder vehicles, 7 six-cylinder vehicles, and 14 eight-cylinder vehicles. We can create a vector with these numbers and use the chi-square test as before to determine if the number of cylinders is equally distributed.

```
> cylinders <- c(7, 11, 14)
> names(cylinders) <- c("four", "six", "eight")
> cylinders
four   six eight
   7    11    14
> chisq.test(cylinders)

Chi-squared test for given probabilities

data:  cylinders
X-squared = 2.3125, df = 2, p-value = 0.3147
```

The degrees of freedom, again, are based on the number of categories, not the sample size, but the sample size is still important. With larger samples, the deviations from expectation may be larger, making the chi-square test more powerful.

When the expected values are unequal, we must provide a vector of expected proportions under the null hypothesis in addition to observed values. Assume we took a random sample of 500 people in a given city and found their blood types to be distributed in the fashion shown in in Table 7-1. The expected proportions are based on the U.S. population values.

Table 7-1. *Distribution of ABO Blood Types*

Type	Prop.	Obs.	Exp.
O+	0.374	195	187.0
A+	0.357	165	178.5
B+	0.085	47	42.5
AB+	0.034	15	17.0
O-	0.066	30	33.0
A-	0.063	35	31.5
B-	0.015	8	7.5
AB-	0.006	5	3.0

Let us test the null hypothesis that the blood types in our city are distributed in accordance with those in the U.S. population using an alpha level of .05. Here is the chi-square test. Note we receive a warning that the value of chi square may be incorrect due to the low expected value in one cell.

```
> obs <- c(195, 165, 47, 15, 30, 35, 8, 5)
> exp <- c(0.374, 0.357, 0.085, 0.034, 0.066, 0.063, 0.015, 0.006)
> chisq.test(obs, p = exp)

Chi-squared test for given probabilities

data:    obs
X-squared = 4.1033, df = 7, p-value = 0.7678

Warning message:
In chisq.test(obs, p = exp) : Chi-squared approximation may be incorrect
```

On the basis of the p value of .768, we do not reject the null hypothesis, and we conclude that the blood types in our city are distributed in accordance with those in the population.

7.2 Working with Two-Way Tables

With two-way tables, we have r rows and c columns. To test the null hypothesis that the row and column categories are independent, we can calculate the value of chi square as follows:

$$\chi^2 = \sum_{j=1}^{c}\sum_{i=1}^{r} \frac{\left(O_{ij} - E_{ij}\right)^2}{E_{ij}}$$

(7.2)

The expected values under independence are calculated by multiplying each cell's marginal (row and column) totals and dividing their product by the overall number of observations. As with one-way tables, we can use the table function in R to summarize raw data or we can work with summaries we have already created or located.

The degrees of freedom for a chi-square test with two categorical variables is $(r-1)(c-1)$. The chi-square test for a two-by-two table will thus have 1 degree of freedom. In this special case, we are using the binomial distribution as a special case of the multinomial distribution, and the binomial distribution is being used to approximate the normal distribution. Because the binomial distribution is discrete and the normal distribution is continuous, as we discussed earlier in Chapter 6, we find that a correction factor for continuity improves the accuracy of the chi-square test. By default, R uses the Yates correction for continuity for this purpose.

Assume we have information concerning the frequency of migraine headaches among a sample of 120 females and 120 males. According to the Migraine Research Foundation, these headaches affect about 18% of adult women and 6% of adult men. We have already been given the summary data, so we can use it to build our table and perform our chi-square test as follows. Let's adopt the customary alpha level of .05.

```
> migraine <- matrix(c(19, 7, 101, 113), ncol = 2, byrow = TRUE)
> colnames(migraine) <- c("female", "male")
> rownames(migraine) <- c("migraine", "no migraine")
> migraine <- as.table(migraine)
> migraine
```

```
           female male
migraine       19    7
no migraine   101  113
```

```
> chisq.test(migraine)
```

Pearson's Chi-squared test with Yates' continuity correction

```
data:  migraine
X-squared = 5.2193, df = 1, p- value = 0.02234
```

As you see, we applied the Yates continuity correction. We reject the null hypothesis in favor of the alternative and conclude that there is an association between an adult's sex and his or her frequency of being a migraine sufferer.

It is also possible easily to use the table function to summarize raw data. For example, here is a cross-tabulation of the sexes and SES groups of the students in the hsb dataset. The chi-square test will now have 2 degrees of freedom because we have two rows and three columns. Let us determine if the sexes of the students are associated with the SES level, which we would hope would not be the case.

```
table(hsb$female, hsb$ses)
```

```
     1  2  3
  0 15 47 29
  1 32 48 29
> femaleSES <- table(hsb$female, hsb$ses)
> chisq.test(femaleSES)
```

Pearson's Chi-squared test

```
data:  femaleSES
X-squared = 4.5765, df = 2, p-value = 0.1014
```

I named the table just to reduce the clutter on the command line. As we see, we do not reject the null hypothesis, and we conclude the SES levels and student sex are independent.

CHAPTER 8

■ ■ ■

Descriptive Statistics and Exploratory Data Analysis

In Chapter 8, we look at both numerical summaries (what are known as descriptive statistics) and graphical summaries related to exploratory data analysis (EDA). We discuss the topic of graphics more generally in Chapter 9, and the related topic of data visualization later in our text.

Statistician John Tukey popularized exploratory data analysis in his 1977 book of the same name. To Tukey, there was exploratory data analysis (EDA) and confirmatory data analysis (CDA), much as we talk about exploratory and confirmatory factor analysis today. Before we do any kind of serious analysis, we should understand our data. Understanding the data involves letting the data tell their own story. Tukey presented a number of graphical and semi-graphical techniques for displaying important characteristics of data distributions. He also said once that "An approximate answer to the right problem is worth a good deal more than an exact answer to an approximate problem," a sentiment with which I find myself in total agreement. Tukey pointed out that numerical summaries of data focus on the expected values, while graphical summaries focus on the unexpected.

Tukey wrote something that sounds quite prescient almost 40 years later: "Even when every household has access to a computing system, it is unlikely that 'just what we would like to work with' will be easily enough available" (Tukey, 1977, p. 663).

8.1 Central Tendency

The three commonly reported measures of central tendency are the mean, the median, and the mode. R provides built-in functions for the mean and the median. The built-in R function called mode returns the storage class of an object. The prettyR package provides a function called Mode that returns the modal value of a dataset, if there is one. If there are multiple modes, prettyR will inform you of that fact, but will not identify the actual values. A table can be used for that purpose, however.

8.1.1 The Mean

The mean is technically correctly computed only for scale (interval or ratio) data, as the inequality of intervals for ordinal data make the mean inappropriate. In some cases, we do average ranks, as in certain nonparametric tests, but as a general rule, we should use only the mode or the median to describe the center of ordinal data. The mean for a population or a sample of data is defined as the sum of the data values divided by the number of values. When distinctions are necessary, we will use N to refer to the number of values in a population and n to refer to the number of values in a sample. If we need to identify sub-samples, we will use subscripts as in n_1 and n_2. The built-in function mean will determine the mean for a dataset. Remember if you have missing data, you must set na.rm = TRUE in order for the mean to be calculated.

In addition to being the most obvious measure of central tendency to most people, the mean has several statistical advantages. It uses information from every value in the dataset. It is used in the calculation of additional measures such as standard scores, the variance, and the standard deviation. Perhaps most important, the mean from a sample is an unbiased estimate of the population mean. We examined the distribution of sample means in Chapter 6, and found that with larger samples, the distribution of sample means becomes more normal in shape. The built-in function for the mean is simply mean(). For example, the mean reading score of the 200 students in the hsb dataset is 52.23:

```
> mean(hsb$read)
[1] 52.23
```

One disadvantage of the mean is its sensitivity to extreme values. Because every value in the dataset contributes to the value of the mean, extreme values "pull" the mean in their direction. Consider a very small sample of n = 3 where one person is unemployed, one earns in the mid five figures, and the third is a billionaire. The mean salary might be quite high in that case! The next measure we will discuss, the median, is more robust than the mean in this regard.

8.1.2 The Median

The median can be used with ordinal, interval, or ratio data. It is the value separating the dataset into halves. The upper half of the data contains values greater than the median, and the lower half contains values lower than the median. The median is also called the second quartile and the 50th percentile. There is intuitive appeal in a middle value dividing the distribution, and the median may be a better index of central tendency than the mean when the data are skewed.

We can locate the median in any set of data by sorting the data from lowest to highest, and finding the value located at the position $(n + 1)/2$ in the ordered data. If there are an odd number of values in the data, the median will be the observed middle value. If there are an even number of data values, the median is computed as the mean of the two middle values. Depending on the actual values in the data, the median may thus be either an observed value or an imputed value. In either case, the median is always the midpoint of the dataset.

As mentioned earlier, the median is insensitive to extreme values. We base its value only on the middle one or two data points. When the data distribution is skewed, the median is often more appropriate than the mean in describing the center of the data. The built-in function is median. Let us find the median value of the reading scores.

```
> median(hsb$read)
[1] 50
```

The fact that the median is lower than the mean of these data indicates that the data are likely to be positively skewed. Let's create a histogram of the reading score data, and use the abline function to draw vertical lines at the positions of the mean and the median to demonstrate this. We will represent the mean with a heavy dashed line using the lwd = 2 argument to control line width, and the lty = 2 argument to control line width. We represent the median with a heavy solid blue line using the col = "blue" argument.

```
> hist(hsb$read)
> abline(v = mean(hsb$read), lty = 2, lwd = 2)
> abline(v = median(hsb$read), col = "blue", lwd = 2)
```

The completed histogram with the vertical lines added is shown in Figure 8-1. As expected, the data are positively skewed, and the high scores exert an influence on the mean, which is pulled in the direction of the skew.

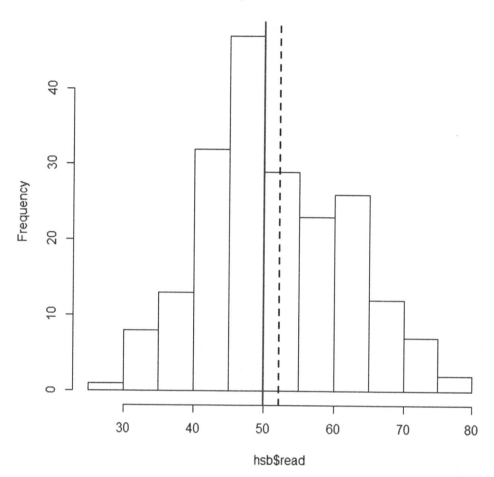

Figure 8-1. *The mean is influenced by extreme values*

8.1.3 The Mode

The mode can be found simply by identifying the most frequently occurring value or values in a dataset. Some datasets have no value that repeats, while other data sets may have multiple modes. Recall the geyser eruption data we used in Chapter 6 to illustrate the central limit theorem were bimodal in nature.

R's built-in mode function returns the storage class of the R object. As we mentioned earlier, the prettyR function Mode will return the mode of a dataset if there is one, but will simply inform you if there are multiple modes. See the following code listing for more details on mode versus Mode.

```
> install.packages("prettyR")
> library(prettyR)
> mode(hsb$read)
[1] "numeric"
> Mode(hsb$read)
[1] "47"

> Mode(mtcars$hp)
[1] ">1 mode"
```

Among many other uses, the table function can be used to identify the values of multiple modes. Using the sort function makes it more obvious which values are the modes. It is convenient to sort the table in descending order – note that the top number is the raw data value and the lower number is the count of how many times that data value shows. Here we have three modes (that show up three times each) of 110, 175, and 180. I've added some spaces for better readability:

```
> sort(table(mtcars$hp), decreasing = TRUE)

110 175 180  66 123 150 245  52  62  65  91  93  95  97 105 109 113 205 215 230
  3   3   3   2   2   2   2   1   1   1   1   1   1   1   1   1   1   1   1   1

264 335
  1   1
```

8.2 Variability

Three common measures of variability are the range, the variance, and the standard deviation. Each has a built-in function in R. The range function returns the minimum and maximum values, so if you want the actual range, you must subtract the minimum from the maximum. The variance function is var, and the standard deviation function is sd.

8.2.1 The Range

The range is easy to compute, requiring the identification of only the maximum and minimum values. It is also intuitively easy to grasp as a measure of how closely together or widely apart the data values are. However, the range is also less informative than other measures of variability in that it tells us nothing else about the data regarding its shape or the nature of the variability. Let us examine the range of the students' reading scores:

```
> range(hsb$read)
[1] 28 76
> max(hsb$read) - min(hsb$read)
[1] 48
```

8.2.2 The Variance and Standard Deviation

The population variance is defined as the average of the squared deviations of the raw data from the population mean:

$$\sigma^2 = \frac{\sum(x-\mu)^2}{N} \tag{8.1}$$

When dealing with sample data, we calculate the variance as shown in equation (8.2). The $n-1$ correction makes the sample value an unbiased estimate of the population variance

$$s^2 = \frac{\sum(x-\bar{x})^2}{n-1} \tag{8.2}$$

where n represents the size of the sample. R's var function returns the variance treating the dataset as a sample, and the sd function returns the sample standard deviation. If you want to treat the dataset as a population, you must adjust these estimates accordingly.

The variance expresses the dispersion in a dataset in squared terms, and as such changes the units of measurement from the original units. Taking the square root of the variance returns the index to the original units of measure. The standard deviation was conceived by Francis Galton in the late 1860's as a standardized index of normal variability.

Examine the use of the built-in functions for the variance and standard deviation of the students' reading and mathematics scores:

```
> var(hsb$read)
[1] 105.1227
> sd(hsb$read)
[1] 10.25294

> var(hsb$math)
[1] 87.76781
> sd(hsb$math)
[1] 9.368448
```

The coefficient of variation (cv) is the ratio of the standard deviation to the mean. For ratio measures, this index provides a standardized index of dispersion for a probability or frequency distribution. We can write a simple function to calculate the cv.

```
> cv <- function(x){
+    cv <- (sd(x)/mean(x))
+    return (cv)
+ }

> cv(mtcars$wt)
[1] 0.3041285

> cv(mtcars$qsec)
[1] 0.1001159
```

8.3 Boxplots and Stem-and-Leaf Displays

Tukey popularized the five-number summary of a dataset. We used the summary() function in Chapter 2 as a way to summarize sample data. As you may recall, this summary adds the mean to the Tukey five-number summary, providing the values of the minimum, the first quartile, the median, the mean, the third quartile, and the maximum. As a refresher, here is the six-number summary of the math scores for the 200 students in the hsb dataset.

```
> summary(hsb$math)
   Min. 1st Qu.  Median    Mean 3rd Qu.    Max.
  33.00   45.00   52.00   52.64   59.00   75.00
```

Tukey conceived of a graphical presentation of the five number summary that he called the box-and-whiskers plot. Today this is more commonly known as the boxplot. The boxplot function in the base R graphics package is quite adequate. The box is drawn around the middle 50% of the data, from the first quartile to the third quartile. The whiskers extend from the first and third quartiles toward the minimum and the maximum, respectively. Values beyond 3/2 of the interquartile range (the difference between the third and first quartile) are considered outliers, and are represented by circles. The command to produce the boxplot is boxplot(hsb$math). The completed boxplot is shown in Figure 8-2.

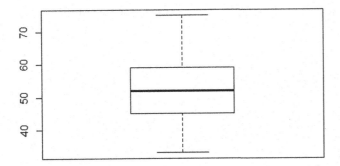

Figure 8-2. *Boxplot of the math scores of 200 students*

Examining the graphical representation of the five-number summary tells a good bit about the data. The location of the median in the box and the relative size of the whiskers tell us whether the distribution is more symmetrical or skewed. When the median is close to the center of the box, and the whiskers are roughly equal in size, the data distribution is more likely to be symmetrical, although these data are not quite symmetrical (the whiskers are not the same length). In Chapter 9, we will begin to use the excellent ggplot2 package written by Hadley Wickham. One of the nice features of ggplot2 is the ability to produce very attractive side-by-side boxplots.

The stem-and-leaf display is a semi-graphical technique suitable for smaller datasets. Stem-and-leaf displays, also called stem plots, are actually displayed in the R console rather than in the R Graphics device. The stems are the leading digits and the leaves are the trailing digits. Using the mtcars dataset provided with R, let us develop a stem-and-leaf display of the miles per gallon:

```
> data(mtcars)
> stem(mtcars$mpg)
```

```
The decimal point is at the |
10 | 44
12 | 3
14 | 3702258
16 | 438
18 | 17227
20 | 00445
22 | 88
24 | 4
26 | 03
28 |
30 | 44
32 | 49
```

The stem-and-leaf display has the advantage that every data point is shown. The display resembles a simple frequency distribution, but provides additional information. For larger datasets, such displays are less helpful than histograms or other visual representations of the data.

8.4 Using the fBasics Package for Summary Statistics

The contributed package fBasics provides a particularly thorough function for descriptive statistics called basicStats. Apart from the mode, this package provides an excellent statistical summary of a vector of data. Here is the use of the basicStats function with the students' math scores.

```
> install.packages ("fBasics")
> library(fBasics)
> basicStats(hsb$math)
              X..hsb.math
nobs           200.000000
NAs              0.000000
Minimum         33.000000
Maximum         75.000000
1. Quartile     45.000000
3. Quartile     59.000000
Mean            52.645000
Median          52.000000
Sum          10529.000000
SE Mean          0.662449
LCL Mean        51.338679
UCL Mean        53.951321
Variance        87.767814
Stdev            9.368448
Skewness         0.282281
Kurtosis        -0.685995
```

References

Chambers, J. M. (2008). *Software for data analysis: Programming in r.* New York, NY: Springer. Hunt, A., & Thomas, D. (1999). *The pragmatic programmer: From journeyman to master.* Reading, MA: Addison Wesley.

Micceri, T. (1989). The unicorn, the normal curve, and other improbable creatures. *Psychological Bulletin, 105* , 156-166.

Ohri, A. (2014). *R for cloud computing: An approach for data scientists.* New York, NY: Springer.

Pace, L. A. (2012). *Beginning R: An introduction to statistical programming.* New York, NY: Apress.

Roscoe, J. T. (1975). *Fundamental research statistics for the behavioral sciences* (2nd ed.). New York, NY: Holt, Rinehart and Winston.

Tukey, J. W. (1977). *Exploratory data analysis.* Reading, MA: Addison Wesley.

University of California, Los Angeles. (2015). *Resources to help you learn and use R.* Retrieved from `http://www.ats.ucla.edu/stat/r/`

Wilkinson, L. (2005). *The grammar of graphics* (2nd ed.). New York, NY: Springer.

CHAPTER 9

■ ■ ■

Working with Graphics

We have obviously been working with graphics since the beginning of this book, as it is not easy to separate statistics and graphics, and perhaps it is impossible to do so. In Chapter 9, we will fill in some gaps and introduce the ggplot2 package as an effective alternative to the graphics package distributed with R.[1]

The ggplot2 package takes some adjustment in one's thinking, as it works very differently from the graphics commands in base R. The payoff is that it can produce beautiful, even stunning, graphics. Although we will occasionally return to the base R's graphics package, we will accomplish the majority of what we do from here on with ggplot2.

To paraphrase John Tukey, descriptive numerical indexes help us see the expected in a set of numbers, but graphics help us see the unexpected. In Chapter 9, we will tie graphics to the visual revelation of data in traditional ways. Later we will broaden the discussion to data visualization and include maps and other ways to allow users to derive meaning and information beyond the traditional graphs and plots.

9.1 Creating Effective Graphics

Graphics can be informative or misleading. Over many years, Yale professor emeritus Edward Tufte has championed the effective visual display of information. Tufte is a statistician and an artist, so his books are worth studying for those who would like to learn and observe the principles of excellent graphical design.[2]

Tufte provides the following principles for good graphics. Graphical displays should

- show the data

- induce the viewer to think about substance rather than methodology, graphic design, the technology of graphic production, or something else

- avoid distorting what the data have to say

- present many numbers in a small space

  - make large datasets coherent

  - encourage the eye to compare different pieces of data

  - reveal the data at several levels of detail, from a broad overview to the fine structure

  - serve a reasonably clear purpose: description, exploration, tabulation, or decoration

  - be closely integrated with the statistical and verbal descriptions of a data set.[1]

---

[1]Edward R. Tufte, *The Visual Display of Quantitative Information* (Columbia, MD: Graphic Press, 2001), at 13.

In addition to Tufte's excellent principles, I will add that it is inappropriate to add three-dimensional effects to two-dimensional graphs, as that introduces both confusion and a false third dimension. Certain packages such as Microsoft Excel will readily allow you to make 3-D bar plots and pie charts, but only data with three actual dimensions should be plotted as such.

9.2 Graphing Nominal and Ordinal Data

Data that are categorical in nature should be represented in bar plots rather than histograms. The visual separation of the bars corresponds to the discrete nature of the categories. Pie charts can also be used to display the relative frequencies or proportions of nominal and ordinal data, but the pie chart is often maligned. Research at Bell Labs indicated that humans are more easily able to judge relative length than relative area, and thus bar plots (also called bar charts) are typically more informative than pie charts. Pie charts are available in base R graphics but not in ggplot2. Bar plots are available in both. In addition to plotting the frequencies for categorical variables, bar plots are also useful for summarizing quantitative data for two or more factors in what are known as clustered bar plots.

The default in base R for the pie chart is a pastel color palette. To produce a pie chart is simple in base R. We will use socioeconomic status (SES) in our hsb data for that purpose; these data record 1 (low), 2 (medium), and 3 (high) SES. First, we will summarize the data using the table function, and then we will produce the pie chart from the table. The completed pie chart appears in Figure 9-1.

```
> ses <- table ( hsb $ ses )
> pie ( ses , main = " Pie Chart ")
```

Pie Chart

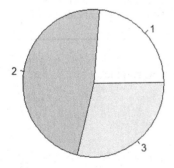

Figure 9-1. *Pie chart of the three levels of student SES*

As an exercise, without looking further at the table or the actual data, try to estimate the relative percentages of the three levels. We will now produce a bar plot using ggplot2. As mentioned, ggplot2 requires a different approach from that of base R. In particular, ggplot2 makes use of *geometric objects* (abbreviated as geom in their source code) and *aesthetics* (abbreviated as aes in their source code). To make the bar plot in ggplot2, we must identify our data source; the variable to summarize; and the type of geometric object that should be used to represent the data, in this case, bars so we use the geometric object bar or, in code, geom_bar(). See that you can build up the plot sequentially and then produce it by typing the name you have given the list. The completed bar plot appears in Figure 9-2. Most people would find it easier to estimate the relative percentages from the length of the bars rather than from relative areas in a pie chart. Notice that we add the factor(ses) command to treat the numeric levels as factors. This would not be required if the three levels were listed as text (e.g., low, medium, and high).

```
> library ( ggplot2 )
> bar <- ggplot ( hsb , aes (x = ses )) + geom_bar()
> bar
```

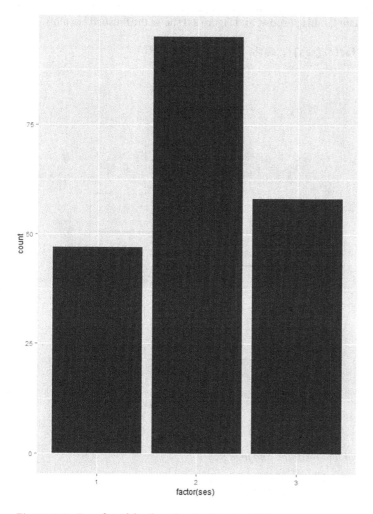

Figure 9-2. *Bar plot of the three levels of student SES*

9.3 Graphing Scale Data

Scale data (interval and ratio) lend themselves to many more kinds of graphics than do nominal and ordinal data. We can generate boxplots, histograms, dotplots, smooth density plots, frequency polygons, scatterplots, and other graphical representations of one or more quantitative variables. We discussed the boxplot in Chapter 8, and we used the base version of R to produce a serviceable boxplot. The boxplot geom in ggplot2 is designed to use a factor with two or more levels to produce side-by-side boxplots, and it is quite good for that purpose. With a little adjustment of the parameters, you can also make an attractive boxplot for a single variable in ggplot2. For that purpose, you would have to use a theme in which certain elements are blank. We will look at the side-by-side boxplots first, and then at how to make a boxplot for a single variable should we need to do that.

9.3.1 Boxplots Revisited

Let's produce side-by-side boxplots of the math scores of the students from the three different SESs. The position of the variable in the aesthetic identifies it as x or y on the plot, so you can omit those labels in most cases. The defaults in ggplot2 are adequate for this purpose, and Figure 9-3 shows the finished boxplots.

```
> boxplots <- ggplot ( hsb , aes( factor(ses) , math )) + geom_boxplot()
> boxplots
```

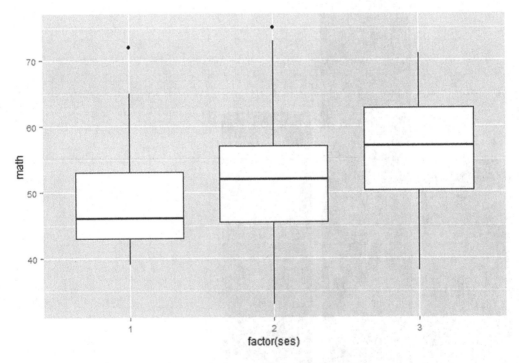

Figure 9-3. *Boxplots of the math scores for low, medium, and high SES*

Although it is a little extra work, we can make a boxplot for a single variable in ggplot2. Let us use a different dataset for some variety. We will use the cars data from the openintro package.

```
> install.packages ("openintro")
> library ( openintro )
> head ( cars )
    type price mpgCity driveTrain passengers weight
1   small  15.9      25      front          5   2705
2 midsize  33.9      18      front          5   3560
3 midsize  37.7      19      front          6   3405
4 midsize  30.0      22       rear          4   3640
5 midsize  15.7      22      front          6   2880
6   large  20.8      19      front          6   3470
```

Recall our discussion of the fact that ggplot2 is designed to use factors for the x axis. When we have a single variable, we must provide a fake x factor. We can remove unwanted x axis labeling by using a theme with element blank() for the axis title, text, and tick marks. Let's do this for the mpgCity variable, again building up the graphic in steps.

```
> mpgBox <- ggplot (cars , aes( factor(0) , mpgCity )) + geom_boxplot()
> mpgBox <- mpgBox + theme ( axis.title.x = element_blank() , axis.text.x = element_blank (),
                             axis.ticks.x = element_blank())
> mpgBox
```

Figure 9-4 shows the completed boxplot. The appearance is slightly different from that of the boxplot we produced using the graphics package in base R.

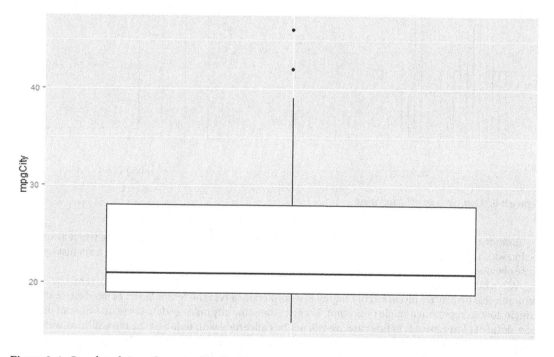

Figure 9-4. *Boxplot of city miles per gallon for 54 cars*

9.3.2 Histograms and Dotplots

In ggplot2, the default is to create histograms with the bins set to the range of the data divided by 30. For larger datasets, this default may be appropriate, but for smaller datasets, it is unlikely to be the best choice. Let's continue with the city MPG data from the cars dataset and create a histogram using the defaults, and then adjust the bin width to something more reasonable. The default number of bins is clearly too many for a dataset with only 54 observations. We can adjust the bin width and change the bars to white bars with black borders by changing our options in ggplot2. In the base version of R, one can use the par() function to create multiple plots in the same graphic viewer window. The ggplot2 package uses a different strategy, including facets for multiple plots (rows or matrices) of plots for similar variables. When the plots are potentially unrelated, we can use the grid.arrange() function from the gridExtra package to easily combine multiple ggplot2 graphs into one. We will create one histogram with the default bin width, and another with a bin width of 5, and then display them side by side (see Figure 9-5 for the finished plots).

```
> install.packages ("gridExtra")
> library ( gridExtra )
> myHist1 <- ggplot (cars , aes ( mpgCity )) + geom_histogram ( fill = " white ", color = "black ")
> myHist2 <- ggplot (cars , aes ( mpgCity )) + geom_histogram ( binwidth = 5, fill = "white",
                                                                color = " black ")
> grid.arrange(myHist1, myHist2, ncol = 2)
stat_bin: binwidth defaulted to range/30. Use 'binwidth = x' to adjust this.
```

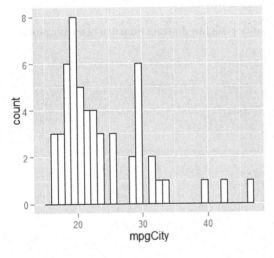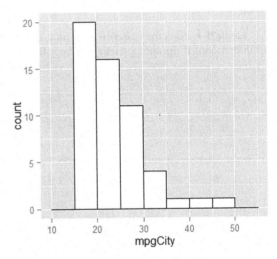

Figure 9-5. *Comparison of histograms*

Examination of the side-by-side plots reveals that the default produced too many bars, whereas setting the bin width to 5 made the histogram more effective. The data are clearly right skewed, as both histograms make obvious.

When datasets are relatively small, a dotplot can be an effective alternative to the histogram. Like the stem-and-leaf display we discussed in Chapter 8, a dotplot preserves the "granularity" of the data, so that a single dot can represent a single data point. Let's use the same city mileage data to create a dotplot using geom_dotplot() in ggplot2. In this case, we will not be concerned with reducing the bin width, as we would want each bin to represent a single data value. We use the table function discussed in Chapter 7 to create a frequency distribution of the data, in order to compare that distribution with the dotplot.

```
> table ( cars $ mpgCity )

16 17 18 19 20 21 22 23 25 28 29 31 32 33 39 42 46
 3  3  6  8  5  4  4  3  3  2  6  2  1  1  1  1  1
> dot <- ggplot (cars , aes ( mpgCity )) + geom_dotplot ()
> dot
stat _ bindot : binwidth defaulted to range / 30. Use 'binwidth = x' to adjust this
```

Figure 9-6 shows the dotplot. As you can see, the dotplot resembles a simple frequency histogram, with each dot representing a single data point. The numbers on the y axis for dotplots are not meaningful in ggplot2.

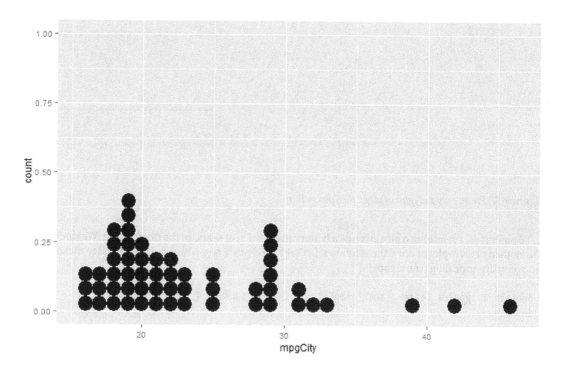

Figure 9-6. *Dotplot of city miles per gallon*

9.3.3 Frequency Polygons and Smoothed Density Plots

A frequency polygon is a type of line graph in which straight-line segments are used to connect the frequencies of data values. Best practice is to anchor such plots to the x axis of the plot rather than having them "float" above the axis, as some statistical software packages do. In ggplot2, geom_freqpoly() is used to produce frequency polygons. We will revert to the bin width of 5 to make the frequency polygon more useful to the reader. Continuing with the city miles per gallon data, we have the following commands to produce the frequency polygon shown in Figure 9-7.

```
> polygon <- ggplot (cars , aes ( mpgCity )) + geom_freqpoly ( binwidth = 5)
> polygon
```

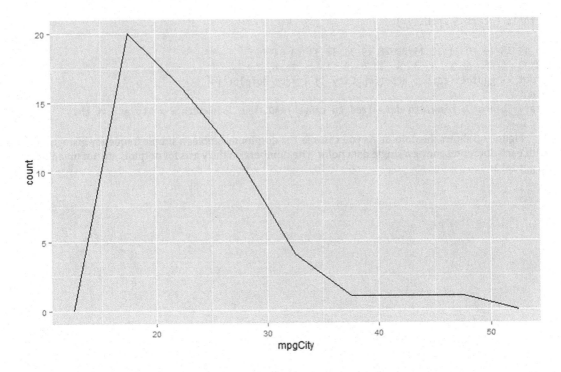

Figure 9-7. *Frequency polygon of city miles per gallon*

Sometimes, smoothing a plot gives us a better idea of the real shape of the distribution. We can create a smoothed density plot of our data as follows. Let's fill the density plot with a gray color just to make it a bit more visually appealing (see Figure 9-8).

```
> density <- ggplot (cars , aes ( mpgCity )) + geom_density ( fill = " gray ")
> density
```

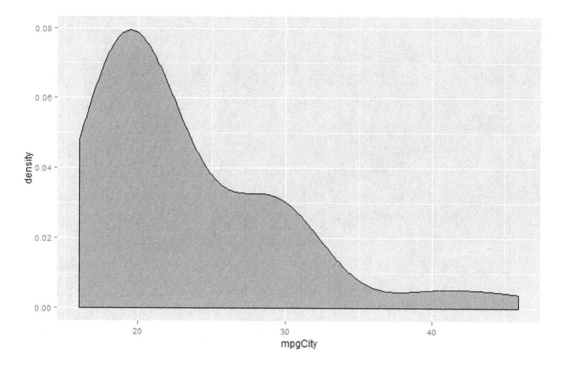

Figure 9-8. *Smoothed density plot of city miles per gallon*

9.3.4 Graphing Bivariate Data

Up to this point, we have been working mostly with a single variable at a time, or with different levels of the same variable used as factors. Often, we have the opportunity to explore the relationships among and between two or more variables, and graphical visualizations of such data are quite helpful. We will limit ourselves here to bivariate data, but you should be aware that R can produce both 2-D and 3-D plots as needed.

When the *x* variable is time, or some index based on time, we can plot the values of *y* over time in a line graph. When both *x* and *y* are continuous variables, we can use points to represent their relationship as a series of (*x*, *y*) pairs. If the relationship is perfectly linear, the points will fit along a straight line. When the relationship is not perfect, our points will produce scatter around a best-fitting line. Let us first examine scatterplots and see that we have the ability in ggplot2 to add the regression line and a confidence region to the scatterplot. We will then examine a hexbin plot in which bivariate data are grouped into hexagonal bins, with shading used to show the overlap in the data, something about which scatterplots do not convey much information.

Let's use ggplot2 to make a scatterplot of the gas mileage of the car and the weight of the car. This should plot a negative relationship, with heavier cars getting lower mileage. To produce the scatterplot, we use geom_point(). As before, we can build up the chart by adding specifications and then plot the final version. The method = lm setting will add the linear regression line, and by default will also add a shaded 95% confidence region. Here is the R code to produce the scatterplot shown in Figure 9-9.

```
> scatter <- ggplot (cars , aes (weight , mpgCity )) + geom_point ()
> scatter <- scatter + geom_smooth ( method = lm)
> scatter
```

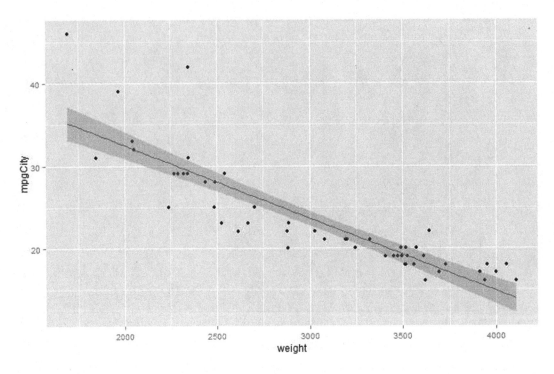

Figure 9-9. *Scatterplot of city miles per gallon and car weight*

If there is more than one observation with the same (*x, y*) coordinates, the points will overlap on the scatterplot. Such overplotting can make seeing the data difficult. If there is a small amount of this, adding some transparency to the points representing the data can help. We can do this in ggplot2 using the alpha argument, which ranges from 0 for complete transparent to 1 for completely opaque (see Figure 9-10 for the results).

```
> scatter <- ggplot (cars , aes (weight , mpgCity )) + geom_point (alpha = .5)
> scatter <- scatter + geom_smooth ( method = lm)
> scatter
```

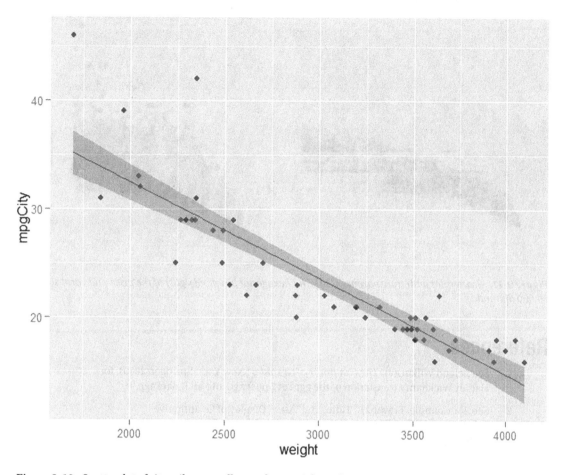

Figure 9-10. *Scatterplot of city miles per gallon and car weight with transparency added for the points*

Another very effective way to show bivariate data is a hexagonal bin plot. Hexagonal bins are shaded to show the frequency of bivariate data in each bin. This plot is a very good way to determine where the data are stacked or overlapped. As before, we can build up the plot by adding elements to the overall list as follows. To show how difficult seeing the data can be with a scatterplot, we use the diamonds dataset built into ggplot2, which has 50,000 observations. We will also use the grid.arrange() function as before to put two plots side by side (shown in Figure 9-11), one a scatterplot and the other a hexagonal bin plot. Note how we can reuse the basic ggplot2 graph data and variable mapping and just present it differently with geom_point() or geom_hex().

```
> install.packages ("hexbin")
> library(hexbin)
> dplot  <- ggplot (diamonds , aes ( price , carat ))
> splot <- dplot + geom_point( alpha = .25 )
> hex <- dplot + geom_hex ()
> grid.arrange ( splot, hex, ncol = 2 )
```

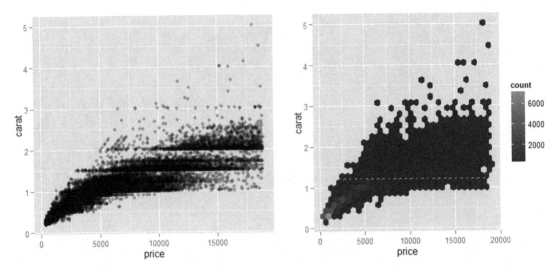

Figure 9-11. *Scatterplot with transparency (left) and hexagonal bin plot (right) of the price and carat size of 50,000 diamonds*

References

1. See Leland Wilkinson, *The Grammar of Graphics* (New York: Springer, 2005), for Hadley Wickham's translation of the ggplot2 package into an R package.

2. See, for example, Edward R. Tufte, The Visual Display of Quantitative Information (Columbia, MD: Graphic Press, 2001), which is considered a classic in the field.

CHAPTER 10

■ ■ ■

Traditional Statistical Methods

Statistics is an evolving, growing field. Consider that, at this moment, there are hundreds of scholars working on their graduate degrees in statistics. Each of those scholars must make an original contribution to the field of statistics, either in theory or in application. This is not to mention the statistics faculty and other faculty members in various research fields who are working on the cutting edge of statistical applications. Add to this total the statistical innovators in government, business, the biomedical field, and other organizations. You get the picture.

The statisticians of the 20th century gave us tools, and we are now in the process of making the tools better. This chapter will provide a quick run-through of the most common statistical procedures and hypothesis tests one might learn in an introductory statistics course, and then we will consider some modern alternatives in Chapter 11.

10.1 Estimation and Confidence Intervals

In this section, we will examine how to produce confidence intervals for means, proportions, and variances. The discussion of confidence intervals will lead directly into the treatment of the most common hypothesis tests.

10.1.1 Confidence Intervals for Means

For reasons we have discussed previously, we commonly use the t distribution to develop confidence intervals for means. We can determine the critical values of t using the qt function, and then we can multiply the critical value of t by the standard error of the mean to determine the width of one-half the confidence interval. Adding this margin of error to the sample mean produces the upper limit of the confidence interval, and subtracting the margin of error from the sample mean produces the lower limit of the confidence interval. The standard deviation of the sampling distribution of means for samples of size n is found as follows:

$$s_x = \frac{s_x}{\sqrt{n}} \tag{10.1}$$

This quantity is known as the standard error of the mean. We then multiply the standard error of the mean by the critical value of t to determine the margin of error. The lower and upper limits of the confidence interval encompass twice the margin of error.

$$(1-\alpha)\times 100\% CI = \bar{x} \pm t_{\alpha/2}\left(s_{\bar{x}}\right) \tag{10.2}$$

The t.test function in R can be used to find a confidence interval for the mean, and it is often used exactly for that purpose. The default is a 95% confidence interval. As you may recall, we must determine the degrees of freedom when finding a critical value of *t* for a confidence interval or hypothesis test. Let us find a 95% confidence interval for the mean science scores of the 200 students in our hsb sample. First, just for fun, let's write a simple function to take the preceding formulas and implement them to get our confidence interval.

```
> CI <- function (x, alpha = .05) {
+    sampMean <- mean (x)
+    stderr <- sd(x)/ sqrt( length (x))
+    tcrit <- qt (1- alpha /2, length (x) - 1)
+    margin <- stderr * tcrit
+    CI <- c( sampMean - margin , sampMean + margin )
+    return (CI)
+ }
> CI( hsb $ science )
[1] 50.46944 53.23056
```

Now, compare the results with those from the one-sample *t*-test. As you see, the function and the *t*-test produced the same confidence limits.

```
> t.test(hsb$ science)

        One Sample t-test

data:  hsb$science
t = 74.061, df = 199, p-value < 2.2e-16
alternative hypothesis: true mean is not equal to 0
95 percent confidence interval:
 50.46944 53.23056
sample estimates:
mean of x
     51.85
```

10.1.2 Confidence Intervals for Proportions

You are probably familiar with journalists announcing that some opinion poll had a margin of error of ± 3 percentage points. For proportions, we use the standard normal distribution, rather than the *t* distribution, to develop confidence intervals. This is because of the relationship between the binomial distribution and the normal distribution we discussed in Chapter 6. Let us define the confidence interval for a sample proportion p^ as follows:

$$(1-\alpha)\times100\%CI = \hat{p} \pm z_{\alpha/2}\sqrt{\frac{\hat{p}(1-\hat{p})}{n}} \tag{10.3}$$

As an example, suppose you wanted to determine a confidence interval for a poll of 200 randomly sampled people in your community of whom 135 expressed support for the death penalty. The sample proportion is 135/200 = .675. Assume it is known from national polls that 63% of the population is in favor of the death penalty. We can calculate a 95% confidence interval and then determine whether our confidence limits "capture" the population proportion.

$$95\%CI = 0.675 \pm 1.96 \sqrt{\frac{0.675(0.325)}{200}} = 0.675 \pm 0.065 \tag{10.4}$$

We see that the lower limit of our confidence interval is thus 0.61, and our upper limit is .74, so the population value is in fact within the bounds of our confidence interval (CI). Of course, R has a built-in function, $prop.test()$, that provides such calculations for us. The confidence interval is slightly different from the preceding one, because the standard error term is based on the hypothesized population proportion rather than the sample proportion. The default for this function is a 95% CI; however, the command was made explicit for readers who wish to use other CI levels. Here, as always, the Help tab on the right-hand side of RStudio is very, ahem, helpful.

```
> prop.test(135,200, conf.level=0.95)

        1-sample proportions test with continuity correction

data:  135 out of 200, null probability 0.5
X-squared = 23.805, df = 1, p-value = 1.066e-06
alternative hypothesis: true p is not equal to 0.5
95 percent confidence interval:
 0.6047423 0.7384105
sample estimates:
    p
0.675
```

10.1.3 Confidence Intervals for the Variance

When we use the t distribution and the standard normal distribution for confidence intervals, the intervals are symmetrical about the estimated value. This is not true when we use the chi-square distribution because the distribution itself is not symmetrical. As mentioned earlier, we can use the chi-square distribution to form a CI around a sample variance. The CI can be constructed as follows[1]:

$$\frac{(n-1)s^2}{X^2_R} < \sigma^2 < \frac{(n-1)s^2}{X^2_L} \tag{10.5}$$

where X^2_L is the left-tailed critical value of chi square and X^2_R is the right-tailed critical value. The degrees of freedom for these values of chi square are $n - 1$. We could write a simple R function to calculate these values, as follows. This is a bare-bones function, and the reader is encouraged to adorn his or her own version with labels and other embellishments. Let us apply our confidence interval function to the variance of the city miles per gallon from the cars dataset we used extensively in Chapter 9.

```
> library ( openintro )

> varInterval <- function (data , conf.level = 0.95) {
+    df <- length ( data ) - 1
+    chi_left <- qchisq ((1 - conf.level )/2, df)
+    chi_right <- qchisq ((1 - conf.level )/2, df , lower.tail = FALSE )
+    v <- var ( data )
+    c(( df * v)/chi_right, (df * v)/ chi_left )
+    }

> var ( cars $ mpgCity )
[1] 43.88015

> varInterval ( cars $ mpgCity )
[1] 31.00787 66.87446
```

As the output shows, the interval is not symmetrical around the point estimate of the population variance, as explained earlier. To find a confidence interval for the sample standard deviation, simply take the square roots of the lower and upper limits of those for the variance.

10.2 Hypothesis Tests with One Sample

You have already learned in Chapter 7 how to do chi-square tests of goodness of fit with a single sample. In addition to testing frequencies, we can also test means and proportions for one sample.

We can test the hypothesis that a sample came from a population with a particular mean by using the one-sample t-test function shown previously for a confidence interval for the sample mean. The value of μ, the population mean is the test value, and the sample value of t is found as:

$$t = \frac{\bar{x} - \mu_0}{s_{\bar{x}}} \tag{10.6}$$

When the null hypothesis that there is no difference between the sample mean and the hypothesized population mean is true, the resulting statistic is distributed as t with $n - 1$ degrees of freedom. To illustrate, let's determine the probability that the city miles per gallon of the car data came from a population with a mean city MPG of 25, adopting a traditional alpha level of 0.05.

```
> t.test ( cars $ mpgCity , mu = 25)

One Sample t-test

data : cars $ mpgCity
t = -1.8694 , df = 53, p- value = 0.06709
alternative hypothesis : true mean is not equal to 25
95 percent confidence interval :
21.50675 25.12288
sample estimates :
mean of x
23.31481
```

We can determine that we should not reject the null hypothesis in three equivalent ways. First, we can examine the confidence interval. The test value of 25 is "in" the confidence interval. Second, we might examine the *p* value and determine that it is greater than .05. Both approaches lead to the same conclusion: namely, we do not reject the null hypothesis. Third, the older critical value method (CVM) would also produce the same conclusion. We would see that our obtained *t* value of −1.87 is lower than the critical value of 2.01 with 53 degrees of freedom.

A special case of the *t*-test arises when we have matched, paired, or repeated measures data. In such cases, we do not have two independent samples but a single sample of difference scores. Our interest is to determine whether the average difference is zero. Failing to recognize the dependent nature of such data means that one is likely to apply a two-sample *t*-test when the appropriate test is a paired-samples test, also known as a dependent or correlated *t*-test. Performing the incorrect test naturally may result in drawing the wrong conclusion(s).

The t.test() function built into R takes as a default argument paired = FALSE that should be swapped to TRUE if two vectors of paired data are input.

To illustrate, let us use the UScrime data from the MASS package. For the 47 states, police expenditure was measured in 1960 and 1959. We will select only the 16 cases from southern states. Let us compare the *t*-test for paired data and the one-sample *t*-test for the same data using the difference scores and testing the hypothesis that the mean difference is zero. Notice it would be incorrect to not explicitly call out paired = TRUE in the first example!

```
> library(MASS)
> pairedPoliceExpenditure <- UScrime [( UScrime $ So == 1) ,]

> t.test ( pairedPoliceExpenditure $ Po1 , pairedPoliceExpenditure $ Po2 , paired = TRUE )

        Paired t-test

data:  pairedPoliceExpenditure$Po1 and pairedPoliceExpenditure$Po2
t = 6.4606, df = 15, p-value = 1.074e-05
alternative hypothesis: true difference in means is not equal to 0
95 percent confidence interval:
 2.680336 5.319664
sample estimates:
mean of the differences
               4
> PolExpenDiffs <- pairedPoliceExpenditure $ Po1 - pairedPoliceExpenditure $Po2
> t.test ( PolExpenDiffs , mu = 0)

        One Sample t-test

data:  PolExpenDiffs
t = 6.4606, df = 15, p-value = 1.074e-05
alternative hypothesis: true mean is not equal to 0
95 percent confidence interval:
 2.680336 5.319664
sample estimates:
mean of x
        4
```

It is clear that the two tests produced exactly the same results, apart from minor labeling differences. The values of t, the degrees of freedom, the p values, and the confidence intervals are identical. Some statistics textbooks do not have a separate presentation of the paired-samples t-test, but those with such sections, in our experience, often confuse students, many of whom have a difficult time understanding the difference between paired and independent samples. The best way to get a feel for this is to (incorrectly) calculate without the `paired = TRUE` and notice the rather stark difference.

10.3 Hypothesis Tests with Two Samples

We can test hypotheses that two independent means or two independent proportions are the same using the `t.test` and `prop.test` functions in base R. For the reasons discussed earlier, we use the standard normal distribution or an equivalent chi-square test to test the difference between proportions.

For each of two independent samples, the number of successes and the number of failures must be at least 5. That is, $np \geq 5$ and $n(1 - p) \geq 5$ for each of the two samples. When that is the case, the statistic shown next follows a standard normal distribution when the null hypothesis is true that the proportions of success in the population are the same for the two samples.

$$z = \frac{\hat{P}_1 - \hat{P}_2}{\sqrt{\dfrac{\overline{Pq}}{n1} + \dfrac{\overline{Pq}}{n2}}} \qquad (10.7)$$

where $\overline{P} = (x_1 + x_2)/(n_1 + n_2)$ and $\overline{q} = 1 - \overline{P}$.

As an example, let us consider comparing the proportions of males and females in favor of the death penalty in two randomly selected samples of 200 each. When we pool the proportions and calculate the z statistic shown previously, the value of z^2 will be equal to the value of χ^2 in the `prop.test` when the continuity correction is not applied. To demonstrate, assume there are 136 men in favor of the death penalty and 108 women in favor. Are these proportions significantly different at an alpha level of 0.05? First, let us use the `prop.test` function both with and without the continuity correction.

```
> prop.test (x = c(136 , 108) , n = c(200 , 200) )

2- sample test for equality of proportions with continuity correction

data : c(136 , 108) out of c(200 , 200)
X- squared = 7.6608 , df = 1, p- value = 0.005643
alternative hypothesis : two . sided
95 percent confidence interval :
0.04039239 0.23960761
sample estimates :
prop 1 prop 2
0.68 0.54

> prop.test (x = c(136 , 108) , n = c(200 , 200) , correct = FALSE )

2- sample test for equality of proportions without continuity correction
```

```
data : c(136 , 108) out of c(200 , 200)
X- squared = 8.2388 , df = 1, p- value = 0.004101
alternative hypothesis : two . sided
95 percent confidence interval :
0.04539239 0.23460761
sample estimates :
prop  1  prop 2
0.68     0.54
```

Note the value of chi square without the continuity correction is 8.2388. The square root of this quantity is 2.8703. For fun, let's create a quick function to perform the same test as a z-test using our previous formula and see if our value of z is in fact the square root of chi square. The results confirm this.

```
> zproptest <- function (x1 , x2 , n1 , n2 , conf.level = 0.95) {
+ ppooled <- (x1 + x2)/(n1 + n2)
+ qpooled <- 1 - ppooled
+ p1 <- x1/n1
+ p2 <- x2/n2
+ zstat <- round (( p1 - p2)/ sqrt (( ppooled * qpooled )/n1 + ( ppooled * qpooled )/n2) ,4)
+ pval <- round (2 * pnorm (zstat , lower.tail = FALSE ) ,4)
+ print ("two - sample z test for proportions ", quote = FALSE )
+ print (c(" valueof z: ",zstat ), quote = FALSE )
+ print (c("p- value : ", pval ), quote = FALSE )
+ }
> zproptest (136 , 108 , 200 , 200)
[1] two - sample z test for proportions
[1] valueof z: 2.8703
[1] p- value : 0.0041
```

The independent-samples t-test has two options. The version most commonly taught in the social and behavioral sciences uses a pooled variance estimate, while statisticians in other fields are more likely to favor the t test that does not make the assumption of equality of variances in the population. The t.test function in R covers both possibilities, and for convenience it provides the ability to use data that are coded by a factor as well as side-by-side data in a data frame or matrix as well as data in two separate vectors.

Because the samples are independent, there is no constraint that the numbers in each sample must be equal. The t-test assuming unequal variances in the population makes use of the Welch-Satterthwaite approximation for the degrees of freedom, thus taking the different variances into account. The t-test assuming equal variances pools the variance estimates, as discussed earlier. We will illustrate both tests. One expedient is simply to test the equality of the two sample variances and choose the appropriate test on the basis of that test.

Let us subset the UScrime data so that we have the southern states in one data frame and the not-southern in another. We will then perform the F test of equality of variances using the var.test function.

```
> southern <- UScrime [(UScrime $ So ==1) ,]
> notSouthern <- UScrime [(UScrime $ So ==0) ,]
> var.test(southern $ Po1 , notSouthern $ Po1)

        F test to compare two variances

data:  southern$Po1 and notSouthern$Po1
```

```
F = 0.56937, num df = 15, denom df = 30, p-value = 0.2498
alternative hypothesis: true ratio of variances is not equal to 1
95 percent confidence interval:
 0.2467857 1.5052706
sample estimates:
ratio of variances
          0.5693726
```

The F test is not significant, so we will use the t-test for equal variances which makes no adjustment to the degrees of freedom and pools the variance estimates. This test has a p value less than 0.05, and thus we believe there is a difference in police expenditures in 1959 for southern versus not-southern states (a quick look at the data via boxplot suggests this makes sense).

```
> t.test(southern $ Po1 , notSouthern $ Po1, var.equal = TRUE)

Two Sample t-test

data:  southern$Po1 and notSouthern$Po1
t = -2.6937, df = 45, p-value = 0.009894
alternative hypothesis: true difference in means is not equal to 0
95 percent confidence interval:
 -40.408529  -5.833406
sample estimates:
mean of x mean of y
 69.75000  92.87097
```

In contrast, the default t-test adjusts the degrees of freedom to account for an inequality of variance. In this case, the two tests produce similar results.

```
> t.test(southern $ Po1 , notSouthern $ Po1)

        Welch Two Sample t-test

data:  southern$Po1 and notSouthern$Po1
t = -2.9462, df = 38.643, p-value = 0.005427
alternative hypothesis: true difference in means is not equal to 0
95 percent confidence interval:
 -38.999264  -7.242671
sample estimates:
mean of x mean of y
 69.75000  92.87097
```

In the next chapter, we will introduce some additional tests which harness some of the compute power possible with the R language and modern computers.

References

1. Mario F. Triola, *Elementary Statistics*, 11th ed. (New York: Pearson Education, 2010).

CHAPTER 11

■ ■ ■

Modern Statistical Methods

Statistics benefited greatly from the introduction of the modern digital computer in the middle of the 20th century. Simulations and other analyses that once required laborious and error-prone hand calculations could be programmed into the computer, saving time and increasing accuracy. We have already used simulations for some demonstrations. In this chapter, we will discuss modern robust alternatives to the standard statistical techniques we discussed in Chapter 10.

As you will recall from our previous discussions, some estimators of population parameters, such as the median, are relatively robust, while others, such as the mean, are less robust, because they are influenced by outliers or the shape of the distribution. Modern robust statistics include an amalgam of procedures that are less sensitive to violations of the standard statistical assumptions than are the traditional techniques we discussed in Chapter 10. Modern techniques include the processes of trimming or Winsorizing estimates such as those of the mean or the variance, bootstrapping, permutation tests, and a variety of rank-based or nonparametric tests (Erceg-Hurn & Mirosevich, 2008). The books and articles by Professor Rand Wilcox of USC are also quite helpful in their presentation of many modern robust alternatives to traditional statistical procedures (for an introduction, see Wilcox, 2010).

We will separate Chapter 11 into the following sections: a discussion of the need for modern statistical methods and some robust alternatives to the traditional t-tests, and then an introduction to both bootstrapping and permutation tests. We will not be looking for a robust alternative to every specific hypothesis test we have discussed thus far but simply for a representation of this more modern approach in contrast to the traditional one.

11.1 The Need for Modern Statistical Methods

The development of traditional statistical procedures and hypothesis tests began at the end of the 19th century and continued into the first half of the 20th century. Even then it was clear that many real datasets did not meet the familiar distributional assumptions of normality, independence, and equality of variance. Many observed data were noted to be skewed in distribution, and nonparametric alternatives were developed, among the first being the Spearman rank correlation as an alternative to the Pearson product-moment correlation we discussed in Chapter 10. Nonparametric tests are so called because they make fewer (if any) assumptions about population parameters than parametric tests, and because in many cases no estimate of a population parameter is being considered.

Many modern statistical procedures are nonparametric in the second sense, as they often do not rely on population parameters but in fact treat a sample as a "pseudo-population" and repeatedly sample with replacement from the original sample in order to generate a distribution of a particular statistic of interest. Resampling techniques can also be used for calculating confidence intervals, not just for familiar statistics but for ones we might create on our own.

The methods of statistics continue to evolve. Data these days are much more ready to become "big" than in any previous era. One of the powerful advantages R provides is the ability to cheaply run many procedures on even comparatively large datasets. The exploratory data analysis promoted by Tukey can now readily go far beyond "just" box-and-whisker plots. Provided the preconditions of particular tests are met, data may be subjected to a battery of procedures to compare and contrast.

11.2 A Modern Alternative to the Traditional *t* Test

The independent-samples t-test is one of the most popular of all statistical procedures. As we have discussed, the t-test assuming unequal variances is available when the data analyst is not willing to assume homoscedasticity. A nonparametric alternative to the independent-samples t-test is the Mann-Whitney U test, for which the data for both groups are converted to ranks. The question arises as to the performance of these alternatives regarding their statistical power when the assumptions of equality of variance and normality of distribution are violated.

Yuen (1974) developed a robust alternative to the independent-samples t-test. Yuen's test makes use of trimmed means and Winsorized variances for both groups. When the trimming amount is zero, the Yuen test produces the same confidence interval for the difference between means as the Welch t-test in base R. Although we can trim means by any amount, it is common to use a 20% trimmed mean as a robust estimator of the population mean. This amounts to trimming the top 20% of the data and the bottom 20% of the data and then calculating the mean of the remaining values. It is worth mentioning that the median is by definition the 50% trimmed mean. Winsorizing is a slightly different process from trimming. Whereas trimming discards data values, Winsorization replaces a certain percentage of the top and bottom values by the scores at given quantiles (e.g., the 5th and 95th percentiles). The unequal-variances t-test has been shown to perform reasonably when both samples are drawn from normal populations but less well when the distributions are not normal and when the sample sizes are different. Rand Wilcox's WRS (Wilcox' Robust Statistics) package is available on GitHub. The package contains many functions (more than 1,100 in fact) for various robust statistical methods, including the Yuen t-test. See the following URL for instructions on how to install WRS or run the commands in the source code distributed with this text (available on `apress.com`).

`https://github.com/nicebread/WRS`

We save an in-depth treatment of the exact mathematical formulae for other authors and texts. We take two groups that differ in sample size, means, and variances. Figure 11-1 shows the kernel density diagrams for the two groups for comparison purposes.

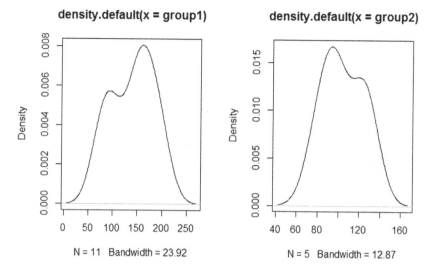

Figure 11-1. *Density plots for two groups of data*

Let us explore these two datasets a bit more, and then compare and contrast the *t*-test with two new tests that are more robust. Of course, from the pictures in Figure 11-1, one would not expect the variance or the means to be the same.

```
> group1 <- c(151, 78, 169, 88, 194, 196, 109, 143, 150, 85, 168)
> group2 <- c(128, 122, 95, 97, 81)
> summary(group1)
   Min. 1st Qu.  Median   Mean 3rd Qu.    Max.
   78.0    98.5   150.0  139.2   168.5   196.0
> var(group1)
[1] 1843.364
>
> summary(group2)
   Min. 1st Qu.  Median   Mean 3rd Qu.    Max.
   81.0    95.0    97.0  104.6   122.0   128.0
> var ( group2 )
[1] 389.3
```

For the sake of reference, let us perform both the *t*-test assuming equal variances and the Welch *t*-test. Notice that the Welch *t*-test gives a p value of less than 0.05.

```
> t.test(group2, group1, var.equal = TRUE)

        Two Sample t-test

data:  group2 and group1
t = -1.6967, df = 14, p-value = 0.1119
alternative hypothesis: true difference in means is not equal to 0
95 percent confidence interval:
 -78.295181   9.131545
sample estimates:
```

```
mean of x mean of y
 104.6000   139.1818


> t.test(group2, group1)

        Welch Two Sample t-test

data:  group2 and group1
t = -2.2074, df = 13.932, p-value = 0.04457
alternative hypothesis: true difference in means is not equal to 0
95 percent confidence interval:
 -68.1984170  -0.9652194
sample estimates:
mean of x mean of y
 104.6000   139.1818
```

Now let us use the Yuen test with a trimming amount of .20 for the means, which is the default. Please see the instructions at the abovementioned GitHub URL (https://github.com/nicebread/WRS) to install WRS or run the downloaded source code.

```
> library ( WRS )
> yuenTest <- yuen ( group2 , group1)
> yuenTest $p.value
[1] 0.1321475
> yuenTest $ci
[1] -83.33050  13.23527
```

Inspection of the results shows that the Yuen test based on trimmed means and Winsorized variances has a more conservative confidence interval, and thus it reduces the chance for a Type I error over either of the two standard *t*-tests for independent groups. As a final consideration in this section, observe the results from the Mann-Whitney U test, which is the test produced by the wilcox.test function in R for independent groups.

```
> wilcox.test ( group2, group1 )

        Wilcoxon rank sum test

data:  group2 and group1
W = 15, p-value = 0.1804
alternative hypothesis: true location shift is not equal to 0
```

There are many other modern statistical tests available for a variety of situations, including robust alternatives to one-sample tests, analysis of variance, and regression. It is always important to examine any necessary preconditions or assumptions to using a particular test (and to examine any specific disclaimers about how R programmers have implemented those tests).

11.3 Bootstrapping

Bootstrapping is simple in logic. Instead of assuming anything about a population, we can sample the same dataset repeatedly. Sampling with replacement allows us to build a distribution of any particular statistic of interest. We are essentially using our sample as a "pseudo-population" when we take multiple resamples with replacement from it.

The "plug-in" principle of bootstrapping means that to estimate a parameter, which is some measurable characteristic of a population, we use the statistic that is the corresponding quantity for the sample. This principle allows us to model sampling distributions when we have little or no information about the population, when the sample data do not meet the traditional assumptions required for parametric tests, and when we create new statistics and want to study their distributions.

To illustrate, let us generate a random sample from a normal distribution with a mean of 500 and a standard deviation of 100. We will take 1,000 observations and then resample from our data 1,000 times with replacement. First, let's bootstrap the mean and then the median to see how this would work. We create the data and find that the mean and standard deviation are close to 500 and 100, respectively. We can use our bootstrapped sample and the quantile function to calculate a confidence interval for the 1,000 means we generated. Note that the population mean of 500 is "in" the confidence interval for the mean of our bootstrapped means. I went back to the base R package and used the abline function to add vertical lines for the two confidence limits (see Figure 11-2).

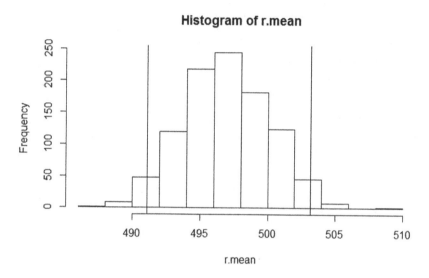

Histogram of r.mean

Figure 11-2. *Histograms for bootstrapped means with confidence limits added*

```
> myData <- rnorm (1000 , 500 , 100)
> resamples <- lapply (1:1000 , function (i) sample ( myData , replace = TRUE ))
> r.mean <- sapply ( resamples, mean )
> ci.mean <- c( quantile (r.mean, 0.025) , quantile (r.mean, 0.975) )
> ci.mean
2.5% 97.5%
491.0863 503.1850

> hist (r.mean )
> abline (v = quantile (r.mean , 0.025) )
> abline (v = quantile (r.mean , 0.975) )

> t.test ( myData )

One Sample t- test
```

```
data : myData
t = 155.2015 , df = 999 , p- value < 2.2e -16
alternative hypothesis : true mean is not equal to 0
95 percent confidence interval :
490.4900 503.0522
sample estimates :
mean of x
496.7711
```

See that the confidence interval for the mean of the original data is virtually the same as the confidence interval for the bootstrapped means.

Finding confidence intervals and standard error estimates for medians is less commonly done than finding these for means. Let us continue with our example and bootstrap the median and the mean for the 1,000 samples from a normal population with a mean of 500 and a standard deviation of 100. We will use the same technique as previously, but this time, we will make a function to combine our procedures. We will pass the dataset and the number of resamples as arguments to the function, and then write the results of the function to an object named boot1. This will allow us to query the object for the output of interest. Let us calculate standard errors for both the mean and the median.

```
> boot.fun <- function (data , num) {
+    resamples <- lapply (1: num , function (i) sample (data, replace=TRUE))
+    r.median <- sapply ( resamples, median )
+    r.mean <- sapply ( resamples, mean )
+    std.err.median <- sqrt ( var (r.median ))
+    std.err.mean <- sqrt (var (r.mean ))
+    rawDataName <-
+    data.frame (std.err.median = std.err.median , std.err.mean = std.err.mean , resamples =
       resamples , medians =r.median , means =r.mean )
+ }
> boot1 <- boot.fun ( myData , 1000)> boot1 <- boot . fun ( myData , 1000)
> boot1 $ std.err.mean
[1] 3.191525
> boot1 $ std.err.median
[1] 4.309543
```

We can see that the medians have a larger standard error than the means. In general, when the data are drawn from a normal distribution with a large sample size, the median will produce a confidence interval about 25% wider than that for the mean.

Figure 11-3 shows the bootstrapped means and medians. The means are clearly the more normally distributed of the two. To produce the histograms, I combined the medians and means into a single data frame and used the ggplot2 and the gridExtra packages to create the side-by-side histograms.

```
> install.packages("gridExtra")
> library ( gridExtra ) > library ( ggplot2 )
> plot1 <- ggplot (boot1, aes (means)) + geom_histogram (binwidth = 1, fill="white",
   color="black")
> plot2 <- ggplot (boot1, aes (medians)) + geom_histogram (binwidth=1, fill ="white",
   color="black")
> grid.arrange (plot1, plot2, nrow = 1)
```

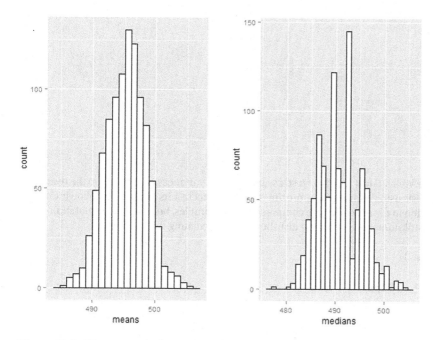

Figure 11-3. *Histograms for bootstrapped means and medians*

11.4 Permutation Tests

Bootstrapping produces a distribution by sampling with replacement. Because the sampling is random, no two bootstraps will produce exactly the same results unless they start with the same seed value. You may recall that permutations are the numbers of ways a set of objects can be ordered or sequenced. Thus when we are comparing means for groups of size n_1 and n_2, it is instructive to determine the number of ways we can divide a total of $N = n_1 + n_2$ objects into two groups of size n_1 and n_2. We can then determine from many possible ways of dividing the data into groups of size n_1 and n_2 the proportion of those samples in which the mean difference is larger in absolute value than the original mean difference. The number of possible permutations increases very quickly as the number of objects increases, and with large samples, it is not necessary to calculate all the permutations. Say we want to compare the means of two different groups, as we have done with the t-test and the Yuen test. To run this as a permutation test, we record the mean difference between the two groups and then combine the data into a single group in order to perform the permutation test.

Permutation tests may be asymptotically valid using the permutational central limit theorem, or they may produce exact p values using Monte Carlo simulation, a network algorithm, or complete enumeration. These features are implemented in the perm package available on CRAN. Let us use a hypothetical dataset of a memory study. The data have the memory recall scores for 20 subjects each from two conditions. Assume in this case the patients were randomly assigned to the conditions, and the memory test was performed after taking the drug or placebo for 30 days.

```
> memory <- read.table("memory_ch11.txt", sep="\t", header = TRUE)
> head ( memory )
  cond recall
1 drug 2.0
2 drug 2.0
3 drug 4.5
4 drug 5.5
```

```
5 drug 6.5
6 drug 6.5
> tail ( memory )
      cond   recall
35 placebo      16
36 placebo      17
37 placebo      20
38 placebo      25
39 placebo      29
40 placebo      30
```

Now, let us perform the Welch t-test and the t-test, assuming equal variances, and compare the results with those of permutation tests using asymptotic approximation and exact results. Note in the following code listing that the permTS function in the perm package compares the two samples, but that the permutation tests use the standard normal distribution instead of the t distribution for calculating the p values.

```
> install.packages("perm")
> library(perm)
> t.test ( recall ~ cond , data = memory )

        Welch Two Sample t-test

data:  recall by cond
t = -2.2552, df = 28.862, p-value = 0.03188
alternative hypothesis: true difference in means is not equal to 0
95 percent confidence interval:
 -8.591498 -0.418502
sample estimates:
   mean in group drug mean in group placebo
            8.930                 13.435

> t.test ( recall ~ cond , data = memory, var.equal = TRUE)

        Two Sample t-test

data:  recall by cond
t = -2.2552, df = 38, p-value = 0.02997
alternative hypothesis: true difference in means is not equal to 0
95 percent confidence interval:
 -8.5490275 -0.4609725
sample estimates:
   mean in group drug mean in group placebo
            8.930                 13.435

> permTS ( recall ~ cond , data = memory )

        Permutation Test using Asymptotic Approximation

data:  recall by cond
Z = -2.1456, p-value = 0.03191
alternative hypothesis: true mean cond=drug - mean cond=placebo is not equal to 0
```

```
sample estimates:
mean cond=drug - mean cond=placebo
                      -4.505

> permTS ( recall ~ cond , data = memory , exact = TRUE )

        Exact Permutation Test Estimated by Monte Carlo

data:  recall by cond
p-value = 0.03
alternative hypothesis: true mean cond=drug - mean cond=placebo is not equal to 0
sample estimates:
mean cond=drug - mean cond=placebo
                      -4.505

p-value estimated from 999 Monte Carlo replications
99 percent confidence interval on p-value:
 0.01251632 0.05338086
```

Note that the *p* values for the all four tests are relatively similar. Interestingly, recent research indicates that the permutation test may not perform well when the data for the groups being compared are not identically distributed. The robust Yuen test we used earlier shows that when the data are trimmed and we use Winsorized variances, the results are not significant. This indicates that the probability of Type I error may have been inflated for all four of our earlier tests.

```
> recall1 <- memory[ memory[,"cond"]=="drug", "recall"]
> recall2 <- memory[ memory[,"cond"]=="placebo", "recall"]
> yuenTest <- yuen ( recall1, recall2 )
> yuenTest $p.value
[1] 0.05191975
> yuenTest $ci
[1] -7.56797807  0.03464473
```

References

Chambers, J. M. *Software for Data Analysis: Programming in r.* New York: Springer, 2008.

Erceg-Hurn, D. M., & Mirosevich, V. M. "Modern robust statistical methods: An easy way to maximize the accuracy and power of your research." *American Psychologist, 63* (7), 591-601 (2008).

Hunt, A., & Thomas, D. *The Pragmatic Programmer: From Journeyman to Master.* Reading, MA: Addison Wesley, 1999.

Micceri, T. "The unicorn, the normal curve, and other improbable creatures." *Psychological Bulletin, 105,* 156-166 (1989).

Ohri, A. *R for Cloud Computing: An Approach for Data Scientists.* New York: Springer, 2014.

Pace, L. A. *Beginning R: An Introduction to Statistical Programming.* New York: Apress, 2012.

Roscoe, J. T. *Fundamental Research Statistics for the Behavioural Sciences* (2nd ed.). New York: Holt, Rinehart and Winston, 1975.

Triola, M. F. *Elementary Statistics* (11th ed.). Boston, MA: Addison-Wesley, 2010.

Tufte, E. R. *The Visual Display of Quantitative Information* (2nd ed.). Cheshire, CN: Graphic Press, 2001.

Tukey, J. W. *Exploratory Data Analysis.* Reading, MA: Addison Wesley, 1977. University of California, Los Angeles. (2015). *Resources to help you learn and use R*. Retrieved from www.ats.ucla.edu/stat/r/.

Wilcox, R. R. *Fundamentals of Modern Statistical Methods* (2nd ed.). New York: Springer, 2010.

Wilkinson, L. *The Grammar of Graphics* (2nd ed.). New York: Springer, 2005.

Yuen, K. K. "The two-sample trimmed t for unequal population variances." *Biometrika, 61,* 165-170 (1974).

CHAPTER 12

■ ■ ■

Analysis of Variance

So far, we have explored hypothesis tests that cope with at most two samples. Now, of course, they could be run multiple times—it would be trivial to extend loops and t.test to run through many iterations. However, that is a proposition fraught with risk. For a given = 0.05, suppose we wish to compare mean staph infection rates for eight regional medical centers. Then there are choose(8,2) = 28 total pairwise comparisons. Thus, the chance of at least one Type I error, supposing our eight samples are independent, is $1 - (.95)^{28} = 0.7621731$ which is rather high. Analysis of variance (ANOVA) compares three or more means simultaneously, thereby controlling the error rate to the nominal 0.05.

Regardless of the precise type, ANOVA is built on the underlying premise that the variance *between* our samples (e.g., the sample means) may be compared with sample variance *within* our samples to determine if it seems reasonable that there is a significant difference between means. An *F-ratio* is built where the *between* variances are divided by the *within* variances. Suppose we have a rather large difference between some of our sample means. This would lead us to suspect at least one of those regional medical centers has an overly high rate of staph infection incidents. However, suppose that the sample standard deviations tend to be rather large—that sort of numerical turbulence would lead us to revise our first-blush instinct toward believing that despite the difference in means, perhaps the centers are all essentially similar. The closer this *F-ratio* is to one, the more support there is for the null hypothesis vis-à-vis sample size(s). Generally, a *p* value is calculated for the *F*-distribution for NHST (null hypothesis significance testing). As we delve into particulars, we caution our readers that the more complex the ANOVA methodology, the more care required in results interpretation.

In this chapter, we will compare the means of three or more groups with one-way ANOVA, followed by the post-hoc comparisons of the Tukey HSD (honest significant difference) criterion. Then, we will delve further into two-way ANOVA, repeated-measures ANOVA, and mixed-model ANOVA.

12.1 Some Brief Background

We leave mathematical explorations of ANOVA to other texts. However, it is essential to know the three requirements for ANOVA methods to hold true. We suppose the samples are random and independent (although we show how to relax this assumption in repeated-measures ANOVA). We also suppose that the populations from which we draw the samples are both normal and have the same variance. The latter two requirements are generally somewhat relaxed, and ANOVA may give practical guidance even in scenarios where the populations are not quite normal or where the variances do not quite match, particularly as long as the distributions are at least symmetrical. More precise definitions of "quite" are controversial and any specific threshold may be misleading in particular cases. If there is concern about whether the assumptions for an ANOVA are met, one approach is to try another test that does not have the same assumptions (e.g., non-parametric tests) to see whether or not the same conclusions are reached using both approaches. Where there are k groups, the default null hypothesis for ANOVA is $H_0: \mu_1 = ... = \mu_k$.

12.2 One-Way ANOVA

With three or more independent samples, we extend the independent-samples *t*-test to the one-way ANOVA. The paired-samples *t*-test is also extended to the repeated-measures ANOVA, in which each observation has three or more repeated measures on the same dependent variable.

Using simulated student final score data (to not run afoul of confidentiality laws), let us suppose our data were randomly drawn and independent (we acknowledge that random draws from education data may be difficult if not impossible/unethical). The alternative hypothesis is that at least one mean is different. Certainly the means in the latter terms look higher (see Figure 12-1). Note that we use the factor() function in order to relevel the factor and enforce chronological order.

```
> myData <- read.table("ANOVA001.txt", sep="\t", header=TRUE)
> myData$Term <- factor(myData$Term, levels = c("FA12", "SP13", "FA13"))
> plot(Score ~ Term, data=myData)
```

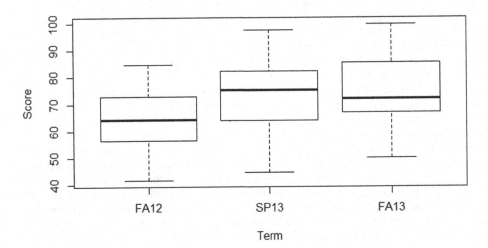

Figure 12-1. *Box-and-whisker plots of the score data for each term*

For an ANOVA run to be legitimate, our data are required to be drawn from normal populations. Visual inspection of the graphs may be a good first place to start (most introductory statistical methods courses often either simply assume normality or simply "eyeball" it). A glance at the histograms in this case may be inconclusive (see Figure 12-2). Notice how we can add color to the histograms depending on which term they are from and also make three separate plots via faceting using facet_wrap() and specifying the variable to facet, in our case by Term. Finally, since we made separate plots by term in addition to adding color, we turn off the automatic legend (by specifying an option to the theme() function) that would be created for color, as that is redundant with the individual plots.

```
> library ( gridExtra )
> library ( ggplot2 )

> ggplot(myData, aes(Score, color = Term)) +
+   geom_histogram(fill = "white", binwidth = 10) +
+   facet_wrap(~ Term) +
+   theme(legend.position = "none")
```

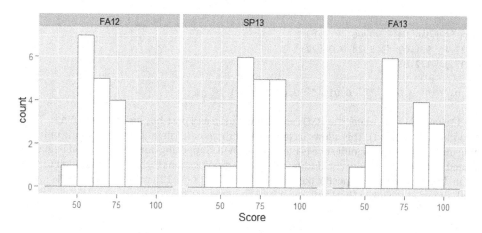

Figure 12-2. *Histograms of the various scores by term looking somewhat normal*

Numerical methods are often preferred to graphical methods. Empirical tests by Razali and Wah (2011) suggest the Shapiro-Wilk (SW) normality test on each level or factor of our data. By using for(), we make the code much cleaner and avoid repeated typing as well as the associated chance for error(s).

```
> for (n in levels(myData$Term)) {
+   test <- with(subset(myData, Term == n), shapiro.test(Score))
+   if (test$p.value < 0.05) {
+     print(c(n, test$p.value))
+   }
+ }
```

As our loop printed no values, we continue to check whether the variances are the same for each sample. The Bartlett test for homogeneity of variances (also called homoscedasticity) is built into R. Bartlett's test is often considered to be sensitive to normality. Since ANOVA requires normality, this is not of particular concern. Levene's Test is another popular test of homoscedasticity, although it would require installing another package.

```
> bartlett.test(Score ~ Term, data = myData)

        Bartlett test of homogeneity of variances

data:  Score by Term
Bartlett's K-squared = 1.199, df = 2, p-value = 0.5491
```

We do not reject the null hypothesis and, having verified or supposed the requirements of one-way ANOVA, may proceed. We run an ANOVA in R using the aov() function and then create a summary of that model using the summary() function. We see that the scores by term are statistically significantly different with a standard alpha of 0.05.

```
> results <- aov(Score ~ Term, data = myData)
> summary(results)
Analysis of Variance Table
```

```
Response: Score
          Df Sum Sq Mean Sq F value  Pr(>F)
Term       2 1123.4  561.69  3.2528 0.04622 *
Residuals 55 9497.3  172.68
---
Signif. codes:  0 '***' 0.001 '**' 0.01 '*' 0.05 '.' 0.1 ' ' 1
```

The command TukeyHSD() calculates the HSDs and is often used as a post-hoc test after ANOVA (when the null hypothesis is rejected). This allows us to see (or perhaps confirm in this case) that the only difference trending toward statistical significance is the FA12 to FA13. Supposing our treatment had begun in SP13, we may need further study before concluding our course modifications a success! In addition to displaying the mean difference between specific pairwise contrasts (FA13 - FA12), we also see the 95% confidence interval, shown as the lower (lwr) and upper (upr) bounds.

```
> TukeyHSD(results)
  Tukey multiple comparisons of means
    95% family-wise confidence level

Fit: aov(formula = Score ~ Term, data = myData)

$Term
                diff         lwr      upr     p adj
SP13-FA12   8.129921 -2.01040487 18.27025 0.1395847
FA13-FA12  10.086237 -0.05408909 20.22656 0.0515202
FA13-SP13   1.956316 -8.31319147 12.22582 0.8906649
```

One-way ANOVA can be extended to a two-way ANOVA by the addition of a second factor, and even higher-order ANOVA designs are possible. We can also use mixed-model ANOVA designs in which one or more factors are within subjects (repeated measures). We explore these more in the next section.

12.3 Two-Way ANOVA

With the two-way ANOVA, we have two between-groups factors, and we test for both main effects for each factor and the possible interaction of the two factors in their effect on the dependent variable. As before, the requirements of normal populations and the same variance hold, and while these should be checked, we suppress those checks in the interest of space. This time, we build a model using data from the MASS package, and use both SES (socioeconomic status) and a language test score as factors to study verbal IQ. We use a completely crossed model and test for main effects as well as interaction. We see significant main effects for both factors but a nonsignificant interaction, as displayed in the ANOVA summary table.

```
> library(MASS)
> twoway <- aov(IQ ~ SES * lang, data = nlschools)
> summary ( twoway )
             Df Sum Sq Mean Sq  F value Pr(>F)
SES           1    982   981.9  372.018 <2e-16 ***
lang          1   2769  2769.1 1049.121 <2e-16 ***
SES:lang      1      8     8.1    3.051 0.0808 .
Residuals  2283   6026     2.6
---
Signif. codes:  0 '***' 0.001 '**' 0.01 '*' 0.05 '.' 0.1 ' ' 1
```

Since the interaction of SES x lang is not significant, we may want to drop it and examine the model with just the two main effects of SES and lang. We could write out the model formula again and rerun it, but we can also update existing models to add or drop terms. It does not make much difference with a simple model as shown in this example, but with more complex models that have many terms, rewriting all of them can be tedious and complicate the code. In the formula, the dots expand to everything, so we update our first model by including everything on the left-hand side of the ~ and everything on the right-hand side, and then subtracting the single term we want to remove, SES x lang. If we had wanted to add a term, we could do that to using + instead of -.

```
> twoway.reduced <- update(twoway, . ~ . - SES:lang)
> summary ( twoway.reduced )
             Df Sum Sq Mean Sq F value Pr(>F)
SES           1    982   981.9   371.7 <2e-16 ***
lang          1   2769  2769.1  1048.2 <2e-16 ***
Residuals  2284   6034     2.6
---
Signif. codes:  0 '***' 0.001 '**' 0.01 '*' 0.05 '.' 0.1 ' ' 1
```

In this case, removing the interaction made little difference and we draw the same conclusions that both SES and language are still significant.

12.3.1 Repeated-Measures ANOVA

The one-way repeated-measures ANOVA is a special case of the two-way ANOVA with three or more measures for the same subjects on the same dependent variable. Suppose we measured fitness level on a scale of 0 to 10 for six research subjects who are participating in a supervised residential fitness and weight loss program. The measures are taken on the same day and time and under the same conditions for all subjects every week. The first four weeks of data are as shown below. Note that we must explicitly define the subject id and the time as factors for our analysis. To convert some of the variables to factors within the data frame, we use the within() function, which tells R that everything we do within the curly braces should be done within the data frame referenced.

```
> repeated <- read.table("repeated_fitness_Ch12.txt", sep = " ", header = TRUE)
> repeated
   id time fitness
1   1    1       0
2   1    2       1
3   1    3       3
4   1    4       4
5   2    1       1
6   2    2       2
7   2    3       4
8   2    4       5
9   3    1       2
10  3    2       3
11  3    3       3
12  3    4       5
13  4    1       3
14  4    2       4
15  4    3       4
16  4    4       5
```

```
17  5  1     2
18  5  2     3
19  5  3     3
20  5  4     4
21  6  1     2
22  6  2     3
23  6  3     3
24  6  4     5
```

```
> repeated <- within(repeated, {
+    id <- factor ( id )
+    time <- factor ( time )
+ })
```

> results <- aov (fitness ~ time + Error (id / time), data = repeated)

```
> summary ( results )

Error: id
          Df Sum Sq Mean Sq F value Pr(>F)
Residuals  5  8.333   1.667

Error: id:time
          Df Sum Sq Mean Sq F value   Pr(>F)
time       3   28.5   9.500    28.5 1.93e-06 ***
Residuals 15    5.0   0.333
---
Signif. codes:  0 '***' 0.001 '**' 0.01 '*' 0.05 '.' 0.1 ' ' 1
```

We see that the effect of time is significant. A *means plot* makes this clearer (see Figure 12-3). We use the ggplot2 stat_summary() function to calculate the means for the six subjects for each week and to plot both points and lines. Note that since we converted time into a factor before, but here we want to use it as a numerical variable for the x axis, we convert back to a number using the as.numeric() function.

```
> library(ggplot2)
> meansPlot <- ggplot(repeated, aes (as.numeric(time) , fitness)) +
+    stat_summary(fun.y = mean , geom ="point") +
+    stat_summary (fun.y = mean , geom = "line")
> meansPlot
```

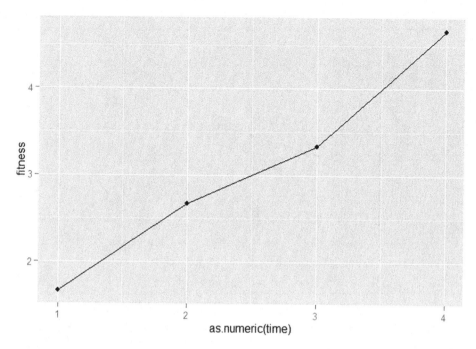

Figure 12-3. *Means plot for fitness over time*

stat_summary() function, using a different summary function and the point-range geom rather than just points (see Figure 12-4).

```
> meansPlot2 <- ggplot(repeated, aes (as.numeric(time) , fitness)) +
+    stat_summary(fun.data = mean_cl_normal, geom ="pointrange") +
+    stat_summary (fun.y = mean , geom = "line")
> meansPlot2
```

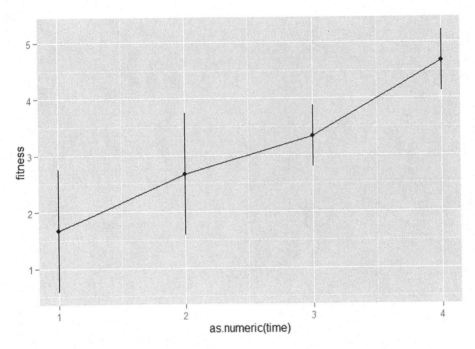

Figure 12-4. *Means plot with 95% confidence intervals for fitness over time*

12.3.2 Mixed-Model ANOVA

A mixed-model ANOVA, as mentioned earlier, must have at least one within-subjects (repeated-measures) factor, and at least one between-groups factor. Let's take a simple example, that of a design in which groups of older and younger adults are taught a list of 20 five-letter words until they can recall the list with 100% accuracy. After learning the list, each subject attempts to recall the words from the list by listening to the target words and 20 additional five-letter distractor words randomly chosen by a computer under three different conditions: no distraction (the subject listens with eyes closed and pushes a button if he or she recognizes the word as being on the list), simple distraction (the subject performs the same task with open eyes and background music), or complex distraction (the subject performs the same task while engaged in a conversation with the experimenter). The data are as follows. We read the data from a CSV file and allow R to assign the string variables to factors (the default):

```
> mixedModel <- read.csv("mixedModel.csv")
> str ( mixedModel )
'data.frame':   24 obs. of  4 variables:
 $ id   : Factor w/ 8 levels "A","B","C","D",..: 1 1 1 2 2 2 3 3 3 4 ...
 $ age  : Factor w/ 2 levels "old","young": 2 2 2 2 2 2 2 2 2 2 ...
 $ distr: Factor w/ 3 levels "h","l","m": 2 3 1 2 3 1 2 3 1 2 ...
 $ score: int  8 5 3 7 6 6 8 7 6 7 ...
> mixedModel
   id   age distr score
1   A young     l     8
2   A young     m     5
3   A young     h     3
4   B young     l     7
```

```
5   B  young   m   6
6   B  young   h   6
7   C  young   l   8
8   C  young   m   7
9   C  young   h   6
10  D  young   l   7
11  D  young   m   5
12  D  young   h   4
13  E  old     l   6
14  E  old     m   5
15  E  old     h   2
16  F  old     l   5
17  F  old     m   5
18  F  old     h   4
19  G  old     l   5
20  G  old     m   4
21  G  old     h   3
22  H  old     l   6
23  H  old     m   3
24  H  old     h   2
```

The ez package makes it easier to perform ANOVA for a variety of designs, including the mixed-model ANOVA. We will use the ezANOVA() function, which will also perform the traditional test of the sphericity assumption, along with appropriate corrections if sphericity cannot be assumed, after producing the standard ANOVA summary table. The table lists the specific effect, followed by the numerator and denominator degrees of freedom for each test, the F value, p value, and stars if the p value is less than .05. One other useful output, labeled "ges," is the generalized η^2, a measure of the size or magnitude of each effect, beyond its statistical significance.

```
> install.packages ("ez")
> library (ez)
> ezANOVA ( mixedModel , score , id , distr , between = age )
$ANOVA
       Effect DFn DFd          F            p p<.05        ges
2         age   1   6 15.7826087 0.007343975     * 0.54260090
3       distr   2  12 19.5000000 0.000169694     * 0.64084507
4   age:distr   2  12  0.2142857 0.810140233       0.01923077

$`Mauchly's Test for Sphericity`
      Effect         W         p p<.05
3      distr 0.5395408 0.2138261
4  age:distr 0.5395408 0.2138261

$`Sphericity Corrections`
      Effect       GGe      p[GG] p[GG]<.05       HFe         p[HF] p[HF]<.05
3      distr 0.6847162 0.001321516         * 0.8191249 0.0005484227         *
4  age:distr 0.6847162 0.729793578           0.8191249 0.7686615724
```

We see that we have significant effects for the age and distraction condition, but no significant interaction. Mauchly's test for sphericity is not significant, suggesting that the results meet the sphericity assumption for mixed-model ANOVAs, and we can also see that the p values corrected for the (nonsignificant) lack of sphericity, labeled p[GG] and p[HF] for the Greenhouse-Geisser correction and Huynh-Feldt correction, respectively, are essentially the same as in the uncorrected ANOVA summary table. An interaction plot, which is quite easy to produce using the base R graphics package, shows the nature of these effects (see Figure 12-5). We can use the with() function to reference the three variables from within the mixedModel data frame, without typing its name each time. The plot (Figure 12-5) shows that younger adults have better recall than older adults at all three levels of distraction, and the fact that all three lines are virtually parallel agrees with the nonsignificant interaction found from the ANOVA.

```
> with(mixedModel, interaction.plot (age , distr , score ))
```

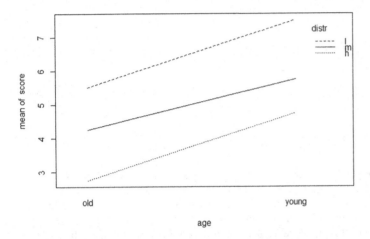

Figure 12-5. *Interaction plot for age and distraction condition*

References

Razali, N. M., & Wah, Y. B. "Power comparisons of Shapiro-Wilk, Kolmogorov-Smirnov, Lilliefors and Anderson-Darling tests." *Journal of Statistical Modeling and Analytics, 2*(1), 21-33 (2011).

CHAPTER 13

■ ■ ■

Correlation and Regression

Discovering a relationship of some sort between various data can often be a powerful model to understand the links between different processes. We generally consider the variable Y to be an outcome or dependent on an independent or input variable X. A statistician would speak of the regression of Y on X while a mathematician would write that Y is a function of X. In this chapter and the next, we are going to take our time to properly explore both the underlying logic and the practice of employing linear regression. Our goal is to avoid what is occasionally called "mathyness" and focus on several practical, applied examples that still allow for the correct sorts of ideas to be living in your head.

In this chapter, we limit our discussion to only two variable (bivariate) data. We will consider correlation (along with covariance), proceed to linear regression, and briefly touch on curvilinear models. Along the way, we'll explore helpful visualizations of our data, to better understand confidence and prediction intervals for these regression models.

In the next chapter, we will delve even further into regression, leaving behind our single-input, single-output restriction.

13.1 Covariance and Correlation

Our goal is to quickly look at pairs of data and determine their degree (if any) of linear relationship. Consider the cars dataset from the openintro package:

```
> library ( openintro )
> attach ( cars )
> head(cars)
     type price mpgCity driveTrain passengers weight
1    small  15.9      25      front          5   2705
2  midsize  33.9      18      front          5   3560
3  midsize  37.7      19      front          6   3405
4  midsize  30.0      22       rear          4   3640
5  midsize  15.7      22      front          6   2880
6    large  20.8      19      front          6   3470
```

It would perhaps make sense that the weight of a car would be related to the miles per gallon in the city (mpgCity) that a car gets. In particular, we might expect that as weight goes up, mpg goes down. Conversely, we might just as well model this type of data by saying that as mpg goes up, weight goes down. There is no particular attachment, statistically speaking, for mpg to be the dependent Y variable and weight to be the independent input X variable. A visual inspection of the data seems to verify our belief that there may be an inverse relationship between our Y of mpg and our X of weight (see Figure 13-1).

```
> plot(mpgCity ~ weight, data = cars)
```

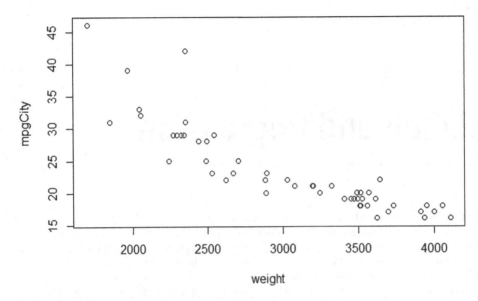

Figure 13-1. *Weight vs. mpgCity scatterplot*

All the same, as before with ANOVA (analysis of variance), we prefer numeric means over visual inspections to make our case. We have data pairs (x, y) of observations. X, the weight, is the input or predictor or independent variable while Y, our `mpgCity`, is the response or criterion or dependent or output variable. If we take the mean of X and the mean of Y and adjust the variance formula just a bit, we get *covariance*:

$$\sigma_{xy} = \frac{\sum(x - \mu_x)(y - \mu_y)}{N} \text{ for population or } s_{xy} = \frac{\sum(x - \bar{x})(y - \bar{y})}{n-1} \text{ for sample data.}$$

In our case of course, we simply use R code to find covariance:

```
> with(cars, cov(x = weight, y = mpgCity))
[1] -3820.3
```

The main point of this is that covariance is a rather natural extension of variance—multiplication (or more precisely *cross product*) is an excellent way to get two variables to relate to each other. The chief complaint against covariance is that it has units; in our case, these units are weight-mpgs per car. If we divided out by the individual standard deviations of X and Y, then we get what is known as the *Pearson product-moment correlation coefficient*. It is scaleless or unitless, and lives in the real number line interval of [-1, 1]. Zero indicates no linear association between two variables, and -1 or +1 indicates a perfect linear relationship. Looking at our data in the scatterplot in Figure 13-1, we would expect any straight-line or linear model to have negative slope. Let's take a look at the R code to calculate correlation:

```
> with(cars, cor (weight, mpgCity, method="pearson" ))
[1] -0.8769183
```

The `cor.test()` function provides a significance test for the correlation coefficient. As we might suspect, the correlation is highly significant with 52 degrees of freedom. We've included some additional function parameters, to gently remind our readers that R often has many options that may be used, depending on your precise goals. As always, `?cor.test` is your friend!

```
> with(cars, cor.test(weight, mpgCity, alternative="two.sided",
+                     method="pearson", conf.level = 0.95))

        Pearson's product-moment correlation

data:  weight and mpgCity
t = -13.157, df = 52, p-value < 2.2e-16
alternative hypothesis: true correlation is not equal to 0
95 percent confidence interval:
 -0.9270125 -0.7960809
sample estimates:
      cor
-0.8769183
```

Having determined that we may reject the null hypothesis, and thus believing that weight and mpg are in fact negatively, linearly correlated, we proceed to our discussion of linear regression.

13.2 Linear Regression: Bivariate Case

We have already covered a good bit about bivariate data, including the addition of the regression line to a scatterplot. Nonetheless, the linear model $\hat{y} = b_0 + b_1 x$ is sample estimate of a linear relationship between x and y, where b0 is the y-intercept term and b1 is the regression coefficient.

In the bivariate case, the test for the significance of the regression coefficient is equivalent to the test that the sample data are drawn from a population in which the correlation is zero. This is not true in the case of multiple regression, as the correlations among the predictors must also be taken into account.

We can obtain the intercept and regression (slope) terms from the lm() function. As in ANOVA, we will use a formula to specify the variables in our regression model. A look into the help file for the fitting linear models function reveals that Y data are also sometimes called a response variable while X may also be referred to as a term.

```
> model <- lm( mpgCity ~ weight )
> model

Call :
lm( formula = mpgCity ~ weight )

Coefficients :
( Intercept )          weight
   50.143042        -0.008833
```

At this point, it is instructive to look once again at our scatterplot, this time with the least-squares regression line (Figure 13-2). It is worth noting that there do appear to be some outliers to our data—this is not a perfect linear model. One could imagine a better curve to "connect all the dots." This leads to an interesting question, namely, How "good" is our model? The truth is, good may be defined in a number of ways. Certainly, a linear model is very good in terms of compute time (both to discover and to use). On the other hand, notice that very few of our plotted dots actually touch our regression line. For a given weight in our range, an interpolation based on our line seems likely to be mildly incorrect. Again, a numerical methodology to begin to quantify a good fit based on training data is indicated.

```
> with(cars, plot(mpgCity ~ weight))
> abline(model, col = "BLUE")
```

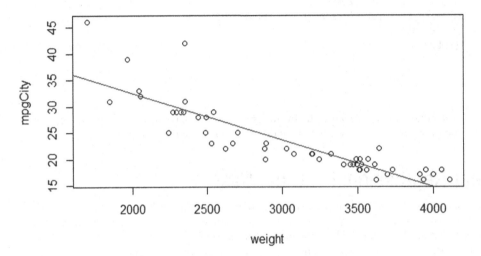

Figure 13-2. *Weight vs. mpgCity scatterplot with blue regression line*

We find a more detailed summary of our linear model by using summary(). There is a great deal of information shown by this command (see the output below). Briefly, R echoes the function call, what we typed to create the model. This is followed by a summary of the residuals. Residuals are defined as $e = y - \hat{y} = y - (b_0 + b_1 x)$, that is, it is the difference between the expected value, $\hat{y}$, and whatever value is actually observed. Residuals are zero when a point falls exactly on the regression line. R provides a summary showing the minimum value, the first quartile (25th percentile), median (50th percentile), third quartile (75th percentile), and maximum residual.

The next part shows the coefficients from the model, often called b or B in textbooks and papers, which R labels as Estimate, followed by each coefficients' standard error, capturing uncertainty in the estimate due to only having a sample of data from the whole population. The t value is simply the ratio of the coefficient to the standard error, $t = b_0 / SE_{b_0}$, and follows the t distribution we learned about in earlier chapters in order to derive a p value, shown in the final column.

At the bottom, R shows the residual standard error and the standard deviation of residual scores, and of particular note is the R-squared (the square of the correlation). R-squared is a value between [0, 1] which is also called the coefficient of determination. It is the percentage of total variation in the outcome or dependent variable that can be accounted for by the regression model. In other words, it is the amount of variation in the response/dependent variable that can be explained by variation in the input/ term variable(s). In our case, 76.9% of the variation in mpgCity may be explained by variation in weight. Contrariwise, 23.1% of the variation in mpg is not explainable by the variation in weights, which is to say that about a fourth of whatever drives mpg is not weight related. We may be looking for a better model!

■ **Warning**   Correlation is not causation! There is a large difference between an observational analysis, such as what we have just performed, and a controlled experiment.

```
> summary (model)

Call :
lm(formula = mpgCity ~ weight, data = cars)

Residuals :
      Min        1Q      Median        3Q        Max
   -5.3580   -1.2233    -0.5002    0.8783    12.6136

Coefficients :
                 Estimate     Std.  Error   t  value  Pr (>|t|)
( Intercept )  50.1430417   2.0855429          24.04  <2e -16 ***
weight         -0.0088326   0.0006713         -13.16  <2e -16 ***
---
Signif . codes :    0   ***   0.001    **   0.01    *   0.05    .   0.1   1

Residual standard error : 3.214 on 52 degrees of freedom
Multiple R- squared : 0.769 , Adjusted R- squared : 0.7645
F- statistic : 173.1 on 1 and 52 DF , p- value : < 2.2e -16
```

As we mentioned earlier, the test of the significance of the overall regression is equivalent to the test of the significance of the regression coefficient, and you will find that the value of *F* for the test of the regression is the square of the value of *t* used to test the regression coefficient. Additionally, the residual standard error is a measure of how far, on average, our y values fall away from our linear model regression line. As our y axis is miles per gallon, we can see that we are, on average, "off" by 3.2 mpg.

We can also calculate a confidence interval for our regression model. The confidence interval describes the ranges of the means of y for any given value of x. In other words, if we shade a 95% confidence interval around our regression line, we would be 95% confident that the true regression line (if we had a population's worth of data values) would lie inside our shaded region. Due to the nature of the mathematics powering regression, we will see that the middle of our scale is more stable than closer to the ends (Figure 13-3). Conservative statistics tends to embrace *interpolation*—using a linear regression model to only calculate predicted values inside the outer term values.

```
> library(ggplot2)
> p1 <- ggplot(cars, aes(weight, mpgCity)) +
+   geom_point() +
+   stat_smooth(method = lm) +
+   ggtitle("Linear Regression of MPG on Weight") +
+   theme_bw()
> p1
```

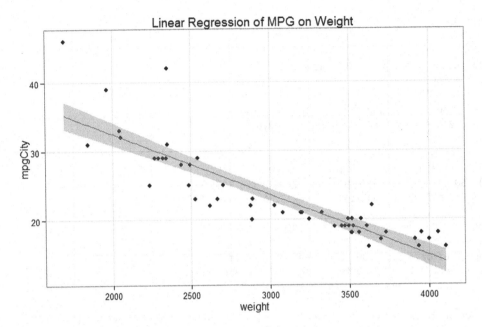

Figure 13-3. *95% Confidence interval shading on our regression line*

Diagnostic plots of the fitted data points and the residuals are often very useful when we examine linear relationships. Let us use ggplot2 to produce a plot of the residuals vs. the fitted values, as well as a normal Q-Q plot for the same data. First, we make the plot of the residuals vs. fitted values. We add a smoothed fit line and a confidence region, as well as a dashed line at the intercept, which is zero for the standardized residuals. The plots appear in Figures 13-4 and 13-5.

```
> p2 <- ggplot(model , aes(.fitted , .resid )) +
+   geom_point() +
+   stat_smooth( method ="loess") +
+   geom_hline( yintercept = 0, col ="red", linetype = "dashed") +
+   xlab(" Fitted values ") +
+   ylab(" Residuals ") +
+   ggtitle(" Residual vs Fitted Plot ") +
+   theme_bw()
> p2
```

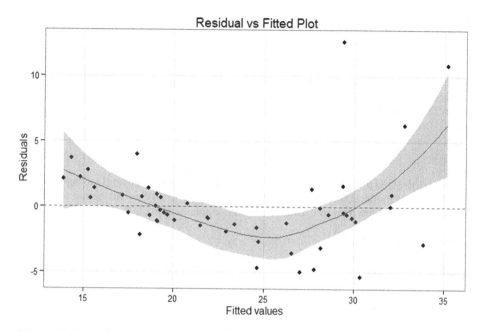

Figure 13-4. *Residuals vs. fitted values for the linear model*

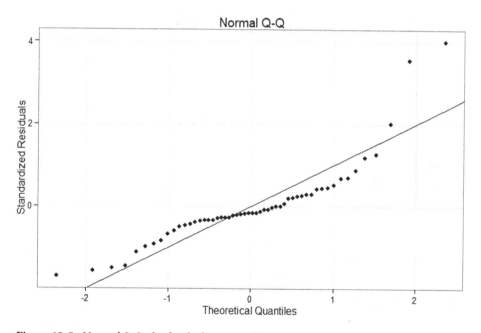

Figure 13-5. *Normal Q-Q plot for the linear model*

The normal Q-Q plot is constructed in a similar fashion, as follows. Figure 13-5 shows the finished plot.

```
> p3 <- ggplot(model , aes(sample = .stdresid)) +
+    stat_qq() +
+    geom_abline(intercept = 0, slope = 1) +
+    xlab(" Theoretical Quantiles ") +
+    ylab (" Standardized Residuals ") +
+    ggtitle(" Normal Q-Q ") +
+    theme_bw ()
> p3
```

A quick examination of the Q-Q plot indicates that the relationship between weight and mileage may not be best described by a linear model. These data seem left skewed. We can also use a histogram as before to visualize whether the residuals follow a normal distribution, as a supplement to the Q-Q plot.

```
> p4 <- ggplot(model , aes(.stdresid)) +
+    geom_histogram(binwidth = .5) +
+    xlab(" Standardized Residuals ") +
+    ggtitle(" Histogram of Residuals ") +
+    theme_bw()
> p4
```

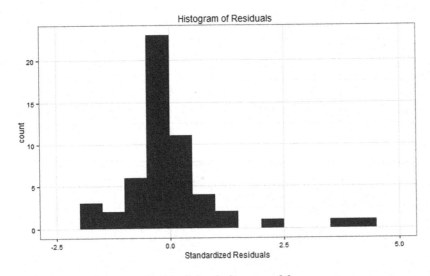

Figure 13-6. *Histogram of residuals for the linear model*

By saving the graphs in R objects along the way, we can put all our results together into a panel of graphs to get a good overview of our model. Note that we can extract output from the model summary. In the example that follows, we extract the estimated R^2 value, multiply by 100 to make it a percentage, and have R substitute the number into some text we wrote for the overall title of the graph, using the sprintf(), which takes a character string and where we write the special %0.1f which substitutes in a number, rounding to the first decimal. Note that we could have included more decimals by writing %0.3f for three decimals. Figure 13-7 shows the results.

```
> library(gridExtra)
> grid.arrange(p1, p2, p3, p4,
+   main = sprintf("Linear Regression Example, Model R2 = %0.1f%%",
+                  summary(model)$r.squared * 100),
+   ncol = 2)
```

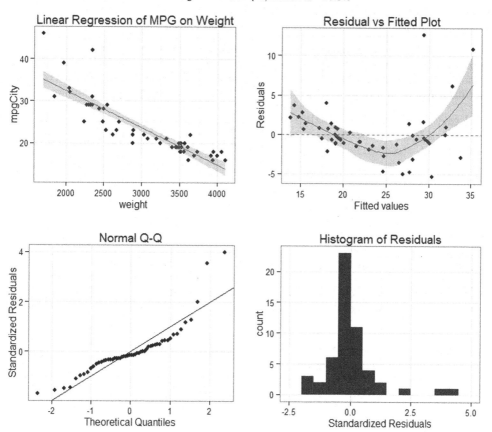

Figure 13-7. *Regression summary and overview panel graph*

13.3 An Extended Regression Example: Stock Screener

Data on stocks are readily enough available for download, and the process may be quite instructive. The usual sorts of disclaimers about being wise before randomly buying stocks apply. We will first explore the linear regression between the closing share price for a particular telecommunications company and day (technically just an indexing of date). We'll progress to trying our hand at a curvilinear model, which will both wrap up this chapter and motivate the next chapter's *multiple* regression.

Note that for simple and multiple linear regression, an assumption is that the observations are independent, that is, the value of one observation does not influence or is not associated with the value of any observation. With stock data or time series data, this assumption is obviously violated, as a stock's price on one day will tend to be related to its price on the day before, the next day, and so on. For the moment, as we introduce regression, we will ignore this fact, but readers are cautioned that time series analysis requires some additional methods beyond simple regression.

Unlike some other languages, R starts indexing at 1 rather than 0. As you rapidly move on to more advanced techniques in R, the temptation to repurpose code from the Internet will be strong. While it may even be wise to not reinvent the wheel, you must be canny enough to watch for things such as different indices.

We have included in this text's companion files the same data we used to run the following code. We also include the code to download stock data "fresh" from the Internet. It is possible that fresh data may not fit our next two models as well as the data we selected; we were choosy in our data. We also edited the first column (with the date data) to be an index. We used Excel's fill handle to do that surgery quickly and intuitively.

```
> sData=read.csv(file="http://www.google.com/finance/historical?output=csv&q=T",header=TRUE)
> write.csv(sData, "stock_ch13.csv", row.names=FALSE) #some edits happen here in Excel
> sData <- read.csv("stock_ch13.csv", header = TRUE)
> head(sData)
  Index  Open  High   Low Close   Volume
1     1 35.85 35.93 35.64 35.73 22254343
2     2 35.59 35.63 35.27 35.57 36972230
3     3 36.03 36.15 35.46 35.52 31390076
4     4 35.87 36.23 35.75 35.77 28999241
5     5 36.38 36.40 35.91 36.12 30005945
6     6 36.13 36.45 36.04 36.18 47585217
```

We create a plot of the closing stock price by year with a linear model fit to the plot with the following code to create Figure 13-8. It is perhaps not too difficult to see that a linear fit is perhaps not the best model for our stock.

```
> plot(Close ~ Index, data = sData)
> abline(lm(Close ~ Index, data = sData))
```

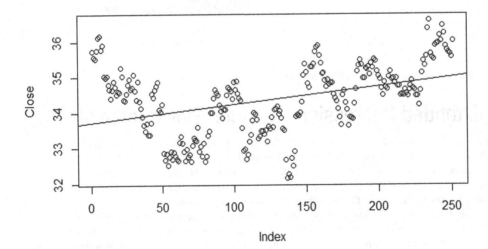

Figure 13-8. *Closing value in United States Dollars (USD) over the last 251 days of a telecommunication stock*

Despite our graph in Figure 13-8 not fitting very well to a linear model, the model does have statistically significant linearity, seen in the regression analysis between day and closing stock price. As we see in our analysis, 14% of the variability in our closing stock price is accounted for by knowing the date.

```
> results <- lm(Close ~ Index, data = sData)
> summary(results)

Call:
lm(formula = Close ~ Index, data = sData)

Residuals:
     Min      1Q   Median      3Q     Max
-2.28087 -0.68787  0.03499  0.65206  2.42285

Coefficients:
             Estimate Std. Error t value Pr(>|t|)
(Intercept) 33.726751   0.114246 295.211  < 2e-16 ***
Index        0.005067   0.000786   6.446 5.91e-10 ***
---
Signif. codes:  0 '***' 0.001 '**' 0.01 '*' 0.05 '.' 0.1 ' ' 1

Residual standard error: 0.9023 on 249 degrees of freedom
Multiple R-squared:  0.143,    Adjusted R-squared:  0.1396
F-statistic: 41.55 on 1 and 249 DF,  p-value: 5.914e-10
```

13.3.1 Quadratic Model: Stock Screener

Let us see if we can account for more of the variability in closing stock prices by fitting a *quadratic* model to our dataset. We are getting near multiple regression territory here, although, technically, we are not adding another term to our mix simply because we will only square the index predictor. Our model will fit this formula:

$$y = b_0 + b_1 x + b_2 x^2$$

We still save multiple input terms for Chapter 14. We could create another variable in our dataset that was a vector of our squared index values, a common practice in curve-fitting analysis that creates a second-order equation. However, R's formula interface allows us to use arithmetic operations right on the variables in the regression model, as long as we wrap them in $I()$, to indicate that these should be regular arithmetic operations, not the special formula notation. Ultimately, this is still a linear model because we have a linear combination of days (index) and days (index) squared. Putting this all together in R and repeating our regression analysis from before yields:

```
> resultsQ <- lm(Close ~ Index + I(Index^2), data = sData)
> summary(resultsQ)

Call:
lm(formula = Close ~ Index + I(Index^2), data = sData)

Residuals:
     Min      1Q   Median      3Q     Max
-1.69686 -0.55384  0.04161  0.56313  1.85393
```

```
Coefficients:
             Estimate Std. Error t value Pr(>|t|)
(Intercept) 3.494e+01  1.387e-01 251.868  <2e-16 ***
Index      -2.363e-02  2.542e-03  -9.296  <2e-16 ***
I(Index^2)  1.139e-04  9.768e-06  11.656  <2e-16 ***
---
Signif. codes:  0 '***' 0.001 '**' 0.01 '*' 0.05 '.' 0.1 ' ' 1

Residual standard error: 0.7267 on 248 degrees of freedom
Multiple R-squared:  0.4463,    Adjusted R-squared:  0.4419
F-statistic: 99.96 on 2 and 248 DF,  p-value: < 2.2e-16
> resultsQ <- lm(Close ~ Index + IndexSQ)
```

Our quadratic model is a better fit (again, we save for another text a discussion about the risks of overfitting) than our linear model. The quadratic model accounts for approximately 44% of the variation in closing stock prices via our Index and Index^2 predictor(s). Using the predict() function, we produce predicted stock closing prices from the quadratic model, and save them into a new variable called predQuad, into our data frame sData so that we may use the lines() function to add the curved line in Figure 13-9.

```
> sData$predQuad <- predict(resultsQ)
> plot(Close ~ Index, data = sData, main = "quadratic model")
> abline(results)
> lines(sData$predQuad, col="blue")
```

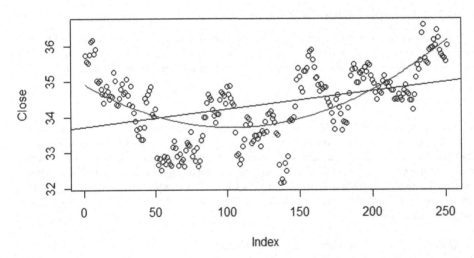

quadratic model

Figure 13-9. *Quadratic (curve) and linear (straight) regression lines on scatterplot*

We may also call R's plot() function on resultsQ to see four diagnostic plots based on the distances between predicted values of stock closing prices (which is what our blue line traces) vs. the observed or training values (we call these *residuals*). Of interest is that R actually has several versions of the plot() function. To be precise, we are using plot.lm(). However, since our object is of the class lm, R is clever enough to use the correct version of our function without us explicitly calling it. R will plot Figures 13-10 through 13-13 one at a time for us.

```
> class(resultsQ)
[1] "lm"

> plot(resultsQ)
Hit <Return> to see next plot:
Hit <Return> to see next plot:
Hit <Return> to see next plot:
Hit <Return> to see next plot:
```

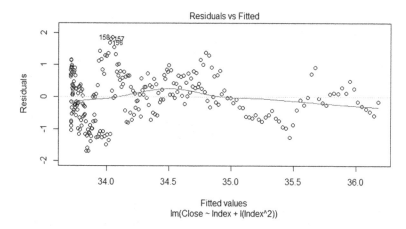

Figure 13-10. *Residuals vs. fitted values*

The normal Q-Q plot shows that excepting a few outliers, our quadratic model is a fairly good fit. Days 156, 157, and 158 show up in the plot as being less-than-ideal residuals, but overall the residuals appear to follow a normal distribution.

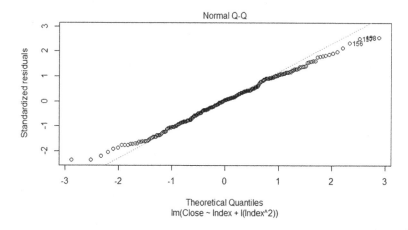

Figure 13-11. *Normal Q-Q plot for the quadratic model shows good fit*

The plot of the standardized residuals against the fitted values can help us see if there are any systematic trends in residuals. For example, perhaps the lower the fitted values, the higher the residuals, which might alert us that our model is fitting poorly in the tails.

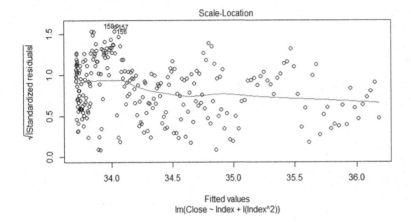

Figure 13-12. *Scale-Location plot*

The final plot shows the standardized residuals against the leverage. Leverage is a measure of how much influence a particular data point has on the regression model. Points with low leverage will not tend to make a big difference on the model fit, regardless of whether they have a large or small residual. R shows the Cook's distance as a dashed red line, values outside this may be concerning. We do not see the Cook's distance line in the graph in Figure 13-13 because it is outside the range of data, a good sign that all our residuals fall within it.

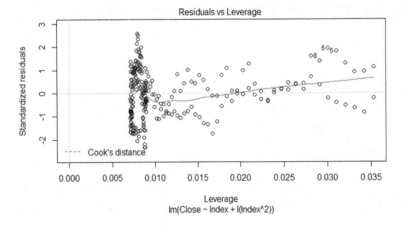

Figure 13-13. *Residuals vs. leverage plot*

13.3.2 A Note on Time Series

One feature of time series data, such as stock prices, is that the value at time *t* is often associated with the value at time *t* - 1. We can see this from the graphs of the data where there appear to be some cyclical effects in stock prices. One common type of time series analyses is *AutoRegressive Integrated Moving Average* (ARIMA) models. ARIMA models can incorporate seasonality effects as well as autoregressive processes, where future values depend on some function of past values. A very brief example of a simple ARIMA model fit to the stock data is shown in the code that follows and in Figure 13-14. Although we will not cover time series analysis in this introductory book, interested readers are referred to Makridakis, Wheelwright, and Hyndman (1998) for an excellent textbook on time series and forecasting.

```
> install.packages("forecast")
> library(forecast)
> m <- auto.arima(sData$Close)

> pred <- forecast(m, h = 49)

> plot(Close ~ Index, data = sData, main = "ARIMA Model of Stock Prices",
+       xlim = c(1, 300), ylim = c(30, 42))
> lines(fitted(m), col = "blue")
> lines(252:300, pred$mean, col = "blue", lty = 2, lwd = 2)
> lines(252:300, pred$lower[, 2], lty = 2, lwd = 1)
> lines(252:300, pred$upper[, 2], lty = 2, lwd = 1)
```

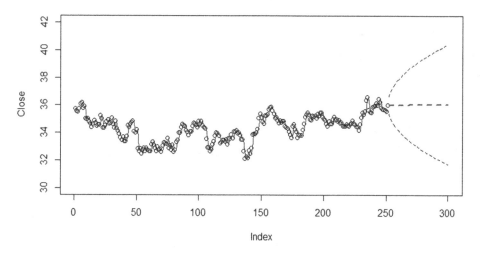

ARIMA Model of Stock Prices

Figure 13-14. ARIMA model of closing stock prices with forecasting and 95% confidence intervalsI

13.4 Confidence and Prediction Intervals

For our regression model(s), we can graph the confidence intervals (CIs) and prediction intervals (PIs). The *t* distribution is used for CI and PI to adjust the standard error of the estimate. In the summary() function we called on our linear results from our stock data, R provides the standard error of the estimate (R calls this *residual standard error*) near the end of the output:

Residual standard error: 0.9023 on 249 degrees of freedom.

Notice that this is in y-axis units (in this case USD) and estimates the population standard deviation for y at a given value of x. This is not the most ideal fit, since +/- $0.90 doesn't do much for stock portfolio estimation! Repeating the calculation on the quadratic model is somewhat better. Recall that earlier, our model yielded Residual standard error: 0.7267 on 248 degrees of freedom.

We show the code for the linear model, have the code for both models in this text's companion files, and show both linear and quadratic models in Figures 13-15 and 13-16, respectively.

```
> conf <- predict(results, interval = "confidence")
> pred <- predict(results, interval = "prediction")
Warning message:
In predict.lm(results, interval = "prediction") :
  predictions on current data refer to _future_ responses

> colnames(conf) <- c("conffit", "conflwr", "confupr")
> colnames(pred) <- c("predfit", "predlwr", "predupr")

> intervals <- cbind(conf, pred)
> head(intervals)
   conffit  conflwr  confupr  predfit  predlwr  predupr
1 33.73182 33.50815 33.95549 33.73182 31.94069 35.52294
2 33.73688 33.51455 33.95922 33.73688 31.94592 35.52784
3 33.74195 33.52095 33.96295 33.74195 31.95116 35.53275
4 33.74702 33.52735 33.96668 33.74702 31.95639 35.53765
5 33.75208 33.53375 33.97042 33.75208 31.96162 35.54255
6 33.75715 33.54014 33.97416 33.75715 31.96684 35.54746
> intervals <- as.data.frame(intervals)

> plot(Close ~ Index, data = sData, ylim = c(32, 37))
> with(intervals, {
+   lines(predLin)
+   lines(conflwr, col = "blue")
+   lines(confupr, col = "blue")
+   lines(predlwr, col = "red")
+   lines(predupr, col = "red")
+ })
```

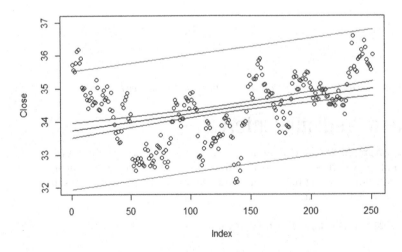

Figure 13-15. *Linear fit to sData with CI and PI lines*

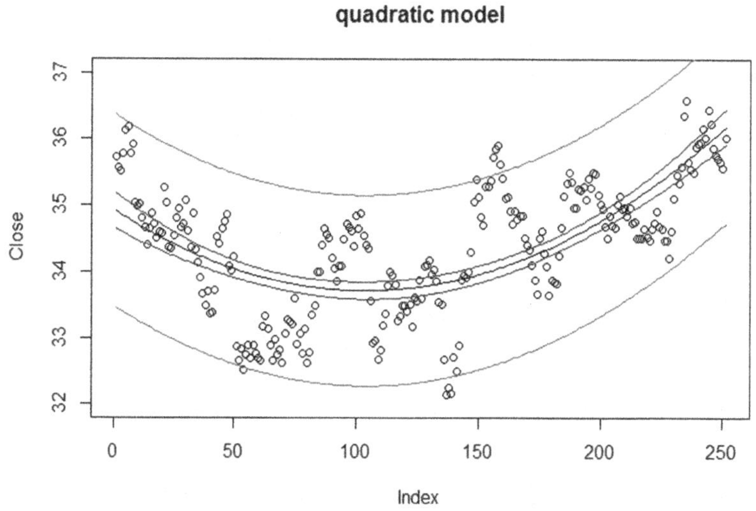

Figure 13-16. *Quadratic fit to sData with CI lines*

Either way, as interesting as these data are, perhaps the authors' choices to remain in academia rather than pursue careers on Wall Street are self-explanatory. Of course, if we were to extend our model with more relevant predictors beyond only time, a more useful model might be uncovered. This is the heart of multiple regression, which we explore in the next chapter.

References

Makridakis, S., Wheelwright, S. C., & Hyndman, R. J. *Forecasting Methods and Applications* (3rd ed.). New York: John Wiley & Sons, 1998.

■ ■ ■

CHAPTER 14

Multiple Regression

The idea of multiple regression is that rather than just having a single predictor, a model built on multiple predictors may well allow us to more accurately understand a particular system. As in Chapter 13, we will still focus overall on linear models—we will simply have a new goal to increase our number of predictors. Also as before, we save for other texts a focus on the behind-the-scenes mathematics; our goal is to conceptually explore the methods of using and understanding multiple regression. Having offered this caveat, however, doesn't free us from taking just a little bit of a look at some of the math that power these types of models.

14.1 The Conceptual Statistics of Multiple Regression

In the previous chapter, we stated simply that our general model was $\hat{y} = b_0 + b_1 x$. This was mostly true. To get just a shade more technical, our model was $\hat{y} = b_0 + b_1 x$ while we hoped to be finding the true equation of $y = B_0 + B_1 X + \varepsilon$. In other words, if we had access to an entire population worth of data, we would find y and it would have been predicted by a single input predictor x, up to some error ε which we would assume as a precondition was independent of our input x and normally distributed about zero. For simple regression, this was perhaps not vital as a fine point to focus on understanding. For multiple predictors, however, we will want to have some techniques to determine which predictors are more or less valuable to improving our model.

This decision of which predictors to include becomes an important part of multiple regression because our formula can be quite a bit more complicated. In multiple regression, we hope to find the true equation of $y = B_0 + B_1 X_1 + B_2 X_2 + \ldots + B_k X_k + \varepsilon$. By using our training data from a limited number of k predictors, we find our regression equation $\hat{y} = b_0 + b_1 x_1 + b_2 x_2 + \ldots + b_k x_k$. Once we remove the restriction of having only a single predictor, one of the questions we'll have to answer is which predictors we should use. We will want to ensure that we reward simpler models over more complex models. Another question that we will need to consider is whether any of our predictors will have an interaction with each other.

Consider the following example, where we wish to study how students succeed at learning statistics. In Chapter 13, we would perhaps have considered how many hours a student studies a week as a predictor for final course score. However, some students arrive at an introductory statistics course fresh out of high school, while other arrive after a decade in the workforce, and still others have already taken calculus and differential equations. So, while *hours per week of study (S)* may well be one useful predictor, we may also wish to add *months since last mathematics course (M)* as well as *highest level of mathematics completed (H)* and *percent of book examples read (P)* to our mix of predictors. Looking at this example, let us talk through how a model should work.

These all sound useful enough, but it may well turn out that some of them are fairly useless as predictors once we build our model. Furthermore, while studying is all well and good, the fact is that study can be thought of as deliberate practice. Practicing incorrect methods would be a terrible idea, and yet it may well happen. On the other hand, a student who reads her textbook examples cautiously is perhaps less likely to practice incorrect methods. In terms of our equation, we start out imagining that

$y = B_0 + B_S S + B_M M + B_H H + B_P P + \varepsilon$ may make a good model. Yet, as mentioned, perhaps incorrect study is a bad idea. We would like to code into our formula the interaction of reading textbook examples with study. We do this through multiplication of the study hours and percent of textbook read predictors: $y = B_0 + B_S S + B_M M + B_H H + B_P P + B_{SP}(S * P) + \varepsilon$. This interaction term answers the question, "Does the effect of hours per week of study depend on the percent of book examples read?" or equivalently, "Does the effect of percent of book examples read depend on the number of hours per week of study?" Two-way interactions can always be interpreted two ways, although typically people pick whichever variable makes most sense as having the "effect" and which one makes most sense as "moderating" or modifying the effect. Later on in an extended example, we will show how to determine if an interaction predictor may be warranted. Of course, we have already seen such interactions somewhat in Chapter 13, where we made a variable interact with itself to create a polynomial model.

Although each predictor may be important on its own, due to overlap, we may find that not all variables are uniquely predictive. For example, in a sample of college seniors, highest level of mathematics completed (H) and months since last mathematics course (M) may be correlated with each other as students who took math most recently may have been taking it their whole undergraduate and thus have a higher level as well. In this case we may want to drop one or the other in order to simplify the model, without much loss in predictive performance. One of the first ways we can evaluate performance in R is by observing the Adjusted R-squared output of the linear model. Recall from the prior chapter that in the summary() function of linear models, near the end of that output, it gave both *Multiple R-squared* and *Adjusted R-squared* values (which in that chapter were the same), and we stated:

R-squared is a value between [0, 1] which is also called the coefficient of determination. It is the percentage of total variation in the outcome or dependent variable that can be accounted for by the regression model. In other words, it is the amount of variation in the response/dependent variable that can be explained by variation in the input/ term variable(s).

Adjusted R-squared is calculated from the Multiple R-squared value, adjusted for the number of observations and the number of predictor variables. More observations make the adjustment increase, while more predictors adjust the value down. The formula is given here:

$$Adjusted\ R^2 = 1 - \left[\frac{n-1}{n-(k+1)}\right]\left(1 - Multiple\ R^2\right)$$

To round out this brief, conceptual discussion of the ideas we're about to see in action, we make a brief note about standard error. Recall from Chapter 13 that we also claimed *"the residual standard error is a measure of how far, on average, our y values fall away from our linear model regression line."* Regression assumes that the error is independent of the predictor variables and normally distributed. The way in which the regression coefficients are calculated makes the errors independent of the predictors, at least linearly. Many people focus on whether the outcome of regression is normally distributed, but the assumption is only that the errors or residuals be normally distributed. Graphs of the residuals are often examined as a way to assess whether they are normally or approximately normally distributed.

As we explore multiple regression through the gss2014 data introduced in prior chapters, we will examine several predictors that we *could* use, and explain how a cautious look at various graphs and R package outputs will help us create a more powerful model through multiple predictors.

14.2 GSS Multiple Regression Example

Recall that our General Social Survey (GSS) data include behavioral, attitudinal, and demographic questions. For our purposes, we will focus on nine items of age in years, female/male sex, marital status, years of education (educ), hours worked in a usual week (hrs2), total family income (income06), satisfaction with finances (satfin), happiness (happy), and self-rated health. Our goal, by the end of the extended example, will be to use multiple predictors to determine total family income.

We will also use several packages, so to focus on the analysis, we will install and load all those packages now. We will also load the GSS2012 file we downloaded in an earlier chapter as an SPSS file and then call out just the reduced dataset of the nine variables we mentioned earlier and name it gssr ("r" for reduced) as follows (note, R often gives some warnings about unrecognized record types when reading SPSS data files, these are generally ignorable):

```
> install.packages(c("GGally", "arm", "texreg"))
> library(foreign)
> library(ggplot2)
> library(GGally)
> library(grid)
> library(arm)
> library(texreg)
> gss2012 <- read.spss("GSS2012merged_R5.sav", to.data.frame = TRUE)
> gssr <- gss2012[, c("age", "sex", "marital", "educ", "hrs2", "income06", "satfin",
"happy", "health")]
```

In our gssr dataset we have 4,820 observations on nine variables. Of these, age, education, hours worked in a typical week, and income are all numeric variables, yet they are not coded as such in our data frame. We use the within() function to take in our data, recode these categories as numeric data, and then save those changes. As always, data munging may well take a fair bit of time. The following code does this:

```
> gssr <- within(gssr, {
+    age <- as.numeric(age)
+    educ <- as.numeric(educ)
+    hrs2 <- as.numeric(hrs2)
+    # recode income categories to numeric
+    cincome <- as.numeric(income06)
+ })
```

With our data in a data frame and organized into usable data types, we are ready to begin deciding which of our eight possible predictors might best allow us to estimate total family income. As a first pass, we might consider that income may be predicted by age, by education, and by hours worked per week.

14.2.1 Exploratory Data Analysis

We are ready to perform some exploratory data analysis (EDA) on our numeric data using ggpairs(). Our goal is to see if any of the values we just forced to be numeric (and thus easy to graph and analyze) might make good predictors. This code will give a convenient, single image that shows the correlations between each of our potential predictors, the bar graph of each individual predictor, and a scatterplot (and single variable regression line) between each pair of variables. Along the diagonal, we'll have our bar graphs, while the lower triangle will have scatterplots.

```
> ggpairs(gssr[, c("age", "educ", "hrs2", "cincome")],
+          diag = list(continuous = "bar"),
+          lower = list(continuous = "smooth"),
+          title = "Scatter plot of continuous variables")
stat_bin: binwidth defaulted to range/30. Use 'binwidth = x' to adjust this.
stat_bin: binwidth defaulted to range/30. Use 'binwidth = x' to adjust this.
stat_bin: binwidth defaulted to range/30. Use 'binwidth = x' to adjust this.
stat_bin: binwidth defaulted to range/30. Use 'binwidth = x' to adjust this.
There were 19 warnings (use warnings() to see them)
```

Our plan is to use age, education, and usual hours worked weekly as predictors for total family income. As such, the right-most column correlations in Figure 14-1 are of interest. Recall that correlation yields an output between [-1, 1]. The further a variable is from 0, the more interesting we consider it as a potential predictor. Education seems to have a positive correlation with income, which makes sense. As education increases, income might increase. Age and income, on the other hand, seem to have a very weak relationship.

This weak relationship may be readily seen in the scatterplots of the lower triangle of our Figure 14-1. It may be difficult to see in the textbook plot due to size, but run the previous code in R and you will see that the lower right income vs. age scatterplot has a rather boring linear regression line. For any particular income, there are many possible ages that could get there. Contrast this with the income vs. education scatterplot; the regression line shows that higher incomes are related to more educations. Something to notice about these scatterplots is that there a dot for each of our 4,820 observations. Since education is measured in years, and income is binned data (and thus segmented), these scatterplots do not quite show the whole picture. That is because it is not easy to see, without the regression line, that there are many more dots at the (educ, cincome) (20, 25) mark then there are at the (20, 10) mark. Now, with the regression line, one supposes that must be true to pull that line up. In just a bit, we'll discuss the idea of jitter to make those differences a shade easier to see.

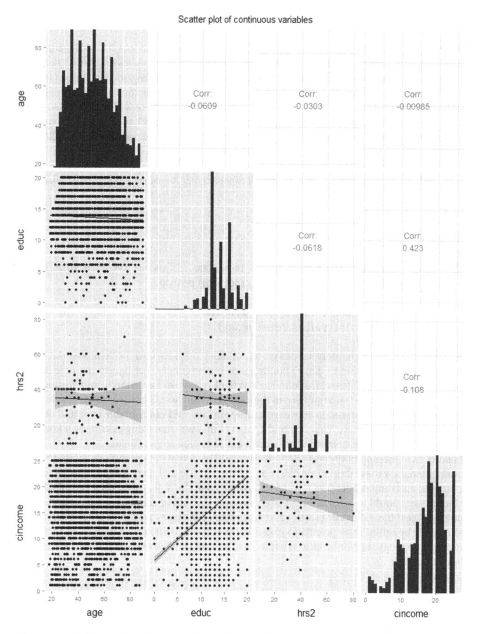

Figure 14-1. *Correlations, bar graphs, and scatterplots of age, education, hours worked in usual week, and incomeZ*

While we are seeking higher correlations between our potential predictor variables and income, low correlations between our predictors are desirable. The fact that education and hours per week have so little in common with a correlation of -0.0618 and a fairly flat regression line in the (educ, hrs2) scatterplot gives us hope that adding hours into the mix of predictors would be bringing something new to the multiple regression.

Spend some time looking over Figure 14-1. It really has quite a lot of data packed inside one set of charts and graphs.

From Figure 14-1, we decide that education may be a good first predictor for income. The GSS actually allows respondents to select from a range of total family income, then codes those ranges into bins. The higher the bin, the more income the respondent's family unit makes in a year. Looking one last time at that scatterplot, recall that we pointed out that a single dot on that chart might well be secretly many dots packed directly on top of each other. In the R package ggplot2, we can include a geometric objected aptly titled *jitter* to introduce just a little wiggle to our data values. This will allow us to visually unpack each dot, so that all 4,820 observations (less some 446 rows of missing data) are more visible. We see the code for this as follows:

```
> ggplot(gssr, aes(educ, cincome)) +
+   # use jitter to add some noise and alpha to set transparency to more easily see data
+   geom_jitter(alpha = .2) +
+   stat_smooth() +
+   theme_bw() +
+   xlab("Years of Education") +
+   ylab("Income Bins")
geom_smooth: method="auto" and size of largest group is >=1000, so using gam with formula:
y ~ s(x, bs = "cs"). Use 'method = x' to change the smoothing method.
Warning messages:
1: Removed 446 rows containing missing values (stat_smooth).
2: Removed 446 rows containing missing values (geom_point).
```

While we've used ggplot2 in prior chapters, let us take a moment to explore how the syntax works. The function call ggplot(data, more_arguments_here) builds a plot incrementally. The data in our case is replaced with the call to our actual data, gssr. Most often in this book, we make an aesthetic map through the aes(x, y, ...) function call as one last argument to the ggplot() function. Since we kept the order that aes() was expecting for x and y, in the code above we simply put our predictor variable educ and our dependent cincome into the function. As we'd already told ggplot() that we were using gssr data, it knew where to look for educ and cincome without more complex row call tags such as gssr$educ.

Next, ggplot2 allows us to incrementally add additional layers. The actual data points are geometric objects, which we want jittered for these data so we call geom_jitter(). The alpha argument is available for most geometric objects, and ranges from 0 to 1, where 0 indicates that the object should be completely transparent, and 1 indicates it should be completely opaque. A value of .2 will be more transparent than opaque. Every geometric object has a default statistic (and vice versa), although that can be overridden as we do in the preceding code by calling stat_smooth() to create the smoothed line in our image. We wrap up the plot with an overall graph theme (bw for black and white, in this example) and explicitly label the x and y axis. Figure 14-2 shows the result.

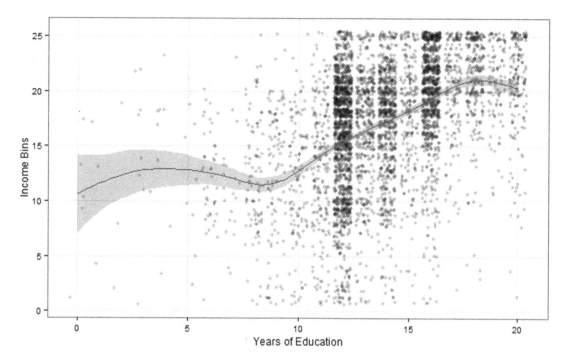

Figure 14-2. *Scatterplot of income vs. years of education (with jitter)*

Looking at Figure 14-2, thanks to jittering, we can see the density of our data values. This shows well why higher education had such a higher correlation with higher income (and the smooth line helps demonstrate this as well). By having a better sense of where our data are located, we can collapse our data. Few people have less than 9 years of education. Furthermore, as we can see from the smooth line, there is not much benefit from more than perhaps 18 years of education. We again reduce our data, not removing columns as we did before, but rather recoding education to a new set of values that trims our data if it is below 9 or above 18. The functions pmin() and pmax() return the parallel minimum or maximum. They operate on each element of a vector or variable. In our example, we first ask for the maximum of either years of education or 9, and then the minimum of years of education or 18.

```
> gssr <- within(gssr, {
+   reduc <- pmin(pmax(educ, 9), 18)
+ })
```

From here, we may redraw our plot, and see an updated graph that more clearly highlights education's expected contribution to our multiple regression model:

```
> ggplot(gssr, aes(reduc, cincome)) +
+   geom_jitter(alpha = .2) +
+   stat_smooth() +
+   theme_bw() +
+   xlab("Years of (Recoded) Education") +
+   ylab("Income Bins")
geom_smooth: method="auto" and size of largest group is >=1000, so using gam with formula:
y ~ s(x, bs = "cs"). Use 'method = x' to change the smoothing method.
```

```
Warning messages:
1: Removed 446 rows containing missing values (stat_smooth).
2: Removed 446 rows containing missing values (geom_point).
```

Running the foregoing code yields the updated graph seen in Figure 14-3. We have a fairly straight line, with only a bit of wiggle near what might be the "less than high school" or "more than high school" breaks. Notice we have cautiously relabeled our graph to call out that we have chosen to recode the education data. Any time data are trimmed or otherwise altered, best practice is to call it by a different title inside the code and to purposefully mention such a thing has been done via graph labels on any images.

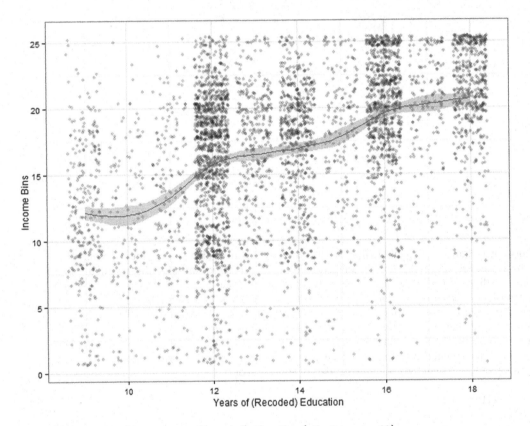

Figure 14-3. *Income bins vs. years of (recoded) education (min. 9 to max. 18)*

14.2.2 Linear Model (the First)

Now that we have explored our data somewhat, we are ready to begin building our linear model. Just as in Chapter 13, we start with a simple model:

```
> m <- lm(cincome ~ reduc, data = gssr)
> summary( m )

Call:
lm(formula = cincome ~ reduc, data = gssr)

Residuals:
     Min       1Q   Median       3Q      Max
-20.1731   -3.2061   0.7609   3.7609  12.6784

Coefficients:
             Estimate Std. Error t value Pr(>|t|)
(Intercept)   3.47003    0.42634   8.139 5.14e-16 ***
reduc         0.98351    0.03049  32.256  < 2e-16 ***
---
Signif. codes:  0 '***' 0.001 '**' 0.01 '*' 0.05 '.' 0.1 ' ' 1

Residual standard error: 5.127 on 4372 degrees of freedom
  (446 observations deleted due to missingness)
Multiple R-squared:  0.1922,    Adjusted R-squared:  0.192
F-statistic:  1040 on 1 and 4372 DF,  p-value: < 2.2e-16
```

We see that our p values are significant for our adjusted education data. However, our education data can only account for 19.2% of the total variance in income. There is definitely room for improvement here! Notice as mentioned earlier that the *Multiple R-squared* is the same as the *Adjusted R-squared* for the single variable case.

It is also important to note that of our 446 deleted values, not all of them have fully missing data. Some are missing education, others miss only income, and of course some are missing both. It is a worthy topic for another time how to handle missing data through more elegant means than list-wise deletion (where cases missing any variable in a regression are removed) for *missingness*.

Just as we did in the last chapter, we will take a look at our graphs to see if this model makes sense as seen from the following code leading to Figure 14-4:

```
> par(mfrow = c(2, 2))
> plot( m )
```

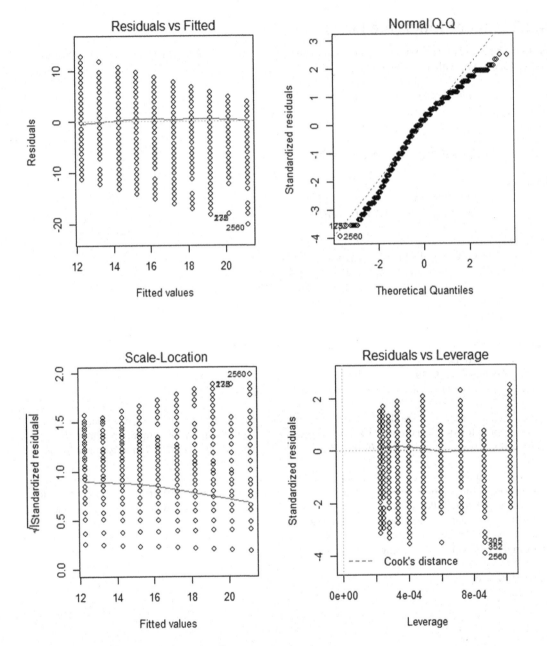

Figure 14-4. *The four plot(m) graphs all at once*

We can see (perhaps clearly enough from the Normal Q-Q plot) that our residuals look normal enough, except for some odd behavior in the tails.

14.2.3 Adding the Next Predictor

It seems that years of education may well be a good predictor for total family income. However, it still only accounts for 19.2% of the total variance found in income. Returning to our collected data, we next explore if sex makes a difference, starting, as always, with a graph for our EDA generated from the following code and seen in Figure 14-5:

```
> ggplot(gssr, aes(reduc, cincome)) +
+   geom_jitter(alpha = .2) +
+   stat_smooth() +
+   theme_bw() +
+   xlab("Years of (Recoded) Education") +
+   ylab("Income Bins") +
+   facet_wrap(~ sex)
geom_smooth: method="auto" and size of largest group is >=1000, so using gam with formula:
y ~ s(x, bs = "cs"). Use 'method = x' to change the smoothing method.
geom_smooth: method="auto" and size of largest group is >=1000, so using gam with formula:
y ~ s(x, bs = "cs"). Use 'method = x' to change the smoothing method.
Warning messages:
1: Removed 178 rows containing missing values (stat_smooth).
2: Removed 268 rows containing missing values (stat_smooth).
3: Removed 178 rows containing missing values (geom_point).
4: Removed 268 rows containing missing values (geom_point).
```

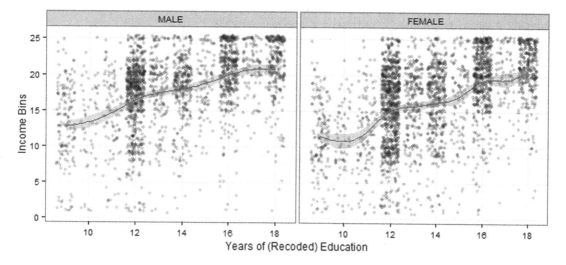

Figure 14-5. *Income vs. years of (recoded) education broken out by sex of survey respondent*

Since our income values for both male and female at 18 years of education are roughly similar (by inspection), yet our initial values for income seem lower, we believe that sex may well be interacting with education. We update our model accordingly, and use a new operator '.' which means *everything*. So we write .~.*sex as shorthand for "everything our model used to have on the left-hand side, while on the right-hand side, include sex and interactions with sex as variables." In R, this sort of update follows this format: a*b = a + b + a*b where it gives the main effects of a, of b, and of a interacting with b. Note that R uses the colons, ":" to indicate the interaction of two variables, although mathematically, it is the multiplication of two variables and in writing typically indicated by "*" or "x" as in "education x sex". You can see the specifics in the summary() function call that follows:

```
> m2 <- update(m, . ~ . * sex)
> summary( m2 )

Call:
lm(formula = cincome ~ reduc + sex + reduc:sex, data = gssr)

Residuals:
     Min      1Q  Median      3Q     Max
-20.4990 -2.8145  0.8855  3.5010 13.5891

Coefficients:
                 Estimate Std. Error t value Pr(>|t|)
(Intercept)       5.34540    0.62202   8.594  < 2e-16 ***
reduc             0.89742    0.04446  20.186  < 2e-16 ***
sexFEMALE        -3.45342    0.84833  -4.071 4.77e-05 ***
reduc:sexFEMALE   0.16023    0.06066   2.641  0.00829 **
---
Signif. codes:  0 '***' 0.001 '**' 0.01 '*' 0.05 '.' 0.1 ' ' 1

Residual standard error: 5.087 on 4370 degrees of freedom
  (446 observations deleted due to missingness)
Multiple R-squared:  0.2054,    Adjusted R-squared:  0.2048
F-statistic: 376.5 on 3 and 4370 DF,  p-value: < 2.2e-16
```

In the summary, we see that while we now have three prediction variables, namely, our adjusted education variable, our dummy-coded sex variable, and our education * sex interaction, we have now accounted for 20.5% of income variability through our model. Our p values remain significant, courtesy of our rather large N even though the additional variance accounted for in this model is only around 1%.

We close out this section by visualizing our predicted results. The function expand.grid() creates a data frame from all possible combinations of factors, in this case the reduc values from 9 to 18 and the levels of gssr$sex data from our gssr dataset. Using the predict() function, we create $\hat{y}$ data and graph it in Figure 14-6.

```
> newdata <- expand.grid(reduc = 9:18, sex = levels(gssr$sex))
> head(newdata)
  reduc  sex
1     9 MALE
2    10 MALE
3    11 MALE
4    12 MALE
5    13 MALE
6    14 MALE

> newdata$yhat <- predict(m2, newdata = newdata)

> ggplot(newdata, aes(reduc, yhat, colour = sex)) +
+   geom_line(size=1.5) +
```

```
+    theme_bw() +
+    xlab("Recoded Years of Education") +
+    ylab("Income Bin")
```

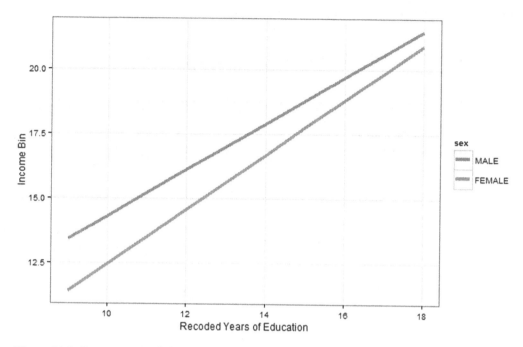

Figure 14-6. *Income vs. recoded years of education broken out by male/female sex*

As can be seen in Figure 14-6, sex seems to have an effect on income. This effect appears larger with lower education, although it is not a dramatic interaction.

14.2.4 Adding More Predictors

As we add more predictors beyond our initial group, we have ever more aspects to consider. Do we need to simply add the new predictors into our model or must we include interactions? This requires some cautious looks at the graphs and at the summary data. We turn to age as that seemed the weakest correlation of our data set. In the code that follows, we see what should now be fairly familiar:

```
> p <- ggplot(gssr, aes(age, cincome)) +
+    geom_jitter(alpha = .2) +
+    stat_smooth() +
+    theme_bw() +
+    xlab("Age in Years") +
+    ylab("Income Bins")
> p
geom_smooth: method="auto" and size of largest group is >=1000, so using gam with formula:
y ~ s(x, bs = "cs"). Use 'method = x' to change the smoothing method.
Warning messages:
1: Removed 470 rows containing missing values (stat_smooth).
2: Removed 470 rows containing missing values (geom_point).
```

The resulting graph in Figure 14-7 shows what appears to be a quadratic effect of age. Notice that this also explains why the age correlation was weak! Correlation only looks for linear effects, and this is quadratic. We left a breadcrumb for this near the start of our discussion where we noted age had a weak correlation; notice too that the geom_jitter() function is very helpful in seeing how a straight-line average would perhaps give a very incorrect picture of the effect age has on income.

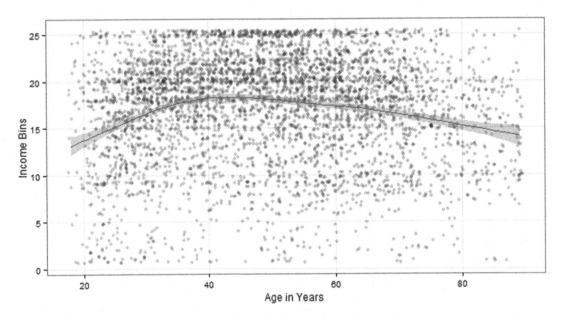

Figure 14-7. *Income vs. age (in years) showing a quadratic fit to the data*

Age seems to have good things to say about income, but do we need to consider whether the effect of age differs by sex? Again, we use the facet_wrap() function to sort by male and female:

```
> p2 <- p + facet_wrap(~ sex)
> p2
geom_smooth: method="auto" and size of largest group is >=1000, so using gam with formula:
y ~ s(x, bs = "cs"). Use 'method = x' to change the smoothing method.
geom_smooth: method="auto" and size of largest group is >=1000, so using gam with formula:
y ~ s(x, bs = "cs"). Use 'method = x' to change the smoothing method.
Warning messages:
1: Removed 186 rows containing missing values (stat_smooth).
2: Removed 284 rows containing missing values (stat_smooth).
3: Removed 186 rows containing missing values (geom_point).
4: Removed 284 rows containing missing values (geom_point).
```

As seen in Figure 14-8, the quadratic shapes of the graphs are approximately the same. Furthermore (and again we are doing this simply by visual inspection), there does not seem to be anything special about male vs. female income by age beyond what we already knew about their incomes in general.

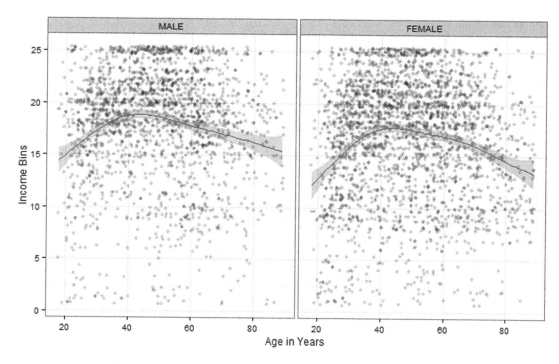

Figure 14-8. *Income vs. male age in years and female age in years*

Since the age effect is quadratic, we update our model to include both age and age squared (we did this in the last chapter with time on our stock example). Note that to use regular arithmetic operators inside an R formula, we wrap them in another function, I(), which is just the identity function.

```
> m3 <- update(m2, . ~ . + (age + I(age^2)))
> summary( m3 )

Call:
lm(formula = cincome ~ reduc + sex + age + I(age^2) + reduc:sex, data = gssr)

Residuals:
     Min       1Q   Median       3Q      Max
-19.0198  -2.7655   0.8147   3.4970  12.9333
```

```
Coefficients:
                 Estimate Std. Error t value Pr(>|t|)
(Intercept)    -1.2387081  0.8546644  -1.449  0.14731
reduc           0.8620941  0.0439172  19.630  < 2e-16  ***
sexFEMALE      -3.4718386  0.8372444  -4.147 3.44e-05  ***
age             0.3023966  0.0260673  11.601  < 2e-16  ***
I(age^2)       -0.0028943  0.0002505 -11.555  < 2e-16  ***
reduc:sexFEMALE 0.1650542  0.0598623   2.757  0.00585  **
---
Signif. codes:  0 '***' 0.001 '**' 0.01 '*' 0.05 '.' 0.1 ' ' 1

Residual standard error: 5.003 on 4344 degrees of freedom
  (470 observations deleted due to missingness)
Multiple R-squared:  0.2289,     Adjusted R-squared:  0.228
F-statistic: 257.9 on 5 and 4344 DF,  p-value: < 2.2e-16
```

In this update, we see again that our p value is significant and that our predictors now explain 22.8% of our variability in income. This is from the Adjusted R-squared, which is a good sign that these are useful predictors to have in our model. We haven't checked our four plots from our regression model recently, so we again run the code for that and view the resulting two-by-two grid in Figure 14-9.

```
> par(mfrow = c(2, 2))
> plot(m3)
```

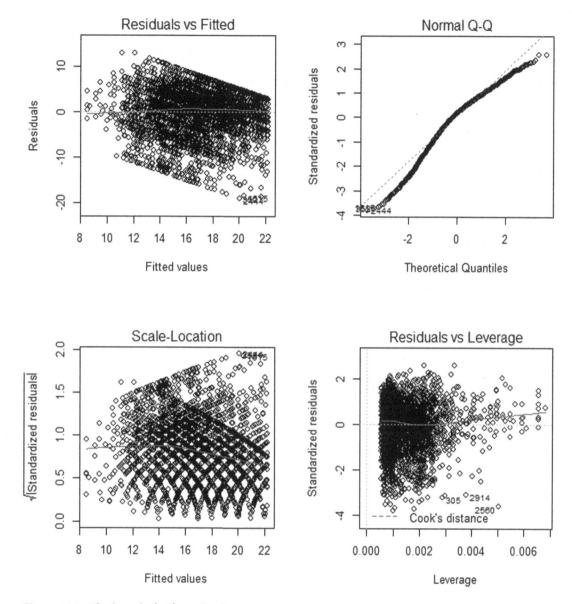

Figure 14-9. *The four plot(m3) graphs all at once*

Again, we see that the normal residuals precondition holds near the middle of our data, but less so at the tails. As we added more predictors, more predicted values are possible and thus our graphs that at first had very clear "bands" in the residuals vs. fitted values are now more dispersed.

As for our last additions, we use our model to create our prediction lines. This time, we will not only get our lines, but we will include standard errors for our confidence intervals. The 95% confidence intervals for the average predicted value can be obtained as approximately $\hat{y} \pm 1.96 * SE$ or precisely $\hat{y} + Z_{\alpha=.025} * SE$ and $\hat{y} + Z_{\alpha=.975} * SE$, which can be obtained in R as qnorm(.025) and qnorm(.975), respectively. However, rounded to two decimals these are +/- 1.96, which is sufficient precision for visual inspection. This time, we select only certain levels of education attainment in three-year increments from our chosen interval. Following is the code for both these steps:

```
> newdata <- expand.grid(age = 20:80, reduc = c(9, 12, 15, 18), sex = levels(gssr$sex))
> head(newdata)
  age reduc  sex
1  20     9 MALE
2  21     9 MALE
3  22     9 MALE
4  23     9 MALE
5  24     9 MALE
6  25     9 MALE

> newdata <- cbind(newdata, predict(m3, newdata = newdata, se.fit = TRUE))

> head(newdata)
  age reduc  sex      fit   se.fit   df residual.scale
1  20     9 MALE 11.41034 0.3165924 4344       5.003214
2  21     9 MALE 11.59407 0.3070684 4344       5.003214
3  22     9 MALE 11.77202 0.2983259 4344       5.003214
4  23     9 MALE 11.94417 0.2903586 4344       5.003214
5  24     9 MALE 12.11053 0.2831553 4344       5.003214
6  25     9 MALE 12.27111 0.2767002 4344       5.003214
```

Next, we run the code to plot our new model's newdata. This time, we let linetype = sex which cycles through different lines types depending on sex. Last time, we did the same process with color (although that may not have been clear in the printed version of this text). The code that follows includes a new geometric object, geom_ribbon(), which shows our confidence intervals. Also the plot will set education constant and contrast income vs. age in years. This is a sort of two-dimensional way to code in the fact that age, sex, and education have us in at least three dimensions (ignoring the addition of interaction predictors). Finally, we include some code to remove the legend's title, move the legend to the lower part of the graph, and make the legend larger.

```
> ggplot(newdata, aes(age, fit, linetype = sex)) +
+   geom_ribbon(aes(ymin = fit - 1.96 * se.fit,
+                   ymax = fit + 1.96 * se.fit), alpha = .3) +
+   geom_line(size=1.5) +
+   theme_bw() +
+   theme(
+     legend.title = element_blank(), # get rid of legend title
+     legend.position = "bottom", # move legend to bottom of graph
+     legend.key.width = unit(1, "cm")) + # make each legend bigger
+   xlab("Age in Years") +
+   ylab("Income Bin") +
+   facet_wrap(~ reduc)
```

We see the result of the preceding code in Figure 14-10. Each panel of the graph has the years of education at the top, although R is only showing the values, not the variable name or anything to tell us those numbers represent years of education (i.e., what a figure legend is for!).

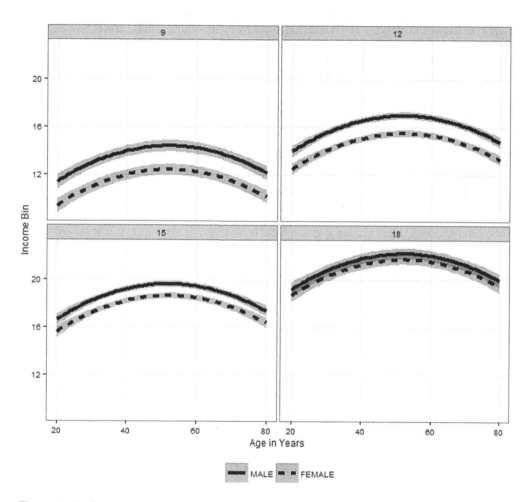

Figure 14-10. *Income vs. age in years for males and females segmented by adjusted education data*

We see in Figure 14-10 that while there is a significant difference in both the model and the confidence intervals around the model for male and female income, by the upper end of educational attainment, that difference becomes less extreme with the overlap of the shaded confidence intervals (as always, trusting a visual inspection is risky, we ran View(newdata) and looked at the actual confidence intervals to confirm)— not entirely comforting, but perhaps better than might have been.

14.2.5 Presenting Results

We turn our attention now to preparing our results for final presentation. We have increased our predictive ability by 3.58%. Of course, with a dataset as rich as the GSS data, we might be tempted to carry on our efforts. After all, we certainly haven't used all possible predictors (including the usual hours worked per week). Indeed, an inspection of Figure 14-1, which has a slightly counterintuitive linear regression line, makes the authors wonder if there is not a quadratic shape to that effect as well. It certainly seems possible that income would be low for both part-time and over-full-time workers, while the highest earners might work typical jobs more generally. Still, we are confident that there is enough here for the interested reader to continue adding predictors.

Using the coef() and confint() functions, we extract the coefficients and confidence intervals from our final m3 model and cbind() them together.

```
> coef(m3)
      (Intercept)           reduc         sexFEMALE              age          I(age^2)
reduc:sexFEMALE
     -1.238708083     0.862094062      -3.471838551      0.302396558      -0.002894312
0.165054159
> confint(m3)
                        2.5 %          97.5 %
(Intercept)      -2.914286341    0.436870176
reduc             0.775993915    0.948194210
sexFEMALE        -5.113264804   -1.830412297
age               0.251291337    0.353501778
I(age^2)         -0.003385371   -0.002403252
reduc:sexFEMALE   0.047693534    0.282414783

> output <- cbind(B = coef(m3), confint(m3))
> output
                          B          2.5 %          97.5 %
(Intercept)     -1.238708083   -2.914286341    0.436870176
reduc            0.862094062    0.775993915    0.948194210
sexFEMALE       -3.471838551   -5.113264804   -1.830412297
age              0.302396558    0.251291337    0.353501778
I(age^2)        -0.002894312   -0.003385371   -0.002403252
reduc:sexFEMALE  0.165054159    0.047693534    0.282414783
```

We see that looks somewhat messy, so we round the output.

```
> round(output, 2)
                     B  2.5 % 97.5 %
(Intercept)      -1.24 -2.91   0.44
reduc             0.86  0.78   0.95
sexFEMALE        -3.47 -5.11  -1.83
age               0.30  0.25   0.35
I(age^2)          0.00  0.00   0.00
reduc:sexFEMALE   0.17  0.05   0.28
```

It can be helpful to standardize variables to help make them more interpretable. Gelman (2008) recommends scaling by 2 standard deviations (SD). This is readily enough done with the arm package we installed and included earlier. Running the model again with the standardize() function not only scales the regression inputs but also mean centers variables to make interactions more interpretable.

```
> z.m3 <- standardize(m3, standardize.y = TRUE)
```

Now coefficients for continuous variables represent the effect on SDs of income bin per 2 SD change in the predictor roughly equivalent to going from "low" to "high" (i.e., one extreme to the other). For a binary variable like sex, the coefficient is the difference between sexes.

```
> round(cbind(B = coef(z.m3), confint(z.m3)), 2)
                 B 2.5 % 97.5 %
(Intercept)   0.07  0.05   0.09
z.reduc       0.43  0.40   0.46
c.sex        -0.11 -0.13  -0.08
z.age         0.05  0.02   0.07
I(z.age^2)   -0.30 -0.35  -0.25
z.reduc:c.sex 0.07  0.02   0.13
```

Writing a generic (and reusable) function to format output, and then calling it on the m3 data yields

```
> regCI <- function(model) {
+   b <- coef(model)
+   cis <- confint(model)
+   sprintf("%0.2f [%0.2f, %0.2f]",
+           b, cis[, 1], cis[, 2])
+ }

> regCI(m3)
[1] "-1.24 [-2.91, 0.44]"  "0.86 [0.78, 0.95]"   "-3.47 [-5.11, -1.83]"
[4] "0.30 [0.25, 0.35]"    "-0.00 [-0.00, -0.00]" "0.17 [0.05, 0.28]"
```

Showing the raw and standardized estimates side by side, we note that on raw scale the squared age term is hard to read because age has such a big range. The effect of changing a single year squared was very small, but standardized, the coefficient is much larger matching the importance of age we saw in the graphs.

```
> data.frame(
+   Variable = names(coef(m3)),
+   Raw = regCI(m3),
+   Std. = regCI(z.m3))
          Variable             Raw                  Std.
1      (Intercept)  -1.24 [-2.91, 0.44]   0.07 [0.05, 0.09]
2            reduc   0.86 [0.78, 0.95]    0.43 [0.40, 0.46]
3       sexFEMALE  -3.47 [-5.11, -1.83]  -0.11 [-0.13, -0.08]
4              age   0.30 [0.25, 0.35]    0.05 [0.02, 0.07]
5          I(age^2)  -0.00 [-0.00, -0.00] -0.30 [-0.35, -0.25]
6 reduc:sexFEMALE    0.17 [0.05, 0.28]    0.07 [0.02, 0.13]
```

We can also make nice summaries of models using the texreg package. It creates a little bit prettier model output using the layout of coefficients (standard error) and *p* values as asterisks. We use an additional argument to put the coefficient and standard error on the same row. If we had many models, we might leave this off, in which case the standard error would go on a new line below the coefficient, making more room across the page for extra models.

```
> screenreg(m3, single.row = TRUE)
```

```
========================================
                     Model 1
----------------------------------------
(Intercept)       -1.24 (0.85)
reduc              0.86 (0.04) ***
sexFEMALE         -3.47 (0.84) ***
age                0.30 (0.03) ***
I(age^2)          -0.00 (0.00) ***
reduc:sexFEMALE    0.17 (0.06) **
----------------------------------------
R^2                0.23
Adj. R^2           0.23
Num. obs.       4350
RMSE               5.00
========================================
*** p < 0.001, ** p < 0.01, * p < 0.05
```

We can also show the iterative model process as a nice summary for this example. It has captured most the results we would want or need to report, including all the coefficients, whether an effect is statistically significant, the number of observations, raw and adjusted R-squared, and the residual standard error, here labeled RMSE for root mean square error. Note that there are options available to control the format of output, including customizing model names to be more informative than the default 1, 2, 3, customizing the row labels, how many digits to round to, whether to include confidence intervals, and many more. The interested reader is referred to the open access journal article on the package by Leifeld (2013).

```
> screenreg(list(m, m2, m3), single.row = TRUE)
```

```
================================================================================
                     Model 1            Model 2            Model 3
--------------------------------------------------------------------------------
(Intercept)       3.47 (0.43) ***    5.35 (0.62) ***   -1.24 (0.85)
reduc             0.98 (0.03) ***    0.90 (0.04) ***    0.86 (0.04) ***
sexFEMALE                           -3.45 (0.85) ***   -3.47 (0.84) ***
reduc:sexFEMALE                      0.16 (0.06) **     0.17 (0.06) **
age                                                     0.30 (0.03) ***
I(age^2)                                               -0.00 (0.00) ***
--------------------------------------------------------------------------------
R^2               0.19               0.21               0.23
Adj. R^2          0.19               0.20               0.23
Num. obs.      4374               4374               4350
RMSE              5.13               5.09               5.00
================================================================================
*** p < 0.001, ** p < 0.01, * p < 0.05
```

14.3 Final Thoughts

Multiple linear regression works well when there is a rich set of data that has many options for predictor or independent variables. As noted earlier in our discussion about the Adjusted R-squared value, larger n can be helpful, particularly when each predictor by itself only explains a small amount of variance. Multiple regression also supposes that the response variable is numeric and continuous. This worked well enough in our GSS data where annual, total family income was used as a response.

This would work less well if we attempted to use income06 to predict sex, on the other hand. Such a categorical, qualitative variable can be better explained through logistic regression or logit models. We will explore models for categorical outcomes, such as logistic regression, in the next chapter.

References

Gelman, A. "Scaling regression inputs by dividing by two standard deviations." *Statistics in Medicine, 27*(15), 2865–2873 (2008).

Gelman, A., & Su, Y-S. arm: Data Analysis Using Regression and Multilevel/Hierarchical Models, 2015. R package version 1.8-6. Available at: http://CRAN.R-project.org/package=arm.

Leifeld, P. (2013). "texreg: Conversion of statistical model output in R to LaTeX and HTML tables." *Journal of Statistical Software, 55*(8), 1–24. Available at: www.jstatsoft.org/v55/i08/.

R Core Team. (2015). foreign: Read Data Stored by Minitab, S, SAS, SPSS, Stata, Systat, Weka, dBase, ... R package version 0.8-65. http://CRAN.R-project.org/package=foreign.

Schloerke, B., Crowley, J., Cook, D., Hofmann, H., Wickham, H., Briatte, F., Marbach, M., &Thoen, E. GGally: Extension to ggplot2, 2014. R package version 0.5.0. Available at: http://CRAN.R-project.org/package=GGally.

CHAPTER 15

■ ■ ■

Logistic Regression

The linear regressions we have been exploring have some underlying assumptions. First and foremost is that response and prediction variables should have a linear relationship. Buried in that assumption is the idea that these variables are *quantitative*. However, what if the response variable is *qualitative or discrete*? If it is binary, such as measuring whether participants are satisfied or not satisfied, we could perhaps dummy-code satisfaction as 1 and no satisfaction as 0. In that case, while a linear regression may provide some guidance, it will also likely provide outputs well beyond the range of [0,1], which is clearly not right. Should we desire to predict more than two responses (e.g., not satisfied, mostly satisfied, and satisfied), the system breaks down even more.

Fortunately, logistic regression provides a mechanism for dealing with precisely these kinds of data. We will start off this chapter going into just enough mathematical background that we can understand when to use logistic regression and how to interpret the results. From there, we will work through a familiar dataset to understand the function calls and mechanisms R has in place to perform such calculations.

15.1 The Mathematics of Logistic Regression

First of all, apologies for the amount of mathematics we are about to go through. This is a methods text, and yet, to properly understand the results of logistic regression, it helps to understand where this all starts. If you are already familiar with logarithms, odds, and probability, feel free to move on to the example. If not, we will keep this as high level as possible, again saving for statistics texts and our appendix the precise reasoning.

At its heart, the advances of modern mathematics are powered by the idea of functions. In mathematics as in R, functions map input values to unique output values. That is, if we input the same information to the same function, we expect the same output. One of the more fascinating functions discovered over the years is the logarithmic function. It has many useful properties; perhaps one of the most impressive is that it converts the multiplication of large numbers into the addition of smaller values. This was terribly useful in computations of early navigation because multiplying large numbers is generally difficult while summing small numbers is comparatively easy.

$$\log(MN) = \log(M) + \log(N)$$

Another useful feature of a logarithm is that it is the inverse function of an exponent. In a once popular movie, the protagonist claimed there were three steps to any good magic trick. The final step was that one had to undo the magic and make things right again. That is the power of inverses. We can map our inputs from our world into a more convenient place where it is easy to solve. However, once we have exploited the easy-to-solve feature, we need to take our results back into our world. We will see throughout our example in this section that we often take our answers and go to some pains to pull them back into "our" world. The fact that we are performing a conversion on our data also means we must be cautious with our interpretation of results.

Our goal is to model dummy-coded quantitative information. If we had a function that took inputs that were continuous variables and forced the outputs to live between 0 and 1, we might well be fairly happy. Fortunately, such a function exists. It is called the logistic function and for a single predictor X is as follows:

$$P(X) = \frac{e^{B_0 + B_1 X}}{1 + e^{B_0 + B_1 X}}$$

We will let R worry about how to discover the coefficients; our focus here is that there are exponents on the right-hand side, and that the foregoing function's range of outputs is trapped between 0 and 1 regardless of the input values. We also care about understanding how to interpret our logistic regression results. A little bit of algebraic manipulation on our function tells us that

$$\frac{P(Y)}{1 - P(Y)} = e^{B_0 + B_1 X}$$

The left-hand side of our equation is the odds. As anyone who attends the Kentucky Derby knows, odds and probability are related, but they are not quite the same. Suppose we know from television that four out of five dentists recommend a particular brand of gum. Then the probability of a dentist recommending this gum is 4/5 which would be $P(Y) = 0.8$. However, our odds would be 4 to 1 which in the foregoing ratio would be 4 since $\frac{0.8}{1 - 0.8} = 4$. Odds can live between 0 and infinity. Still, while we can understand the left-hand side, the right-hand side is not as nice as it might be. Remember, logarithms and exponents are inverses. If we take (or compose) both sides of our equation with a logarithm, we get a left-hand side of *logarithmic odds* or *log odds* or simply *logit*. The right-hand side becomes a linear model.

$$log\left(\frac{P(Y)}{1 - P(Y)}\right) = B_0 + B_1 X$$

As we interpret our coefficients from the example model we are about to meet, it will often be convenient to talk about the logit or log odds. If we want to convert to odds, then we may simply take the exponent of logit. Thus, while statistical work often discusses probability, when doing logistic regression, we tend to speak in terms of odds instead. As visible from the preceding equation, this is a linear model. Much of what we calculate will be quite similar to the single and multivariate linear regressions we have already performed, just on the log odds scale!

As a final note, logistic regression assumes that our dependent variable is categorical, that there is a linear relationship between the predictor and response variables in the logistic space (not necessarily in the "real world" space, indeed in some examples we will see decidedly nonlinear probabilities, even though they are linear on the log odds scale), that our predictor variables are not perfectly collinear, and that we have a fairly large dataset (we use z-scores rather than t-scores). Things that we used to require (such as normal distribution for response variable or normal distribution for errors) are no longer required, which is rather convenient.

15.2 Generalized Linear Models

Previously, we talked about linear models. Now we will introduce the generalized linear model (GLM). GLMs, as you might expect, are a general class of models. The expected value of our outcome, Y, is $E(Y)$, which is the mean or μ. GLMs then take the following form:

$$\eta = B_0 + B_1 X$$
$$g(\mu) = \eta$$

The first part should look very familiar, except we have replaced $\hat{y}$ with η. η is called the *linear predictor*, because it is always on a linear scale. $g()$ is called the *link function*. Link functions are functions that link the linear predictor to the original scale of the data, or "our" world. Finally, we will define one more function:

$$h() = g()^{-1}$$

$h()$ is the inverse link function, the function that takes us back to "our" world from the linear world. So $g()$ takes us from our world to a linear world, and $h()$ takes us back again. With that said, more or less as long as we can (1) find a suitable link function so that on that scale, our outcome is a linear function of the predictors, (2) we can define an inverse link function, and (3) we can find a suitable distribution, then we can use a GLM to do regression.

For example, linear regression is very simple. It assumes that $g(Y) = Y$ and that $h(g(Y)) = Y$, in other words, the link and inverse link functions are just the identity function—no transformation occurs, and it assumes the data come from a Gaussian distribution. We have already talked about another link function, although we did not call it that. For logistic regression, $g(Y) = \log\left(\dfrac{P(Y)}{1 - P(Y)}\right)$ and $h(\eta) = \dfrac{e^{\eta}}{e^{\eta} + 1}$, and we assume the data follow a binomial distribution. There are many other distributions and link functions we could choose from. For example, we could fit a log normal model, but using a log link function, but still assuming the data follow a Gaussian distribution, such as for income data which cannot be zero. We will see in R how we specify the distribution we want to assume, and the link function.

15.3 An Example of Logistic Regression

We will use our familiar gss2012 dataset, this time attempting to understand when satisfaction with finances (satfin) occurs. Suppose satfin is a dependent variable, and recall this dataset has age in years (age), female vs. male (sex), marital status (marital), years of education (educ), income divided into a number of bins where higher bin number is higher income (income06), self-rated health (health), and happiness (happy). We explore the dataset to find predictors for financial satisfaction. Also, as before, we will make our library calls first, read our data, and perform some data management. We will also for simplicity's sake drop all missing cases using the na.omit() function. Handling missing data (in more reasonable ways than dropping all cases missing any variable) is definitely an important topic. In the interest of keeping our focus on logit models, we save that topic for a future book.

```
> library(foreign)
> library(ggplot2)
> library(GGally)
> library(grid)
> library(arm)
> library(texreg)

> gss2012 <- read.spss("GSS2012merged_R5.sav", to.data.frame = TRUE)
> gssr <- gss2012[, c("age", "sex", "marital", "educ", "income06", "satfin",
                      "happy", "health")]
> gssr <- na.omit(gssr)

> gssr <- within(gssr, {
+    age <- as.numeric(age)
+    educ <- as.numeric(educ)
+    cincome <- as.numeric(income06)
+ })
```

Our `gssr` data have 2,835 observations after fully removing every row that had missing data for any of our eight variables. Notice that while age and education were already text numbers that we have forced to be numeric, the `income06` variable was descriptive, so we have created a new column named `cincome` to hold a numeric value for those titles (e.g., "150000 OR OVER" becomes "25"). Recalling that we have deleted the n/a responses from our data, we take a first look at the `satfin` data in Figure 15-1 generated by the following code:

```
> ggplot(gssr, aes(satfin)) +
+   geom_bar() +
+   theme_bw()
```

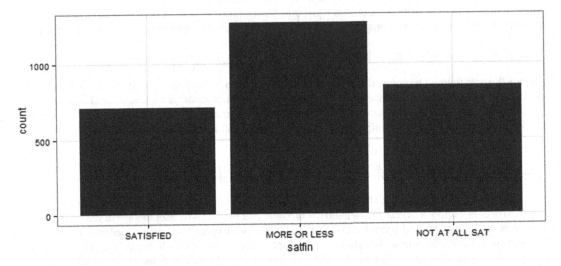

Figure 15-1. *Bar graph* `satfin` *levels vs. count*

For our first pass at logistic regression, we wish to focus only on satisfied vs. not fully satisfied. We create a new variable named `Satisfied` to append to our `gssr` dataset which we code to 1 for satisfied responses to `satfin` and 0 otherwise. We also look at a table of those results in the code that follows:

```
> gssr$Satisfied <- as.integer(gssr$satfin == "SATISFIED")
> table(gssr$Satisfied)

   0    1
2122  713
```

15.3.1 What If We Tried a Linear Model on Age?

These data now seem to satisfy our requirements for running logistic regression. In particular, having financial satisfaction or not fully having financial satisfaction is a qualitative variable and some 2,835 observations seem to be a large dataset. Suppose we select age as a potential predictor for `Satisfied`. We take a moment to consider a normal linear model. This has the advantage of not only seeing (with real data) why we would want such a creature as logistic regression but also seeing what data that are not normal might look like in the usual plots for exploratory data analysis (EDA). We fit the linear model, generate our plots, and see from Figure 15-2, particularly the Normal Q-Q plot, that a linear model is not the way to go. Of course, none of these four graphs looks anything like the linear model results we saw in the last two chapters. These diagnostics show marked non-normality of the data along with other violations of assumptions.

```
> m.lin <- lm(Satisfied ~ age, data = gssr)

> par(mfrow = c(2, 2))
> plot(m.lin)
```

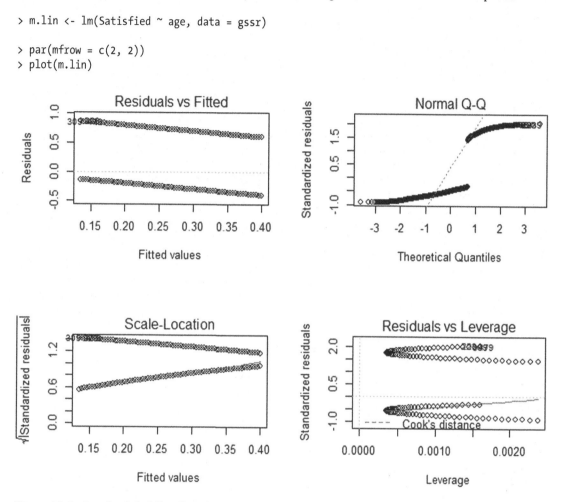

Figure 15-2. *Standard plot() call on the linear model Satisfied ~ age*

15.3.2 Seeing If Age Might Be Relevant with Chi Square

Earlier, we learned of the chi-square tests for categorical data, such as these. If we converted our age variable (much as we did with satfin) into a discrete variable, we could do a chi-square test. Of course, to do so, we would have to pick some level cut-off for age and recode it; here we create a new variable that is 1 if age is ≥ 45 and 0 if age is < 45. Creating a contingency table and running the test shows highly significant results. By the way, when assigning output to a variable for use later, wrapping the whole statement in parentheses is a simple trick to get the output to print, without too much extra typing.

```
> gssr$Age45 <- as.integer(gssr$age >= 45)

> (tab <- xtabs(~Satisfied + Age45, data = gssr))
         Age45
Satisfied    0    1
        0  940 1182
        1  249  464
> chisq.test(tab)
         Pearson's Chi-squared test with Yates' continuity correction
data:  tab
X-squared = 18.88, df = 1, p-value = 1.392e-05
```

The fact that these results are significant does lend weight to our hypothesis that age may well make a good predictor for satisfaction. What if we prefer to leave age as a continuous variable? We turn to logistic regression, which in R uses the GLM and the glm() function. One of the virtues of using R is that the usual functions are often quite adept at determining what sorts of data and data structures are being passed to them. Thus, we will see many similarities between what we have done and what we do now for logit models. We start with our new function and our old friend, the summary() function. You will see that glm() works very similarly to lm() except that we have to use an additional argument, family = binomial(), to tell R that the errors should be assumed to come from a binomial distribution. If you would like to see what other families can be used with the glm() function, look at the R help page for the ?family. You will see that linear regression is actually a specific case of the GLM and if you wanted to, you could run it using the glm() function. You can also use different link functions for each distribution. We did not have to tell R that we wanted to use a logit link function, because that is the default for the binomial family, but if we wanted to, we could have written family = binomial(link = "logit").

15.3.3 Fitting a Logistic Regression Model

```
> m <- glm(Satisfied ~ age, data = gssr, family = binomial())

> summary(m)

Call:
glm(formula = Satisfied ~ age, family = binomial(), data = gssr)

Deviance Residuals:
    Min      1Q   Median      3Q     Max
-1.0394  -0.7904  -0.6885  1.3220  1.9469

Coefficients:
             Estimate Std. Error z value Pr(>|z|)
(Intercept) -2.086915   0.142801 -14.614  < 2e-16 ***
age          0.019700   0.002621   7.516 5.64e-14 ***
---
Signif. codes:  0 '***' 0.001 '**' 0.01 '*' 0.05 '.' 0.1 ' ' 1

(Dispersion parameter for binomial family taken to be 1)

    Null deviance: 3197.7  on 2834  degrees of freedom
Residual deviance: 3140.4  on 2833  degrees of freedom
AIC: 3144.4

Number of Fisher Scoring iterations: 4
```

The summary() function is quite as it has been. It starts off echoing the model call and then provides a summary of the residuals. Recall from our earlier discussion of the theory that these estimates are log odds or logits. In other words, a one-year increase in age is associated with a 0.019700 increase in the log odds of being financially satisfied. We'll spend some effort in a moment to convert that number into something more intuitively meaningful. For now, just keep in mind that our outcome is in log odds scale. Also notice that, again as mentioned, we have z values instead of t values. Logistic regression (as a specific case of GLM) relies on large-number theory and this is the reason we need to have a large sample size, as there is no adjustment for degrees of freedom. The p values (which are significant) are derived from the z values. The intercept coefficient is the log odds of being satisfied for someone who is zero years old. Notice that this is outside the minimum value for our age predictor, and thus it is a somewhat meaningless number. Also notice that log odds can be negative for odds between 0 and 1. This can also be counterintuitive at first.

Looking at the final outputs of our summary tells us that for the binomial model we're using, dispersion is taken to be fixed. The null deviance is based on the log likelihood and is for an empty model; the residual deviance is based on the log likelihood and is for the actual model. These two numbers can be used to give an overall test of model performance/fit similar to the F test for linear models, but in this case it is called a likelihood ratio test (LRT) and follows the chi-square distribution.

To perform a LRT, we first fit a null or empty model which has only an intercept. To test constructed models against null models in R (or to test any two models against each other, for that matter), the generally agreed upon function call is anova(). It is somewhat confusing as we should not interpret its use to mean we are doing an ANOVA (analysis of variance). This function, when given a sequence of objects, tests the models against one another. This function is also part of the reason we opted to remove our rows with null data. It requires the models to be fitted to the same dataset, and the null model will find fewer conflicts than our constructed model. Of note in the code and output that follows is that there is a significant difference between the two models, and thus we believe our model, m, provides a better fit to the data than a model with only an intercept (not a hard bar to beat!).

```
> m0 <- glm(Satisfied ~ 1, data = gssr, family = binomial())
>
> anova(m0, m, test = "LRT")
Analysis of Deviance Table

Model 1: Satisfied ~ 1
Model 2: Satisfied ~ age
  Resid. Df Resid. Dev Df Deviance  Pr(>Chi)
1      2834     3197.7
2      2833     3140.4  1   57.358 3.634e-14 ***
```

As we mentioned previously, the fact that the intercept is fairly meaningless due to being well outside our range of ages might be something to fix to make our model more intuitive. But first, an aside.

15.3.4 The Mathematics of Linear Scaling of Data

If we were to look at a very brief example of just three data points we wished to average, let us say 0, 45, and 45, we would see the arithmetic mean was 30. Now, suppose that we wanted to adjust our x-axis scale in a linear fashion. That is, we might choose to divide all our numbers by 45. If we did that, our new variables would be 0, 1, and 1, and our new average would be 2/3. Of course, we could have simply found our new mean by reducing 30/45 which is of course also 2/3. All this is to say that we might expect linear adjustments to x-axis variables to be well behaved in some convenient fashion. After taking a brief look at Figure 15-3 and the code that created it, notice that linear adjustments of the x axis, while they may change the scale of the x axis, do not change the line really. Here, we make our x-axis conversion by dividing by 5 and adding 3.

```
> x0 <- c(5, 15, 25, 35, 45)
> x1 <- c(4, 6, 8, 10, 12)
> y <- c(0, 10, 20, 30, 40)
> par(mfrow = c(1,2))
> plot(x0,y, type = "l")
> plot(x1,y, type = "l")
```

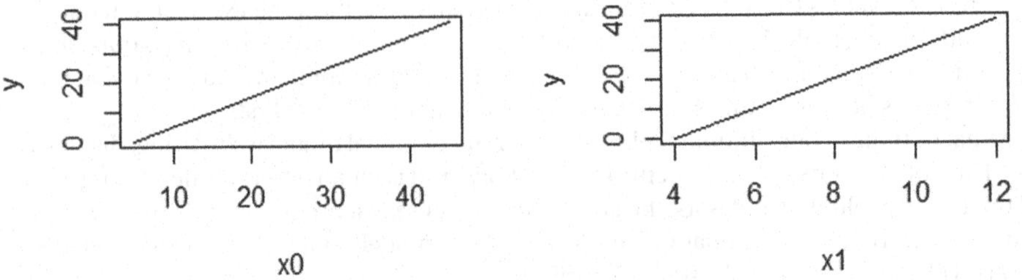

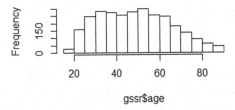

Figure 15-3. *A visual demonstration that linear x-axis rescales don't really change the line*

15.3.5 Logit Model with Rescaled Predictor

Let us take a closer look at our age variable. We can see from Figure 15-4 and the `summary()` code that respondents' ages ranged from 18 to 89 years. We recall from before that our log odds for increase by a single year were rather low. This all leads us to consider changing our predictor scale to something more suitable.

```
> hist(gssr$age)
> summary(gssr$age)
   Min. 1st Qu.  Median    Mean 3rd Qu.    Max.
  18.00   35.00   49.00   49.24   61.00   89.00
```

Histogram of gssr$age

Figure 15-4. *Histogram of age vs. frequency*

A more suitable choice might be to center our age data so that 0 is 18 years of age. This would make our intercept much more useful to us. We also might divide by 10 to be able to discuss how satisfaction changes by decades after reaching adulthood.

Now, with this change, since regression models are invariant to linear transformations of predictors, our model is the same, although our output looks a little different. The intercept is now the log odds of being satisfied at age 18 where our age scale starts and the age effect of 0.19700 is the log odds for a decade increase in age.

```
> gssr$Agec <- (gssr$age - 18) / 10
> m <- glm(Satisfied ~ Agec, data = gssr, family = binomial())
> summary(m)

Call:
glm(formula = Satisfied ~ Agec, family = binomial(), data = gssr)

Deviance Residuals:
    Min      1Q   Median      3Q      Max
-1.0394  -0.7904  -0.6885   1.3220   1.9469

Coefficients:
             Estimate Std. Error z value Pr(>|z|)
(Intercept) -1.73232    0.09895 -17.507  < 2e-16 ***
Agec         0.19700    0.02621   7.516 5.64e-14 ***
---
Signif. codes:  0 '***' 0.001 '**' 0.01 '*' 0.05 '.' 0.1 ' ' 1

(Dispersion parameter for binomial family taken to be 1)

    Null deviance: 3197.7  on 2834  degrees of freedom
Residual deviance: 3140.4  on 2833  degrees of freedom
AIC: 3144.4

Number of Fisher Scoring iterations: 4
```

Often the log odds scale is not very intuitive, so researchers prefer to interpret odds ratios directly; we can convert the coefficients to odds ratios by exponentiation, since logarithm and exponents are inverses.

```
> cbind(LogOdds = coef(m), Odds = exp(coef(m)))
              LogOdds      Odds
(Intercept) -1.7323153 0.1768744
Agec         0.1969999 1.2177439
```

Now we can interpret the effect of age, as for each decade increase in age, people have 1.22 times the odds of being satisfied; they do **not** have 1.22 times the chance or the probability of being satisfied. These are still *odds*. Just not log odds.

We may also be interested in the confidence intervals (CIs). As usual, we take the coefficient and add the 95% confidence intervals. We do this in the log odds scale *first* and *then* exponentiate that result. This is because our method of discovering CIs is predicated around the linear model of the log odds scale (i.e., estimate ± 1.96 x standard error).

```
> results <- cbind(LogOdds = coef(m), confint(m))
Waiting for profiling to be done...
> results
              LogOdds      2.5 %     97.5 %
(Intercept) -1.7323153 -1.9284027 -1.5404056
Agec         0.1969999  0.1457785  0.2485537
```

```
> exp(results)
              LogOdds      2.5 %      97.5 %
(Intercept) 0.1768744 0.1453802 0.2142942
Agec        1.2177439 1.1569399 1.2821696
```

For graphing and interpreting, perhaps the easiest scale is probabilities as odds can still be confusing and depend on the actual probability of an event happening. Let us create a new dataset of ages, across the whole age range, and get the predicted probability of being satisfied for each hypothetical person. We will generate the age dataset, get the predicted probabilities, and then graph it. The predict() function knows we are calling it on m which is an S3 class of type GLM. Thus, we are actually calling predict.glm(), which has as its default type the decision to use the "link" scale, which is log odds. We want a probability scale, which is the original response scale, and thus set the type to "response".

```
> newdat <- data.frame(Agec = seq(0, to = (89 - 18)/10, length.out = 200))
> newdat$probs <- predict(m, newdata = newdat, type = "response")

> head(newdat)
        Agec     probs
1 0.00000000 0.1502917
2 0.03567839 0.1511915
3 0.07135678 0.1520957
4 0.10703518 0.1530043
5 0.14271357 0.1539174
6 0.17839196 0.1548350
```

```
> p <- ggplot(newdat, aes(Agec, probs)) +
+   geom_line() +
+   theme_bw() +
+   xlab("Age - 18 in decades") +
+   ylab("Probability of being financially satisfied")
> p
```

The foregoing code generates Figure 15-5, but notice that it doesn't quite give us what we want. Namely, while the y axis is now in a very intuitive probability scale, the x axis is still in our linearly transformed scale. It would be helpful to rerun the graph making sure to both analyze the code at years that make sense (i.e. 20, 40, 60, and 80 years of age) and label the x axis in such a way that we could see that. The following code makes this happen, and we show Figure 15-6 on the next page contrasted with our earlier image. When we update the labels, we also need to relabel the x axis to make it clear the axis is now in age in years rather than centered and in decades.

```
> p2 <- p +
+   scale_x_continuous("Age in years", breaks = (c(20, 40, 60, 80) - 18)/10,
+   labels = c(20, 40, 60, 80))
> p2
```

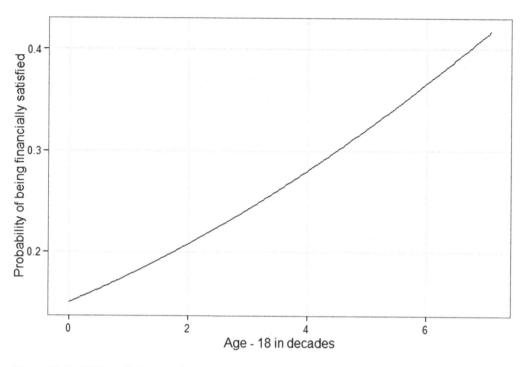

Figure 15-5. *GLM prediction graph on age minus 18 in decades and probability of being financially satisfied*

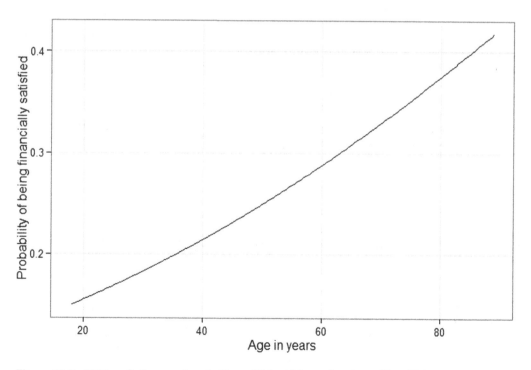

Figure 15-6. *GLM prediction graph as in Figure 15-5 with better breaks and hand labeled for interpretability*

15.3.6 Multivariate Logistic Regression

We turn our efforts now to multivariate logistic regression to improve our logit model. It would seem `cincome` might make a good predictor of income satisfaction and perhaps education, `educ`, also matters. Income does seem to be significant, although the main effect of education is not statistically significant.

```
> m2 <- update(m, . ~ . + cincome + educ)
> summary(m2)

Call:
glm(formula = Satisfied ~ Agec + cincome + educ, family = binomial(),
    data = gssr)

Deviance Residuals:
    Min      1Q   Median      3Q      Max
-1.3535  -0.8009  -0.6029  1.0310   2.7238

Coefficients:
            Estimate Std. Error z value Pr(>|z|)
(Intercept) -4.27729   0.27387  -15.618  <2e-16 ***
Agec         0.24130   0.02836    8.508  <2e-16 ***
cincome      0.10989   0.01049   10.478  <2e-16 ***
educ         0.03045   0.01693    1.799  0.0721 .
---
Signif. codes:  0 '***' 0.001 '**' 0.01 '*' 0.05 '.' 0.1 ' ' 1

(Dispersion parameter for binomial family taken to be 1)

    Null deviance: 3197.7  on 2834  degrees of freedom
Residual deviance: 2955.6  on 2831  degrees of freedom
AIC: 2963.6

Number of Fisher Scoring iterations: 4
```

Perhaps there is an interaction between education and income? Education and income interact when income is zero, higher education is associated with lower log odds of financial satisfaction, but as income goes up, the relationship between education and financial satisfaction goes toward zero.

```
> m3 <- update(m, . ~ . + cincome * educ)
> summary(m3)

Call:
glm(formula = Satisfied ~ Agec + cincome + educ + cincome:educ,family = binomial(),
    data = gssr)

Deviance Residuals:
    Min      1Q   Median      3Q      Max
-1.5182  -0.7865  -0.5904  0.9003   2.8120
```

```
Coefficients:
             Estimate Std. Error z value Pr(>|z|)
(Intercept) -1.391097   0.661266  -2.104 0.035406 *
Agec         0.235217   0.028477   8.260  < 2e-16 ***
cincome     -0.051122   0.036209  -1.412 0.157992
educ        -0.190748   0.050788  -3.756 0.000173 ***
cincome:educ 0.012068   0.002647   4.559 5.13e-06 ***
---
Signif. codes:  0 '***' 0.001 '**' 0.01 '*' 0.05 '.' 0.1 ' ' 1

(Dispersion parameter for binomial family taken to be 1)

    Null deviance: 3197.7  on 2834  degrees of freedom
Residual deviance: 2936.8  on 2830  degrees of freedom
AIC: 2946.8

Number of Fisher Scoring iterations: 4
```

One item of note is that as we add more predictors to our model, unlike with the linear regressions we did in prior chapters, there is not a convenient multiple correlation coefficient (i.e., R^2) term to measure if we are progressing toward a "better" model or not. One possibility we have hinted at before is to have two datasets. We could train our model on the first dataset, and then test our model against the second dataset to determine how far off our predictions might be. There are a variety of methods to do so (e.g., cross-validation), and these methods are not particularly difficult to *code* in R. However, they can be compute intensive. McFadden (1974) suggests an analogous measure using a log likelihood ratio which belongs to a class of measures sometimes labeled *pseudo R-squared*. There are many alternative approaches available and each has various pros and cons, without any single measure being agreed upon as optimal or the "gold standard." McFadden's R^2 is straightforward to calculate, and for now, we show a function implementing McFadden's algorithm.

```
> McFaddenR2 <- function(mod0, mod1, ... ){
+   L0 <- logLik(mod0)
+   L1 <- logLik(mod1)
+   MFR2 <- 1 - (L1/L0)
+   return(MFR2)
+ }
>
> MFR2_1 <- McFaddenR2(m0,m)
> MFR2_2 <- McFaddenR2(m0,m2)
> MFR2_3 <- McFaddenR2(m0,m3)
>
> McFaddenResults <- cbind( c(MFR2_1,MFR2_2,MFR2_3))
> McFaddenResults
          [,1]
[1,] 0.01793689
[2,] 0.07469872
[3,] 0.08161767
```

Our model seems to be improving, so we turn our attention to getting results. Before we start looking at predictions, we take a look at our new predictor variables. Based on those explorations, we build our new data model to pass to our predict() function. In this case, we will see from the summary() function calls (and our intuition) that it makes sense to segment education based on high school, university, and postgraduate levels while we model all income bins and fix age to be the mean age. When generating predictions, it is important to have an eye on how we're going to present those predictions in graphical form. Graphs that are "too complicated" may not clearly convey what is happening in the model. As models become better at uncovering the response variable, they tend to gain predictors and complexity. Only observing certain educational levels and fixing the age to mean age are ways to reduce that complexity somewhat. We want both predicted probabilities based on some choices of inputs to our predictors (with the coefficients from our model) as well as CIs around the predictions. Recall that CIs can be calculated as the model estimates plus or minus 1.96 times standard error. As before, these calculations make sense on linear equations (imagine if we had a predicted probability of zero and subtracted 1.96 x standard error, we would end up with a CI going beyond a probability of zero!). Thus, they must be done first on the log odds scale (the link scale), and then converted to probabilities at the end. To add the CIs, we use the se.fit = TRUE option to get the standard errors, and we get the estimates on the link scale, rather than the response scale.

```
> summary(gssr$educ)
   Min. 1st Qu.  Median    Mean 3rd Qu.    Max.
   0.00   12.00   14.00   13.77   16.00   20.00

> summary(gssr$cincome)
   Min. 1st Qu.  Median    Mean 3rd Qu.    Max.
   1.00   14.00   18.00   17.04   21.00   25.00

> newdat <- expand.grid(
+   educ = c(12, 16, 20),
+   cincome = 1:25,
+   Agec = mean(gssr$Agec))

> newdat <- cbind(newdat, predict(m3, newdata = newdat,
+                                 type = "link", se.fit = TRUE))

> head(newdat)
  educ cincome      Agec       fit    se.fit residual.scale
1   12       1  3.124056 -2.851555 0.1808835              1
2   16       1  3.124056 -3.566276 0.2598423              1
3   20       1  3.124056 -4.280998 0.4206850              1
4   12       2  3.124056 -2.757866 0.1705653              1
5   16       2  3.124056 -3.424317 0.2470500              1
6   20       2  3.124056 -4.090769 0.4002471              1

> newdat <- within(newdat, {
+   LL <- fit - 1.96 * se.fit
+   UL <- fit + 1.96 * se.fit
+ })
```

Recall that to calculate CIs, we had to use the log odds scale. Thus, in our predict() function, we chose type = "link" this time. Then we calculated our lower limit (LL) and our upper limit (UL) for each point. Never forgetting that we are presently in the log odds scale, we can now convert the fitted values (these are what R calls predicted values) and the CIs to the probability scale. In R, the inverse logit function plogis() can be applied to the data. At the same time, ggplot can be employed to visualize the results in a strictly functional fashion. The plot color-codes the three education levels and has shaded probability ribbons. Of note is that provided the error ribbons do not intersect the lines of the other plots, then there is a significant difference between education levels, which allows for relatively easy visual inspection of the level of income at which education makes a statistically significant difference in probability of being satisfied. We see that at various income levels, this seems to be the case, although Figure 15-7 isn't fully clear.

```
> newdat <- within(newdat, {
+    Probability <- plogis(fit)
+    LLprob <- plogis(LL)
+    ULprob <- plogis(UL)
+ })

> p3 <- ggplot(newdat, aes(cincome, Probability, color = factor(educ))) +
+    geom_ribbon(aes(ymin = LLprob, ymax = ULprob), alpha = .5) +
+    geom_line() +
+    theme_bw() +
+    xlab("Income Bins") +
+    ylab("Probability of being financially satisfied")
> p3
```

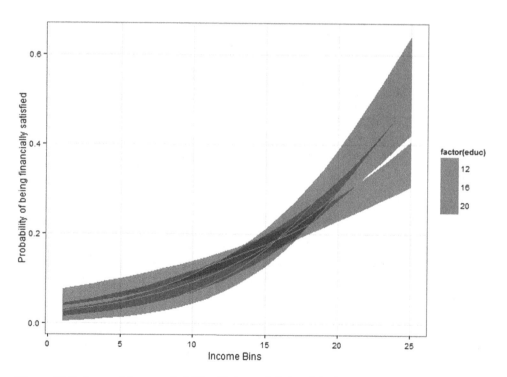

Figure 15-7. Income bin vs. probability of being satisfied with high school, university, and graduate education levels. Not the most attractive graph

While this graph may be functional, it leaves a lot to be desired. It is perhaps difficult to see when the CIs intersect the various education lines. This makes it difficult to see when more or less education might cause statistically significant differences in Satisfaction. We use the scales library here to clean up the y axis. The theme() command increases the size of our legend, and moves it to the bottom of the graph. Notice that in the aes() function the factor(educ) was used for color, fill, and linetype. To remove the factor(educ) and replace it with a nicer label of "Education" for all three of those in our legend, we must change the label in each one. Finally, we force the shown intervals of our Income bins and our y-axis probability via the coord_cartesian() command. Our efforts pay off in Figure 15-8 (be sure to run this code as the printed version of this text won't show the full color picture).

```
> library(scales) # to use labels = percent

Attaching package: 'scales'

The following object is masked from 'package:arm':

    rescale

>
> p4 <- ggplot(newdat, aes(cincome, Probability,
+                          color = factor(educ), fill = factor(educ),
+                          linetype = factor(educ))) +
+    geom_ribbon(aes(ymin = LLprob, ymax = ULprob, color = NULL), alpha = .25) +
+    geom_line(size = 1) +
+    theme_bw() +
+    scale_y_continuous(labels = percent) +
+    scale_color_discrete("Education") +
+    scale_fill_discrete("Education") +
+    scale_linetype_discrete("Education") +
+    xlab("Income Bins") +
+    ylab("Probability of being financially satisfied") +
+    theme(legend.key.size = unit(1, "cm"),
+          legend.position = "bottom") +
+    coord_cartesian(xlim = c(1, 25), ylim = c(0, .65))
> p4
```

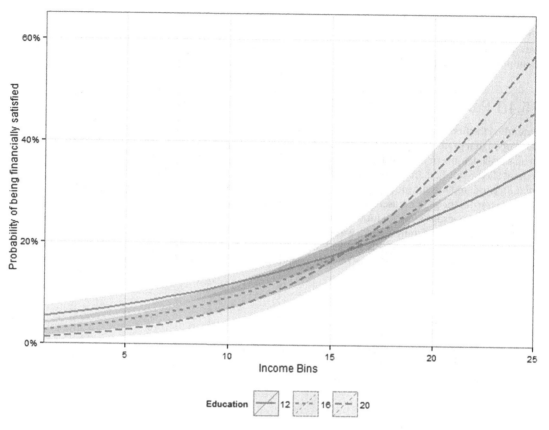

Figure 15-8. A much nicer graph, which more cleanly shows the effects of income and education on Satisfaction

In Figure 15-8, one can readily see that on either side of the 15 Income bin ($25,000 to $29,999), there are places where the confidence bands do not include the other line. Thus, in those regions, it seems education has a more potent effect rather than in the middle where there is overlap for middling income levels. Also notice that the y-axis labels are at last in a very intuitive probability scale and are even written as a percent.

A final thought on this example is that satfin was deliberately recoded to an all-or-nothing Satisfaction variable. The natural extension is to consider if there is a way to make this model work well for nonbinary categorical data. It turns out the answer is indeed in the positive, and the next section explores the topic of ordered logistic regression.

15.4 Ordered Logistic Regression

Our first prediction was binary in nature. One was either fully financially satisfied or recoded to a "not fully satisfied" catch-all variable that had both not at all and more or less financially satisfied. This is often a very useful level of masking to engage. Multiple-choice exam question options (e.g., with options A, B, C, and D where only one is correct) are readily coded to a 25% probability of randomly guessing the correct (i.e., True) answer and a 75% probability of randomly selecting an incorrect (i.e., False) answer. The advantage is that such steps simplify the model. One of the challenges in building good models is that they are meant to be simplifications of the real world. To paraphrase Tukey (1962), "Never let your attraction to perfection prevent you from achieving good enough."

All the same, there are times when more advanced models are required to get any traction on the challenge at hand. In those cases, it can be helpful to recognize that while the overall model is still logistic, we would like some nuances that are more subtle than an all-or-nothing approach. We present two such examples in the next two sections.

15.4.1 Parallel Ordered Logistic Regression

Extending the first example from using predictions of only full financial satisfaction, a model could be developed that predicts *each* level of satisfaction. From the raw gss2012 data, satfin has three levels, not at all satisfied, more or less satisfied, and satisfied. These are ordered in that not at all satisfied < more or less satisfied < satisfied. Installing and loading the VGAM package, which allows fits for many types of models including ordered logistic models, will allow for a more nuanced exploration of financial satisfaction. The first step is to let the gssr dataset know that satfin in fact holds factored, ordered data. The model is built using the VGAM package's vglm() function to create an ordered logistic regression. In this particular function call, the cumulative() family is used; we specify parallel = TRUE, and while glm() used the logit link as well (by default), here it is explicitly stated. Finally, the summary() function is called on this null model. The following commands and output have been respaced somewhat for clarity and space.

```
> install.packages("VGAM")
> library(VGAM)
Loading required package: stats4
Loading required package: splines
> gssr$satfin <- factor(gssr$satfin,
+                       levels = c("NOT AT ALL SAT", "MORE OR LESS", "SATISFIED"),
+                       ordered = TRUE)

> mo <- vglm(satfin ~ 1,
+            family = cumulative(link = "logit", parallel = TRUE, reverse = TRUE),
+            data = gssr)

> summary(mo)

Call:
vglm(formula = satfin ~ 1, family = cumulative(link = "logit",
    parallel = TRUE, reverse = TRUE), data = gssr)

Pearson residuals:
                  Min      1Q  Median      3Q     Max
logit(P[Y>=2]) -1.4951 -1.4951  0.3248  0.8206  0.8206
logit(P[Y>=3]) -0.7476 -0.7476 -0.3036  1.6943  1.6943

Coefficients:
              Estimate Std. Error z value Pr(>|z|)
(Intercept):1  0.84478    0.04096   20.62   <2e-16 ***
(Intercept):2 -1.09063    0.04329  -25.20   <2e-16 ***
---
Signif. codes:  0 '***' 0.001 '**' 0.01 '*' 0.05 '.' 0.1 ' ' 1
```

```
Number of linear predictors:  2
Names of linear predictors: logit(P[Y>=2]), logit(P[Y>=3])
Dispersion Parameter for cumulative family:   1
Residual deviance: 6056.581 on 5668 degrees of freedom
Log-likelihood: -3028.291 on 5668 degrees of freedom
Number of iterations: 1
```

Notice that mo is an empty model. Thus, the only estimates are intercepts for our two levels; one of which is the log odds of being greater than 2 and the other which is log odds of being precisely 3. Since there are only three possibilities, we can solve for the probability of being in any of the three levels. Since this is an empty model, it should match precisely with a proportion table. A handful of function calls to plogis() and some algebra will yield the probability of being satisfied, more or less satisfied, or not satisfied, respectively. The code for this follows:

```
> plogis(-1.09063)
[1] 0.2514997
> plogis(0.84478) - plogis(-1.09063)
[1] 0.4479713
> 1 - plogis(0.84478)
[1] 0.300529
> prop.table(table(gssr$satfin))

NOT AT ALL SAT    MORE OR LESS    SATISFIED
     0.3005291       0.4479718    0.2514991
```

With the null model in place, the model may be updated to explore the effect of age (the adjusted age from earlier) on financial satisfaction.

```
> mo1 <- vglm(satfin ~ 1 + Agec,
+             family = cumulative(link = "logit", parallel = TRUE, reverse = TRUE),
                            data = gssr)

> summary(mo1)
Call:
vglm(formula = satfin ~ 1 + Agec, family = cumulative(link = "logit",
    parallel = TRUE, reverse = TRUE), data = gssr)


Pearson residuals:
                  Min     1Q Median     3Q    Max
logit(P[Y>=2]) -2.048 -1.3060 0.3395 0.8071 0.9815
logit(P[Y>=3]) -0.937 -0.7183 -0.3167 1.2556 2.1670


Coefficients:
              Estimate Std. Error z value Pr(>|z|)
(Intercept):1  0.38898    0.07587   5.127 2.94e-07 ***
(Intercept):2 -1.57479    0.08193 -19.222  < 2e-16 ***
Agec           0.15128    0.02121   7.132 9.91e-13 ***
---
```

```
Signif. codes:  0 '***' 0.001 '**' 0.01 '*' 0.05 '.' 0.1 ' ' 1
Number of linear predictors:  2
Names of linear predictors: logit(P[Y>=2]), logit(P[Y>=3])
Dispersion Parameter for cumulative family:  1
Residual deviance: 6005.314 on 5667 degrees of freedom
Log-likelihood: -3002.657 on 5667 degrees of freedom
Number of iterations: 3
```

Again, the cbind() function along with exponentiation may be used to compare and contrast the log odds with the odds of the coefficients with code and output as follows:

```
> cbind(LogOdds = coef(mo1), Odds = exp(coef(mo1)))
                 LogOdds      Odds
(Intercept):1  0.3889768 1.4754703
(Intercept):2 -1.5747920 0.2070506
Agec           0.1512757 1.1633174
```

Interpreting this, it could be said that for every decade older a person is, that person has 1.16 times the odds of being in a higher financial satisfaction level. To see this graphically, create a new data frame that has 200 values of the adjusted age data. Specifically, ensure that the range of ages is from 0 for 18 to the maximum age of 89 less 18 divided by 10 to adjust the scale. Then, use the predict() function again, which is turning out along with summary() to be very powerful in the number of models it has been built to understand, to ensure that the points are in probability response rather than log odds link. The new dataset that has the created inputs for the predictor variable as well as the resulting output response values may be viewed.

```
> newdat <- data.frame(Agec = seq(from = 0, to = (89 - 18)/10, length.out = 200))
>
> #append prediction data to dataset
> newdat <- cbind(newdat, predict(mo1, newdata = newdat, type = "response"))
>
> #view new data set
> head(newdat)
        Agec NOT AT ALL SAT MORE OR LESS SATISFIED
1 0.00000000     0.4039636    0.4245020 0.1715343
2 0.03567839     0.4026648    0.4250325 0.1723027
3 0.07135678     0.4013673    0.4255589 0.1730738
4 0.10703518     0.4000712    0.4260812 0.1738476
5 0.14271357     0.3987764    0.4265994 0.1746241
6 0.17839196     0.3974831    0.4271134 0.1754034
```

Once the data for a graph is thus acquired, it may be plotted. To use ggplot2, it must be a *long* dataset, and thus the library reshape2 is called along with the function melt(). As with summary(), there is more than one type of melt() function. Regardless of the type, melt() takes an input of data and reshapes the data based on a vector of identification variables aptly titled id.vars. For this particular example, this should be set to id.vars="Agec". Notice the difference between the previous head(newdat) call and the same call on the melted data frame that follows:

```
> library(reshape2)
> newdat <- melt(newdat, id.vars = "Agec")
> head(newdat)
        Agec      variable     value
1 0.00000000 NOT AT ALL SAT 0.4039636
2 0.03567839 NOT AT ALL SAT 0.4026648
3 0.07135678 NOT AT ALL SAT 0.4013673
4 0.10703518 NOT AT ALL SAT 0.4000712
5 0.14271357 NOT AT ALL SAT 0.3987764
6 0.17839196 NOT AT ALL SAT 0.3974831
```

The data are ready to graph with fairly familiar calls to ggplot. The only new aspect of this call is perhaps providing better factor names from the raw names to something a little more reader friendly.

```
> newdat$variable <- factor(newdat$variable,
+                           levels = c("NOT AT ALL SAT", "MORE OR LESS", "SATISFIED"),
+                           labels = c("Not Satisfied", "More/Less Satisfied", "Satisfied"))
>
> p5 <- ggplot(newdat, aes(Agec, value, color = variable, linetype = variable)) +
+   geom_line(size = 1.5) +
+   scale_x_continuous("Age", breaks = (c(20, 40, 60, 80) - 18)/10,
+                       labels = c(20, 40, 60, 80)) +
+   scale_y_continuous("Probability", labels = percent) +
+   theme_bw() +
+   theme(legend.key.width = unit(1.5, "cm"),
+         legend.position = "bottom",
+         legend.title = element_blank()) +
+   ggtitle("Financial Satisfaction")
> p5
```

Figure 15-9 makes it clear that there is little difference in the percentage of people who are more or less satisfied with financial situation across the lifespan, with the bigger changes happening to those who are not satisfied vs. those who are satisfied. One helpful way to better understand the results besides graphs is to look at the *marginal effect*. The marginal effect answers the question: "How much would the probability of being financially satisfied [or any of the levels] change for person i if age increased?" This is valuable because although the model is linear on the log odds scale, it is not linear on the probability scale; the marginal effect is the first derivative of the function on the probability scale. With R, fortunately, it is easy enough to compute as follows:

```
> margeff(mo1, subset = 1)
            NOT AT ALL SAT MORE OR LESS    SATISFIED
(Intercept)    -0.09249320   0.32523987 -0.23274666
Agec           -0.03597124   0.01361342  0.02235782
```

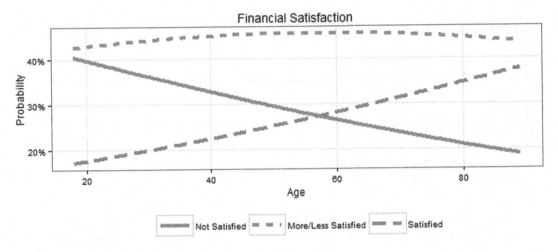

Figure 15-9. *Age vs. probability of three levels of financial satisfaction*

These results show that for person 1, the instantaneous rate of change in probability of being satisfied is .022, whereas there is a larger decrease of -.036 in probability of being not at all satisfied. Another useful sort of effect size is the average marginal effect in the data. That is, it asks the question: "On average in the sample, what is the instantaneous rate of change in probability of being satisfied [or any of the levels] by age?" We can get this by not subsetting the data, then extracting just the Agec term ignoring intercepts, and taking the mean of each row, to get the averages.

```
> rowMeans(margeff(mo1)["Agec", ,])
NOT AT ALL SAT   MORE OR LESS      SATISFIED
  -0.031344533    0.003157332     0.028187201
```

These results show that, on average, a decade change in age is associated with almost no change in being more or less satisfied at .003, about a .028 probability higher chance of being satisfied, and about a .031 probability lower chance of being not satisfied.

As we turn our attention from this example, we call to the reader's attention that while our primary goal was to explore *ordered logistic regression*, we deliberately chose to set one of our variables to be parallel = TRUE. Let us explore what happens if we choose otherwise.

15.4.2 Non-Parallel Ordered Logistic Regression

In the prior example, the use of the parallel argument in the function call assumed the effect of any predictors have exactly parallel (equal) relationship on the outcome for each of the different groups. If we set parallel = FALSE, then the effect of predictors, here Agec, would be allowed to be different for each comparison where the comparisons are being satisfied or more or less satisfied vs. not satisfied, and satisfied vs. more or less satisfied or not satisfied. This is still an *ordered logistic regression*. We are only relaxing the assumption that a predictor has the *same effect* for each level of response. It is a very minor code change, and we show the code for that as well as a summary() as follows:

```
> mo.alt <- vglm(satfin ~ 1 + Agec,
+                 family = cumulative(link = "logit", parallel = FALSE, reverse = TRUE),
+                 data = gssr)
> summary(mo.alt)
```

```
Call:
vglm(formula = satfin ~ 1 + Agec, family = cumulative(link = "logit",
    parallel = FALSE, reverse = TRUE), data = gssr)

Pearson residuals:
                  Min     1Q  Median     3Q    Max
logit(P[Y>=2]) -1.873 -1.3518  0.3296 0.8116 0.9033
logit(P[Y>=3]) -1.051 -0.7022 -0.3234 1.1607 2.3272

Coefficients:
               Estimate Std. Error z value Pr(>|z|)
(Intercept):1   0.50092    0.08565   5.849 4.95e-09 ***
(Intercept):2  -1.70992    0.09842 -17.374  < 2e-16 ***
Agec:1          0.11222    0.02505   4.479 7.50e-06 ***
Agec:2          0.19020    0.02610   7.288 3.15e-13 ***
---
Signif. codes:  0 '***' 0.001 '**' 0.01 '*' 0.05 '.' 0.1 ' ' 1

Number of linear predictors:  2
Names of linear predictors: logit(P[Y>=2]), logit(P[Y>=3])
Dispersion Parameter for cumulative family:   1
Residual deviance: 5997.851 on 5666 degrees of freedom
Log-likelihood: -2998.925 on 5666 degrees of freedom
Number of iterations: 4
```

Note first that, as before, we edited some spaces out for readability. Also notice that this looks very much like our earlier code for a parallel model, excepting Agec:1 and Agec:2. The values for the intercepts have changed, of course, as well. All the prior code and processes we did to discuss log odds vs. odds and to create CIs continues to hold true.

What the preceding code demonstrates is an elegant way to recover essentially the same coefficients without needing to create two variables. Going all the way back to our code near the beginning of this chapter, the non-parallel process in a single step essentially compares satisfied or more or less satisfied with not satisfied as well as compares satisfied with more or less satisfied or not satisfied. To demonstrate this binary logistic model, we could create the two variables from satfin and generate two completely separate models:

```
> gssr <- within(gssr, {
+   satfin23v1 <- as.integer(satfin != "NOT AT ALL SAT")
+   satfin3v12 <- as.integer(satfin == "SATISFIED")
+ })
>
> m23v1 <- glm(satfin23v1 ~ 1 + Agec,
+             family = binomial(), data = gssr)
> m3v12 <- glm(satfin3v12 ~ 1 + Agec,
+             family = binomial(), data = gssr)
```

Now we can explore our models using summary(). As you look through the two models, notice that although not exactly the same, this is essentially what the ordinal logistic model does. There are only very slight differences in the coefficients. It is the job of the researcher to determine if the actual, real-world process makes more sense to model with non-parallel predictor coefficients. Otherwise, we choose to set parallel = TRUE, thereby adding the constraint during parameter estimation that the coefficients for independent predictors be equal. As long as this assumption holds, it provides a simpler or more parsimonious model to the data, as only a single coefficient is needed for age (or all the other predictors we may choose to enter), which can result in a reduced standard error (i.e., it is more likely to have adequate power to detect a statistically significant effect)and is easier to explain to people.

```
> summary(m23v1)

Call:
glm(formula = satfin23v1 ~ 1 + Agec, family = binomial(), data = gssr)

Deviance Residuals:
    Min      1Q   Median      3Q      Max
-1.7525  -1.4600   0.7976   0.8759   0.9719

Coefficients:
            Estimate Std. Error z value Pr(>|z|)
(Intercept)  0.50474    0.08568   5.891 3.83e-09 ***
Agec         0.11104    0.02505   4.432 9.33e-06 ***
---
Signif. codes:  0 '***' 0.001 '**' 0.01 '*' 0.05 '.' 0.1 ' ' 1

(Dispersion parameter for binomial family taken to be 1)

    Null deviance: 3466.1  on 2834  degrees of freedom
Residual deviance: 3446.2  on 2833  degrees of freedom
AIC: 3450.2

Number of Fisher Scoring iterations: 4

> summary(m3v12)

Call:
glm(formula = satfin3v12 ~ 1 + Agec, family = binomial(), data = gssr)

Deviance Residuals:
    Min      1Q   Median      3Q      Max
-1.0394  -0.7904  -0.6885   1.3220   1.9469

Coefficients:
            Estimate Std. Error z value Pr(>|z|)
(Intercept) -1.73232    0.09895 -17.507  < 2e-16 ***
Agec         0.19700    0.02621   7.516 5.64e-14 ***
---
Signif. codes:  0 '***' 0.001 '**' 0.01 '*' 0.05 '.' 0.1 ' ' 1

(Dispersion parameter for binomial family taken to be 1)

    Null deviance: 3197.7  on 2834  degrees of freedom
Residual deviance: 3140.4  on 2833  degrees of freedom
AIC: 3144.4

Number of Fisher Scoring iterations: 4
```

To recap what we have accomplished so far, we remind our readers that one of the underlying reasons for logistic regression is to have qualitative response variables. So far, we have explored examples of such qualitative models that were binary, that were ordered, and, just now, that were ordered as well as having the predictors effect different levels of that ordering in not the same way. We turn our attention now to another possibility, namely, that there are multiple, qualitative outcomes that are not ordered.

15.5 Multinomial Regression

Multinomial regression is related to logistic regression; it is applicable when there are multiple levels of an *unordered* outcome. It is conceptually similar to ordered regression, in that we shy away from binary outcomes, yet these outcomes have no particular order or organization. For example, we might look at predicting marital status, which can be married, widowed, divorced, separated, or never married. We may well have access in the gssr dataset to the types of predictors that could get some traction on marital status. Furthermore, such a very qualitative response perhaps precludes any binary process (although never married vs. married at least once comes to mind for some scenarios). The vglm() function from before has various settings for family, and, for our last example, we will use the multinomial() option. First, some EDA:

```
> table(gssr$marital)

     MARRIED     WIDOWED     DIVORCED     SEPARATED NEVER MARRIED
        1363         209          483            89           691
```

We see that there are definitely plenty of survey participants in each of the response categories. Additionally, it seems reasonable that Agec may have something to do with this as well. After all, it takes time to move through some of these cycles! We build our model and explore the summary() as follows (again with some spacing edits to enhance readability):

```
> m.multi <- vglm(marital ~ 1 + Agec, family = multinomial(), data = gssr)

> summary(m.multi)

Call:
vglm(formula = marital ~ 1 + Agec, family = multinomial(), data = gssr)

Pearson residuals:
                        Min      1Q   Median       3Q     Max
log(mu[,1]/mu[,5]) -8.282 -0.7192 -0.40376  0.89433   1.813
log(mu[,2]/mu[,5]) -9.053 -0.1651 -0.05401 -0.01177  21.453
log(mu[,3]/mu[,5]) -8.086 -0.3927 -0.26479 -0.13968   3.970
log(mu[,4]/mu[,5]) -6.431 -0.1918 -0.07934 -0.06021   8.050

Coefficients:
               Estimate Std. Error z value Pr(>|z|)
(Intercept):1  -1.04159    0.10376 -10.038   <2e-16 ***
(Intercept):2  -8.29667    0.40292 -20.592   <2e-16 ***
(Intercept):3  -2.71498    0.14884 -18.241   <2e-16 ***
(Intercept):4  -3.71948    0.26232 -14.179   <2e-16 ***
Agec:1          0.68608    0.03980  17.240   <2e-16 ***
Agec:2          1.89683    0.08399  22.585   <2e-16 ***
Agec:3          0.87255    0.04817  18.114   <2e-16 ***
Agec:4          0.67009    0.07955   8.424   <2e-16 ***
---
Signif. codes:  0 '***' 0.001 '**' 0.01 '*' 0.05 '.' 0.1 ' ' 1
```

```
Number of linear predictors:  4

Names of linear predictors:
log(mu[,1]/mu[,5]), log(mu[,2]/mu[,5]), log(mu[,3]/mu[,5]), log(mu[,4]/mu[,5])
Dispersion Parameter for multinomial family:   1
Residual deviance: 6374.723 on 11332 degrees of freedom
Log-likelihood: -3187.362 on 11332 degrees of freedom
Number of iterations: 6
```

These results are similar to those in our previous logistic regression models. There are five levels of marital status; the model will compare the first four levels against the last level. Thus, one can think of each intercept and coefficient as a series of four binary logistic regressions. There will always be k - 1 models, where k is the number of levels in the dependent/outcome variable. The reason it is important to use a multinomial model, rather than a series of binary logistic regressions, is that in a multinomial model, each person's probability of falling into any of the category levels must sum to one. Such requirement is enforced in a multinomial model but may not be enforced in a series of binary logistic regressions. Perhaps the last category is not the "best" comparison group. We may readily change it up, and while the coefficients will change (because they are comparing different sets of groups), the model is actually the same (which can be seen from identical log-likelihoods). Perhaps confusingly, VGLM uses 1, 2, 3, and 4 to indicate the first, second, third, and fourth coefficients, regardless of what the reference level is. The software leaves it to us to figure out which specific comparisons 1, 2, 3, and 4 correspond to.

```
> m.multi <- vglm(marital ~ 1 + Agec, family = multinomial(refLevel = 1), data = gssr)

> summary(m.multi)

Call:
vglm(formula = marital ~ 1 + Agec, family = multinomial(refLevel = 1), data = gssr)

Pearson residuals:
                      Min      1Q   Median        3Q     Max
log(mu[,2]/mu[,1]) -1.7895 -0.2320 -0.09909 -0.010393 21.455
log(mu[,3]/mu[,1]) -1.0607 -0.5687 -0.40601 -0.108840  3.891
log(mu[,4]/mu[,1]) -0.4455 -0.2859 -0.10124 -0.056649  8.637
log(mu[,5]/mu[,1]) -1.4390 -0.5711 -0.31163 -0.009688 15.948

Coefficients:
              Estimate Std. Error z value Pr(>|z|)
(Intercept):1 -7.25508    0.39308 -18.457  < 2e-16 ***
(Intercept):2 -1.67339    0.13649 -12.260  < 2e-16 ***
(Intercept):3 -2.67789    0.25766 -10.393  < 2e-16 ***
(Intercept):4  1.04159    0.10376  10.038  < 2e-16 ***
Agec:1         1.21075    0.07520  16.100  < 2e-16 ***
Agec:2         0.18647    0.03581   5.207 1.92e-07 ***
Agec:3        -0.01599    0.07360  -0.217    0.828
Agec:4        -0.68608    0.03980 -17.240  < 2e-16 ***
---
Signif. codes:  0 '***' 0.001 '**' 0.01 '*' 0.05 '.' 0.1 ' ' 1
```

```
Number of linear predictors:  4
Names of linear predictors:
log(mu[,2]/mu[,1]), log(mu[,3]/mu[,1]), log(mu[,4]/mu[,1]), log(mu[,5]/mu[,1])

Dispersion Parameter for multinomial family:  1
Residual deviance: 6374.723 on 11332 degrees of freedom
Log-likelihood: -3187.362 on 11332 degrees of freedom
Number of iterations: 6
```

The probabilities may also be presented (again as before):

```
> newdat <- data.frame(Agec = seq(from = 0, to = (89 - 18)/10, length.out = 200))
> newdat <- cbind(newdat, predict(m.multi, newdata = newdat, type = "response"))
> head(newdat)
        Agec    MARRIED      WIDOWED   DIVORCED  SEPARATED NEVER MARRIED
1 0.00000000 0.2444538 0.0001727253 0.04586190 0.01679599     0.6927156
2 0.03567839 0.2485414 0.0001833658 0.04694004 0.01706710     0.6872681
3 0.07135678 0.2526617 0.0001946343 0.04803671 0.01734014     0.6817669
4 0.10703518 0.2568134 0.0002065657 0.04915198 0.01761503     0.6762130
5 0.14271357 0.2609957 0.0002191969 0.05028588 0.01789169     0.6706075
6 0.17839196 0.2652075 0.0002325665 0.05143843 0.01817004     0.6649515
```

Converting these data into long data allows us to graph it with ggplot2 as seen in Figure 15-10 via the following code:

```
> newdat <- melt(newdat, id.vars = "Agec")

> ggplot(newdat, aes(Agec, value, color = variable, linetype = variable)) +
+   geom_line(size = 1.5) +
+   scale_x_continuous("Age", breaks = (c(20, 40, 60, 80) - 18)/10,
+                      labels = c(20, 40, 60, 80)) +
+   scale_y_continuous("Probability", labels = percent) +
+   theme_bw() +
+   theme(legend.key.width = unit(1.5, "cm"),
+         legend.position = "bottom",
+         legend.direction = "vertical",
+         legend.title = element_blank()) +
+   ggtitle("Marital Status")
```

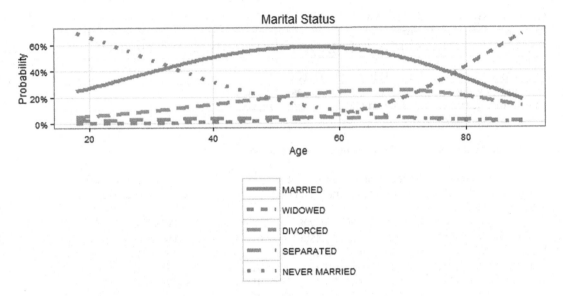

Figure 15-10. *Marital status probability vs. age (relabeled)*

This can also be visualized using an area plot, where at any given age, 100% of the people fall into one of the possible categories. This allows for visualization of how the probability of being in any specific marital status changes across the lifespan, as seen in Figure 15-11 (of course, since this is cross-sectional data, there may also be cohort effects, with people who were 80 years old at the time of the GSS 2012 survey having grown up with a different culture or experience at age 20 than perhaps those people who were 20 at the time of the GSS 2012 survey were experiencing). It is best to run the following code on your own computer, to allow the full color experience:

```
> ggplot(newdat, aes(Agec, value, fill = variable)) +
+   geom_area(aes(ymin = 0)) +
+   scale_x_continuous("Age", breaks = (c(20, 40, 60, 80) - 18)/10,
+                      labels = c(20, 40, 60, 80)) +
+   scale_y_continuous("Probability", labels = percent) +
+   theme_bw() +
+   theme(legend.key.width = unit(1.5, "cm"),
+         legend.position = "bottom",
+         legend.direction = "vertical",
+         legend.title = element_blank()) +
+   ggtitle("Marital Status")
```

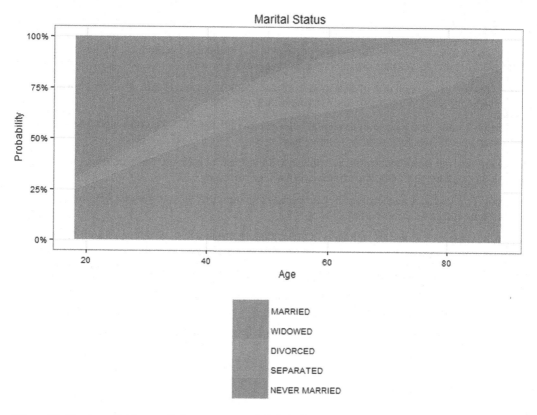

Figure 15-11. *Area plot for marital status vs. age (relabeled)*

The GLM provides a consistent framework for regression even when the outcomes are continuous or discrete and may come from different distributions. In this chapter we have explored a variety of models that can utilize noncontinuous, discrete outcomes, including binary logistic regression, ordered logistic regression for discrete data with more than two levels where there is a clear ordering, and multinomial regression for discrete data with more than two levels where there is not a clear ordering to the levels. We have also seen how nonlinear transformations (such as the inverse logit) can have finicky requirements. For example, we must compute CIs on the log odds scale and then convert back to probabilities. This can raise some challenges. For example, what if we wanted CIs for the average marginal effects in the probabilities we presented? We averaged the probabilities, which was intuitive, but it is not clear how we could obtain CIs not for an individual probability but for the average marginal effect on the probability scale. Problems like this turn out to be tricky and are often not implemented in software. In the next chapter, we will explore some nonparametric tests, and we will also discuss bootstrapping, a powerful tool that can be used to derive CIs and standard errors and conduct statistical inference when we are not sure what the exact distribution of our data is or when we do not know the formula to estimate standard errors or CIs, or they are just not implemented in the software we are using, such as for the average marginal effect on the probability scale.

References

Gelman, G., & Su, Y-S. arm: Data Analysis Using Regression and Multilevel/Hierarchical Models. R package version 1.8-6, 2015. http://CRAN.R-project.org/package=arm.

Leifeld, P. "texreg: Conversion of statistical model output in R to LaTeX and HTML tables. *Journal of Statistical Software, 55*(8), 1–24 (2013). www.jstatsoft.org/v55/i08/

McFadden, D. "Conditional logit analysis of qualitative choice behavior." In P. Zarembka (ed.), *Frontiers in Econometrics, pp.* 105–142, New York: Academic Press, 1974.

R Core Team. foreign: Read Data Stored by Minitab, S, SAS, SPSS, Stata, Systat, Weka, dBase, ... R package version 0.8-65, 2015. http://CRAN.R-project.org/package=foreign.

R Core Team. R: A language and environment for statistical computing. Vienna, Austria: R Foundation for Statistical Computing, 2015. www.R-project.org/.

Schloerke, B., Crowley, J., Cook, D., Hofmann, H., Wickham, H., Briatte, F., Marbach, M., & and Thoen, E. GGally: Extension to ggplot2. R package version 0.5.0, 2014. http://CRAN.R-project.org/package=GGally.

Wickham, H. *ggplot2: Elegant Graphics for Data Analysis.* New York: Springer, 2009.

Wickham, H. scales: Scale Functions for Visualization. R package version 0.2.5, 2015. http://CRAN.R-project.org/package=scales.

Tukey, J. W. (1962). The future of data analysis. The Annals of Mathematical Statistics, 1-67.

CHAPTER 16

■ ■ ■

Modern Statistical Methods II

In this chapter, we explore more of what might be termed *modern* statistics. In particular, we will explore *nonparametric tests* and *bootstrapping*. As with many things, it helps to explore the reasons why such modern methods might be useful in a little depth. We have organized this chapter into three main parts. The first delves philosophically into the reasoning behind the need for these methods, while again avoiding as much mathematics as possible. The second section covers our familiar process of methodologically introducing the packages and function calls for several useful nonparametric tests. Finally, we investigate bootstrapping, with examples highlighting the historically unprecedented power available now through modern computing.

16.1 Philosophy of Parameters

So far, we have primarily focused on analyses that supposed some parameterization of our data. In Chapter 10, we tended to care about the distribution of our data. So for the *t*-test(s) that we performed, it was a requirement or assumption that our data values followed a normal distribution, that the variance of our data followed a chi-squared distribution, and that our data would be independently sampled. In Chapter 12, we explored analysis of variance (ANOVA) and introduced the Shapiro-Wilk (SW) normality test function of shapiro.test(). We also introduced the bartlett.test() function for homoscedasticity. By Chapter 13, we were looking at Normal Q-Q plots to inform as to whether the residuals followed a normal distribution. Thus, so far, most of our statistical analyses have had a requirement of several preconditions or assumptions or *parameters*. The approach used has been to use exploratory data analysis (EDA), find a distribution that matched, and then run a test whose assumptions could be satisfied. Along the way, we sometimes mentioned that some of these analyses were robust enough to cope with minor deviations from their assumptions provided their results were interpreted accordingly.

This chapter explores methods that do not simply relax the normality (or other distribution) assumptions—we may remove them entirely! This is termed *nonparametric statistics*. This becomes important when we have no reason to make parametric assumptions about data, or in fact the data may clearly violate assumptions of standard models. A case in point might be if the Normal Q-Q plot were to show that the residuals of our linear model were clearly not normal. Another feature often present in nonparametric tests is that they are outlier resistant. In other words, if an outlier is appended to a dataset, measures such as the arithmetic mean will be perhaps significantly altered. Often, by their nature, nonparametric tests are somewhat more immune to such changes.

As a final comment before we delve into our usual examples, if an assumption of a test cannot be satisfied, then we cannot trust the conclusions of that test (see Chapter 11, section 11.2)—that is, a *t*-test run on non-normal data might give a significant *p* value when there is no significance (beyond the chance of Type I error) or might give a nonsignificant *p* value when there is in fact significance (beyond the chance of Type II error). Using a nonparametric test can then provide guidance in such cases. Generally, however, the more assumptions that can be found to hold true, the more nuanced the test results can be. Thus, the *traditional* methods, when they hold true, in some sense work "better" or are more powerful than (some of) the modern methods.

16.2 Nonparametric Tests

So far, we have already looked at the function wilcox.test(), which was also called the Mann-Whitney test (see the section "A Modern Alternative to the Traditional t-Test," in Chapter 11). That test was used similarly to two independent sample t-tests, except it removed the assumption that normality was required. In this section, we make extensive use of the coin package. We now explore the Wilcoxon-Signed-Rank test (a substitute for a t-test in paired samples), Spearman's test (a ranked version of Pearson's correlation coefficient), the Kruskal-Wallis test, and a test to measure up to k independent sample data.

We start off by installing the coin package, and loading our libraries.

```
> install.packages("coin")
package 'coin' successfully unpacked and MD5 sums checked

> library(ggplot2)
> library(GGally)
> library(grid)
> library(reshape2)
> library(scales)
> library(coin)
Loading required package: survival
```

16.2.1 Wilcoxon-Signed-Rank Test

As with a paired t-test, it is supposed the data are paired and come from the same population and that each pair is randomly selected. This is a non-parametric test, however. Thus, normality is not required. Furthermore, our data need only be ordinal, not truly continuous. This greatly widens the range of data that may be considered. Suppose we have ten pairs of data measured before and after some treatment. By using the R function call runif(), we can generate random data. By using the set.seed() function call, we can be sure that our pseudo-random data will match your data (and thus we expect to get the same answers). As you can see in Figure 16-1, the data are not normally distributed. Thus, using a paired t-test would not be appropriate. The wilcoxsign_test() may be called, however, as these data definitely fit its criterion. All the same, the null hypothesis is not rejected (expected given the use of random data).

```
> set.seed(4)
> untreated <- runif(10, 20, 75)
> treated <- runif(10,20,75)
> differences = treated - untreated
> xydat <- data.frame(treated, untreated)
> shapiro.test(differences)

        Shapiro-Wilk normality test

data:  differences
W = 0.9352, p-value = 0.5009

> hist(differences)
> wilcoxsign_test(treated ~ untreated,data = xydat)

        Asymptotic Wilcoxon-Signed-Rank Test
```

```
data:  y by x (neg, pos)
         stratified by block
Z = 0.96833, p-value = 0.3329
alternative hypothesis: true mu is not equal to 0
```

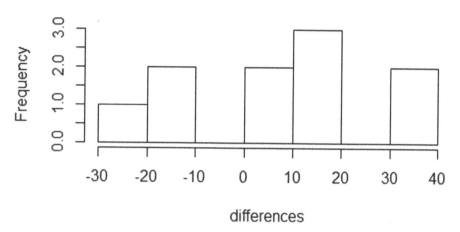

Figure 16-1. *Histogram of differences between two sets of random data showing the data are not normal*

16.2.2 Spearman's Rho

The nonparametric form of Pearson's r is Spearman's Rho. You'll recall that Pearson's r, also called the Pearson product-moment correlation coefficient, was a measure of linear correlation between two variables. Pearson's r also requires interval or ratio level metrics, and it is sensitive to outliers. Spearman's Rho simply seeks to determine if as one variable increases, it is reasonable to say that the other variable either consistently increases or consistently decreases. Spearman's does not require normality, and can work on ranked or ordinal data. Suppose we want to measure wolf pack hierarchy vs. number of elk successfully hunted in a summer. We can readily send our field researchers out into various national parks to collect data. And, imagining a fully funded operation, suppose the actual number of kill-bites delivered (if such a metric exists) per wolf was collectible. Our response data of elk hunted might well be a reasonable type of data. However, pack hierarchy is less precise. While our field researchers may well have a strong sense as to which animals are dominant compared to which members of the pack are not, there really isn't a reason to say that the alpha is ten times more dominant than the beta wolf! We see the results of the test for our invented data, along with a scatterplot in Figure 16-2.

```
> wolfpackH <- c(1:10)
> wolfkills <- c(23, 20, 19, 19, 19, 15, 13, 8, 2, 2)
> spearman_test(wolfkills~wolfpackH)

        Asymptotic Spearman Correlation Test

data:  wolfkills by wolfpackH
Z = -2.9542, p-value = 0.003135
alternative hypothesis: true mu is not equal to 0

> plot(wolfpackH, wolfkills, type="p")
```

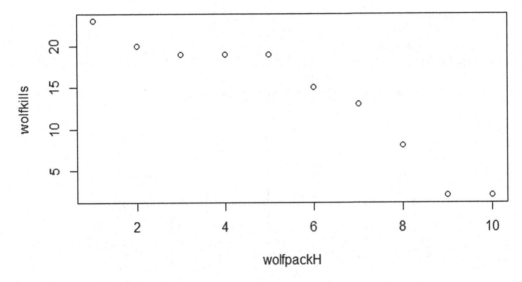

Figure 16-2. *Wolf scatterplot of elk kills vs. pack hierarchy rank*

16.2.3 Kruskal-Wallis Test

The Kruskal-Wallis one-way analysis of variance is another ranked test. It is a nonparametric counterpart to ANOVA. To explore this variety of nonparametric statistics, we'll be examining the mtcars dataset. The volume of an engine's cylinders displaces a certain amount of air, called displacement. To get started, let's look at the distribution of displacement (disp) in Figure 16-3. In looking at the histogram, our data do not appear to be particularly normal.

```
> hist(mtcars$disp)
```

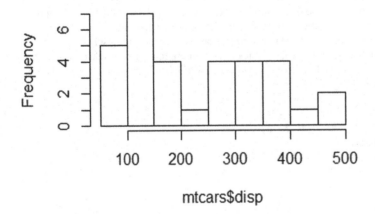

Figure 16-3. *mtcars' displacement vs. frequency histogram*

Next, ANOVA is used to examine whether carburetor predicts displacement; in this case, the results were not statistically significant. However, displacement does not seem to have exactly a normal distribution. In particular, we note that the Normal Q-Q plot has some issues, as seen in Figure 16-4 on the lower left. We could also use a Kruskal-Wallis Rank Sum Test (Hollander & Wolfe, 1973) using the function call kruskal.test(). The Kruskal-Wallis test operates on ranks, rather than on means, so it does not matter what the distribution of the original variable was as everything is converted to ranks.

```
> summary(aov(disp ~ factor(carb), data = mtcars))
            Df Sum Sq Mean Sq F value Pr(>F)
factor(carb)  5 149586   29917   2.382 0.0662 .
Residuals    26 326599   12562
---
Signif. codes:  0 '***' 0.001 '**' 0.01 '*' 0.05 '.' 0.1 ' ' 1
> Data4<-aov(disp ~ factor(carb), data = mtcars)
> plot(Data4)
> kruskal.test(disp ~ factor(carb), data = mtcars)

        Kruskal-Wallis rank sum test

data:  disp by factor(carb)
Kruskal-Wallis chi-squared = 11.868, df = 5, p-value = 0.03664
```

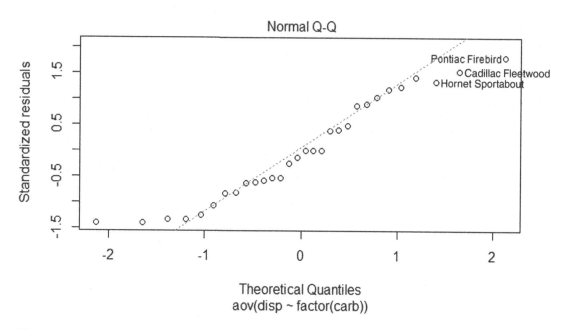

Figure 16-4. *Normal Q-Q plot of the residuals that do not look fully normal*

The kruskal.test() form of this function has few options. More options are available in the coin package version. We utilize the function call kruskal_test() which gives us the same results as the call from base R. The authors recommend performing such double-checks on occasion with packages you are unfamiliar with as a way of checking that you understand how a function works and the quality of the package. It is, of course, not a completely foolproof error-checking methodology, but it can certainly help us understand if there are any differences in notation.

```
> kruskal_test(disp ~ factor(carb), data = mtcars)

        Asymptotic Kruskal-Wallis Test

data:  disp by factor(carb) (1, 2, 3, 4, 6, 8)
chi-squared = 11.868, df = 5, p-value = 0.03664
```

16.2.4 One-Way Test

Carrying on from our Kruskal-Wallis data, we explore the perspective of the oneway_test(). This test is a k-sample permutation test that, unlike Kruskal-Wallis, computes the test statistics on untransformed response variables. As our data of displacements are not already ranked, this may yield alternative insight. The results of the permutation test are closer to the initial ANOVA and suggest that overall carburetor does not have a statistically significant effect, which if your authors knew more about cars might not be surprising.

```
> oneway_test(disp ~ factor(carb), data = mtcars)

        Asymptotic K-Sample Fisher-Pitman Permutation Test

data:  disp by factor(carb) (1, 2, 3, 4, 6, 8)
chi-squared = 9.7381, df = 5, p-value = 0.083
```

One way we can look at the data is by plotting the means and medians. Some of the levels only have one point because the mean and median overlap when there is a single observation. This is not a perfect example since this is a small dataset with only 32 observations. Often, in data analysis, we may consider dropping some levels or collapsing levels. Nevertheless, we close out this section with code to observe this and the plot in Figure 16-5.

```
> p <- ggplot(mtcars, aes(carb, disp)) +
+   stat_summary(fun.y = mean, geom = "point", colour = "black", size = 3) +
+   stat_summary(fun.y = median, geom = "point", colour = "blue", size = 3) +
+   theme_bw()
> p
```

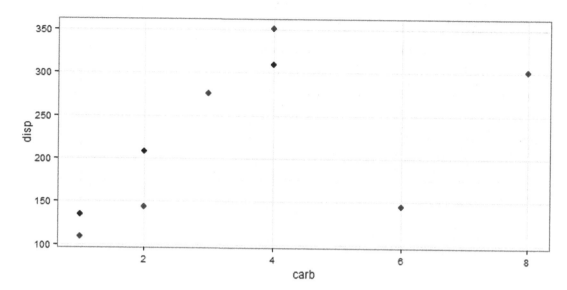

Figure 16-5. *Means and medians of carburators vs. displacement*

16.3 Bootstrapping

One of the primary forces behind many aspects of statistics is the realization that it is not possible to deal with entire populations of data. So, instead, a fair amount of effort is spent projecting sample data as estimators of the population measures. However, as we have seen, not all populations are normal or readily matchable to some other useful mold. Thus, the nonparametric tests can allow for the same process to occur, but without as many preconditions or assumptions.

However, what if one could turn a sample into a population? What if there was some way to randomly draw again and again from a sample, until one's data size was as large as a population? Such a sample would not be as precise as drawing randomly from the actual population. Still, we could presumably use more direct methods rather than the less precise statistical estimates. Methods that attempt to exploit such ideas are generally termed *resampling* methods. The variant we discuss in this section is the bootstrap.

The name *bootstrap* comes from a story about a baron who was trapped in a swamp. Left with few resources, he ended up pulling himself out of the swamp by his own bootstraps (an impressive feat to be sure) and was able to be on his way. Slightly less mythically, we perform our sampling from our sample with replacement, and apply such a process to many different scenarios. We do not exhaustively treat those scenarios in this section; we simply observe several examples that are perhaps very common.

In our R code for this section, we will use the boot package library(boot). The boot package has a function, boot(), which is what we will primarily use for bootstrapping. This function takes as input both data and another function that produces the expected values to be bootstrapped. The function inputted into the boot function call should take a parameter and the indices of the data which boot() will provide for each bootstrapped (re)sample.

```
> library(boot)

Attaching package: 'boot'

The following object is masked from 'package:survival':

    aml

>
```

16.3.1 Examples from mtcars

To start, we can just bootstrap the difference in two means like an independent samples *t*-test. Because the indices are randomly generated, to make the bootstrap reproducible we need to set the random number seed. We return to our mtcars dataset, and again inspect our displacement data. This time, we create a dataset we call bootres where we've drawn 5,000 bootstrap samples to get the distribution of mean differences. We also plot the distribution and observe the quantiles in Figure 16-6.

```
> set.seed(1234)
> ## now we can draw 5,000 bootstrap samples
> ## to get the distribution of mean differences
>
> bootres <- boot(
+   data = mtcars,
+   statistic = function(d, i) {
+     as.vector(diff(tapply(d$disp[i], d$vs[i], mean)))
+   },
+   R = 5000)
> plot(bootres)
```

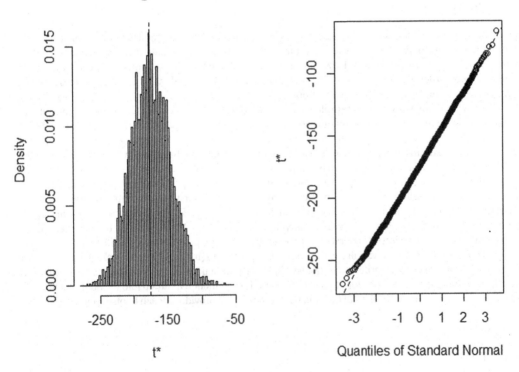

Figure 16-6. *Histogram of 5,000 bootstrapped samples and Normal Q-Q plot*

We can also plot the distribution with an added line for the mean in the raw data. In this case the distribution of mean differences appears approximately normal as we see in Figure 16-7 plotted from the following code.

```
> hist(bootres$t[,1])
> abline(v = bootres$t0, col = "blue", lwd = 3)
```

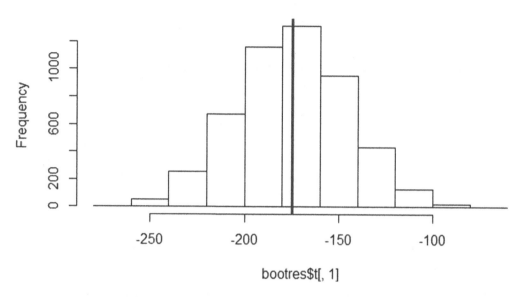

Figure 16-7. *Histogram of bootres with an added line for the mean in the raw data*

The real power of bootstrapping is that bootstrapping works even for items where the distribution is unknown, such as for medians. The distribution of medians appears less normal as seen in Figure 16-8.

```
> set.seed(1234)
> bootres2 <- boot(
+     data = mtcars,
+     statistic = function(d, i) {
+       as.vector(diff(tapply(d$disp[i], d$vs[i], median)))
+     },
+     R = 5000)
>
> hist(bootres2$t[,1], breaks = 50)
> abline(v = bootres2$t0, col = "blue", lwd = 3)
```

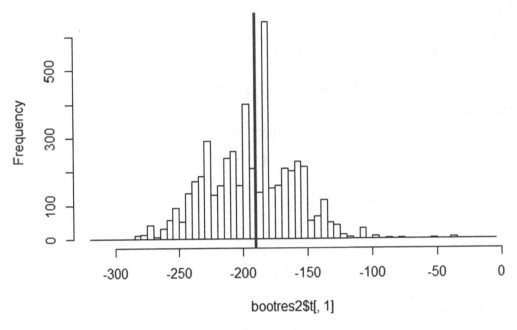

Figure 16-8. *Histogram of bootres2 for medians on displacement from mtcars*

Another simple example is bootstrapping the log of the variance as shown in the following code and in Figure 16-9. We take the log of the variance because variances fall within the bounds of (0, Inf). When log transformed the bounds go from (-Inf, Inf). It is generally better, if possible, to have unbounded variances.

```
> set.seed(1234)
> bootres3 <- boot(
+   data = mtcars,
+   statistic = function(d, i) {
+     as.vector(diff(tapply(d$disp[i], d$vs[i], function(x) log(var(x)))))
+   },
+   R = 5000)
>
> hist(bootres3$t[,1], breaks = 50)
> abline(v = bootres3$t0, col = "blue", lwd = 3)
```

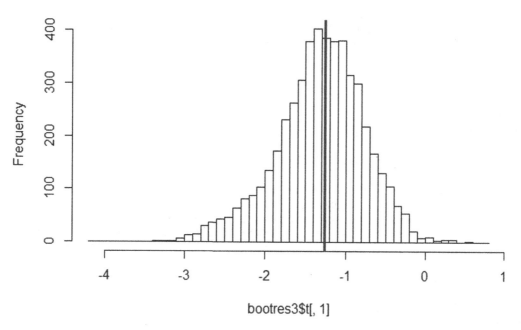

Figure 16-9. *Histogram for log of the variance on displacement from mtcars*

16.3.2 Bootstrapping Confidence Intervals

While looking at the various distributions from the bootstrap samples is helpful, typically we want to summarize the distribution somehow. Most commonly, people report on the estimate and bootstrapped confidence intervals. There are actually several different ways to calculate confidence intervals from bootstrapping.

Typically if we want 95% confidence intervals, we have to work out what the 2.5th and 97.5th percentile of a distribution would be, given the estimated parameters. For example, for a normal distribution we use the estimated mean and variance, and from those we can find the percentiles. In bootstrapping, we can use the "percentile" method to get confidence intervals very easily. Because we actually have (typically) thousands of bootstrap resamples, we actually have a pretty good sample of the distribution we are interested in. Rather than working out assumptions and the math for a particular percentile, we can just find the percentiles we desire (typically 2.5th and 97.5th) empirically. To do this in R, we can use the quantile() function, which calculates quantiles or percentiles. For example (rounded to three decimals):

```
> round(quantile(bootres3$t[,1], probs = c(.025, .975)), 3)
  2.5%  97.5%
-2.586 -0.313
```

We can also do this directly in R using the boot.ci() function with type = "perc" as shown next:

```
> boot.ci(bootres3, type = "perc")
BOOTSTRAP CONFIDENCE INTERVAL CALCULATIONS
Based on 5000 bootstrap replicates

CALL :
boot.ci(boot.out = bootres3, type = "perc")

Intervals :
Level      Percentile
95%    (-2.588, -0.312 )
Calculations and Intervals on Original Scale
```

The reason these estimates are slightly different is that for non-integer order statistics, R interpolates on the normal quantile scale. That is, the .025th percentile may not exactly exist in the bootstrap data, and so R interpolates between the two nearest points to estimate it, and the way that is done in boot.ci() vs. quantile() differs, leading to slightly different results. These would get smaller and smaller as the number of bootstrap resamples increased (if you like as an exercise, try changing from 5,000 to 50,000, which should still only take a few minutes for this simple example, and then rerun and compare the results). Putting these together with our graph, we can visualize it as shown in Figure 16-10.

```
> hist(bootres3$t[,1], breaks = 50)
> abline(v = bootres3$t0, col = "blue", lwd = 3)
> abline(v = quantile(bootres3$t[,1], probs = c(.025)), col = "yellow", lwd = 3)
> abline(v = quantile(bootres3$t[,1], probs = c(.975)), col = "yellow", lwd = 3)
```

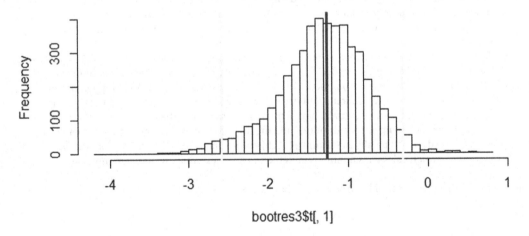

Figure 16-10. Histogram with confidence intervals for log of the variance

Another type of confidence interval is called the "basic" bootstrap. It is actually very similar to the percentile method, but rather than reporting the percentiles directly, these are subtracted from 2x the actual estimate (again rounded by three decimals). Again, we may do this directly in R using the boot.ci() function with type = "basic". We show both sets of code next, and, again, small differences are due to interpolation.

```
> round((2 * bootres3$t0) - quantile(bootres3$t[,1], probs = c(.975, .025)), 3)
 97.5%   2.5%
-2.205  0.068


## directly
> boot.ci(bootres3, type = "basic")
BOOTSTRAP CONFIDENCE INTERVAL CALCULATIONS
Based on 5000 bootstrap replicates

CALL :
boot.ci(boot.out = bootres3, type = "basic")

Intervals :
Level      Basic
95%   (-2.206,  0.070 )
Calculations and Intervals on Original Scale
```

Another type of confidence interval is called the "normal" interval, which assumes the parameter distribution is normal but, instead of using the variance estimate from the model, uses the variance of the bootstrap distribution. The normal interval also adjusts for bias in the bootstrap distribution, which is calculated as the difference between the mean of the bootstrap samples and the actual statistic on the original raw data. Again, we can also do this directly in R using the boot.ci() function with type = "norm" as shown in the following code:

```
> bias <- mean(bootres3$t) - bootres3$t0
> sigma <- sd(bootres3$t[,1])
> ## manually
> round(bootres3$t0 - bias - qnorm(c(.975, .025), sd = sigma), 3)
[1] -2.296 -0.106
> ## directly
> boot.ci(bootres3, type = "norm")
BOOTSTRAP CONFIDENCE INTERVAL CALCULATIONS
Based on 5000 bootstrap replicates

CALL :
boot.ci(boot.out = bootres3, type = "norm")

Intervals :
Level      Normal
95%   (-2.296, -0.106 )
Calculations and Intervals on Original Scale
```

A final approach to confidence intervals in bootstrapping is the bias corrected and accelerated (BCa) confidence interval. This attempts to adjust not only for bias but also for differences in the shape of the bootstrap distribution. The details behind the exact calculation are more complicated and are not discussed here (but see Carpenter & Bithell, 2000). It is easy to obtain the BCa bootstrap confidence intervals in R, and at least in theory these should provide less bias and better coverage (i.e., a nominal 95% confidence interval should include the true value about 95% of the time; if it includes the true value exactly 95% of the time, this is a good sign, if a nominally 95% confidence interval only includes the true value about 80% of the time, we would conclude that the coverage was poor).

```
> boot.ci(bootres3, type = "bca")
BOOTSTRAP CONFIDENCE INTERVAL CALCULATIONS
Based on 5000 bootstrap replicates

CALL :
boot.ci(boot.out = bootres3, type = "bca")

Intervals :
Level       BCa
95%   (-2.384, -0.194 )
Calculations and Intervals on Original Scale
```

So far, we have examined fairly simple examples of statistics we might want to bootstrap. Next, we will examine a more complex case where we could use bootstrapping.

16.3.3 Examples from GSS

In the previous chapter, we built some models for categorical outcomes using the GSS data. We will use that data again and fit an ordered logistic model to it as a preliminary step, and then examine how we might incorporate bootstrapping. We show the code to get the basic model up running below with some cleanup for legibility:

```
> library(foreign)
> library(VGAM)

> gss2012 <- read.spss("GSS2012merged_R5.sav", to.data.frame = TRUE)
> gssr <- gss2012[, c("age", "sex", "marital", "educ", "income06", "satfin", "happy", "health")]
> gssr <- na.omit(gssr)

> gssr <- within(gssr, {
+    age <- as.numeric(age)
+    Agec <- (gssr$age - 18) / 10
+    educ <- as.numeric(educ)
+    # recode income categories to numeric
+    cincome <- as.numeric(income06)
+    satfin <- factor(satfin,
+                     levels = c("NOT AT ALL SAT", "MORE OR LESS", "SATISFIED"),
+                     ordered = TRUE)
+ })
```

```
> m <- vglm(satfin ~ Agec + cincome * educ,
+           family = cumulative(link = "logit", parallel = TRUE, reverse = TRUE), data = gssr)
> summary(m)

Call:
vglm(formula = satfin ~ Agec + cincome * educ, family = cumulative(link = "logit",
    parallel = TRUE, reverse = TRUE), data = gssr)

Pearson residuals:
                   Min      1Q  Median     3Q   Max
logit(P[Y>=2]) -3.651 -0.9955  0.3191 0.7164 2.323
logit(P[Y>=3]) -1.562 -0.6679 -0.3018 0.7138 6.240

Coefficients:
               Estimate Std. Error z value Pr(>|z|)
(Intercept):1  0.964729   0.480847   2.006   0.0448 *
(Intercept):2 -1.188741   0.481270  -2.470   0.0135 *
Agec           0.169257   0.021790   7.768 8.00e-15 ***
cincome       -0.061124   0.027614  -2.213   0.0269 *
educ          -0.182900   0.036930  -4.953 7.32e-07 ***
cincome:educ   0.012398   0.002033   6.098 1.07e-09 ***
---
Signif. codes:  0 '***' 0.001 '**' 0.01 '*' 0.05 '.' 0.1 ' ' 1
Number of linear predictors:  2
Names of linear predictors: logit(P[Y>=2]), logit(P[Y>=3])
Dispersion Parameter for cumulative family:    1
Residual deviance: 5675.892 on 5664 degrees of freedom
Log-likelihood: -2837.946 on 5664 degrees of freedom
Number of iterations: 5
```

Now that we have the basic model, what if we wanted to get bootstrapped confidence intervals for coefficients or predictions from the model? To do this within R, we need to write a function that can be passed to the boot() function that will get all the statistics we are interested in exploring.

```
> model_coef_predictions <- function(d, i) {
+
+   m.tmp <- vglm(satfin ~ Agec + cincome * educ,
+                 family = cumulative(link = "logit", parallel = TRUE, reverse = TRUE),
+                 data = d[i, ])
+   newdat <- expand.grid(
+     Agec = seq(from = 0, to = (89 - 18)/10, length.out = 50),
+     cincome = mean(d$cincom),
+     educ = c(12, 16, 20))
+
+   bs <- coef(m.tmp)
+   predicted.probs <- predict(m.tmp, newdata = newdat,
+                               type = "response")
+
+   out <- c(bs, predicted.probs[, 1], predicted.probs[, 2], predicted.probs[, 3])
+
+   return(out)
+ }
```

Now, this next bit of code may take some time to run on your machine. In fact, in one of the remaining chapters we will discuss ways to wring out more performance from modern computers. At its default settings, R is not the most efficient user of available compute power. To put this into context, we ran this on fairly powerful machines with large amounts of RAM (not so relevant in this case) and multiple cores (potentially relevant but not with this code) and high processing power (more relevant). It took under ten minutes, but over three to run (the author made a brief caffeinated beverage run and offers apologies for less than precise measurement).

```
> set.seed(1234)
> boot.res <- boot(
+    data = gssr,
+    statistic = model_coef_predictions,
+    R = 5000)
```

Again, this code took several minutes to run, but once complete, it gives us quite a bit of information as it has the bootstrapped distributions for each of the model coefficients as well as a variety of predicted probabilities. Of course, we could have just saved the model coefficients, as those are enough to calculate the predicted probabilities.

To start with, we can loop through the results and calculate the 95% BCa confidence intervals for each statistic) and store the results along with the estimate in the original data in a new data frame. Perhaps surprisingly, calculating the confidence intervals for each statistic actually took longer than running the initial bootstrap! To see how this works without taking too much time, you can run just the first few parameters, by replacing *1:length(boot.res$t0)* with *1:6* in the code that follows. On a high-end desktop, this code took over an hour, and may take much longer depending on the specific machine being used. This is due to using the BCa confidence intervals, which are more computationally demanding, and are repeated for each of the statistics of which there are 450 predicted probabilities (three levels of the outcome by 150 observations in our made-up dataset for prediction), and a handful more model coefficients.

```
> boot.res2 <- lapply(1:length(boot.res$t0), function(i) {
+    cis <- boot.ci(boot.res, index = i, type = "bca")
+    data.frame(Estimate = boot.res$t0[i],
+                  LL = cis$bca[1, 4],
+                  UL = cis$bca[1, 5])
+ })
```

Next we can take the results, which currently are a list of data frames where each data frame has a single row, and combine them row-wise.

```
> boot.res2 <- do.call(rbind, boot.res2)
> head(round(boot.res2, 3), 10)
                  Estimate     LL      UL
(Intercept):1        0.965   0.066   1.888
(Intercept):2       -1.189  -2.097  -0.263
Agec                 0.169   0.124   0.213
cincome             -0.061  -0.113  -0.007
educ                -0.183  -0.254  -0.112
cincome:educ         0.012   0.009   0.016
1                    0.434   0.395   0.474
2                    0.428   0.391   0.467
3                    0.422   0.386   0.459
4                    0.417   0.381   0.452
```

We can see that the first six rows give parameter estimates along with confidence intervals, and then the predicted probabilities start. We can use the rep() function to help us label each row of the dataset.

```
> boot.res2$Type <- rep(c("coef", "Not Satisfied", "More/Less Satisfied", "Satisified"),
+                        c(6, 150, 150, 150))
```

Copying the data used from prediction within our function, we can merge the predicted results and confidence intervals from bootstrapping with the values used for prediction to generate a final dataset for graphing or presentation. Note that since we have three levels of the outcome, we need to repeat our newdat object three times. We could have just typed it three times, but that does not scale well (what if you needed to do it 300 times), so we show how to use the rep() function again this time to create a list where each element is a data frame, we then combine row-wise using do.call() and rbind(), before finally column-wise combining it with the bootstrapping results to create a final dataset for presentation.

```
> newdat <- expand.grid(
+    Agec = seq(from = 0, to = (89 - 18)/10, length.out = 50),
+    cincome = mean(gssr$cincom),
+    educ = c(12, 16, 20))
>
> finaldat <- cbind(boot.res2[-(1:6), ], do.call(rbind, rep(list(newdat), 3)))
```

We do this, and graph the results in Figure 16-11 using fairly familiar code as follows:

```
> p<- ggplot(finaldat, aes(Agec, Estimate, colour = Type, linetype = Type)) +
+    geom_ribbon(aes(ymin = LL, ymax = UL, colour = NULL, fill = Type), alpha = .25) +
+    geom_line(size = 1.5) +
+    scale_x_continuous("Age", breaks = (c(20, 40, 60, 80) - 18)/10,
+                       labels = c(20, 40, 60, 80)) +
+    scale_y_continuous("Probability", labels = percent) +
+    theme_bw() +
+    theme(legend.key.width = unit(1.5, "cm"),
+          legend.position = "bottom",
+          legend.title = element_blank()) +
+    facet_wrap(~educ) +
+    ggtitle("Financial Satisfaction")
> p
```

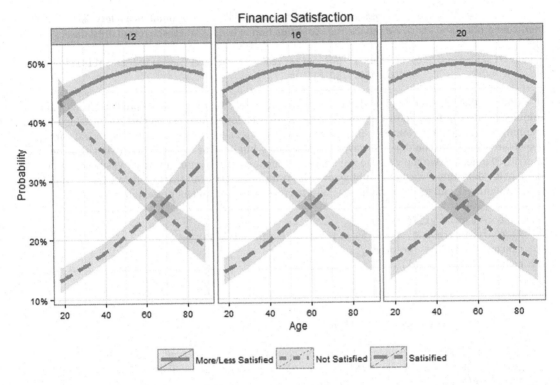

Figure 16-11. *Financial satisfaction plot(s) sorted by years of education*

These results show us that for adults in the average income bin, there is not much difference in financial satisfaction by education level. Conversely, there are large changes across the lifespan.

Finally, let's examine whether there are any differences in the confidence intervals from normal theory vs. bootstrapping. First, we get the estimates and standard errors as a matrix.

```
> (coef.tab <- coef(summary(m)))
                   Estimate  Std. Error   z value      Pr(>|z|)
(Intercept):1   0.96472914  0.480847174   2.006311  4.482304e-02
(Intercept):2  -1.18874068  0.481270087  -2.470007  1.351103e-02
Agec            0.16925731  0.021790024   7.767651  7.995485e-15
cincome        -0.06112373  0.027614421  -2.213471  2.686517e-02
educ           -0.18290044  0.036929590  -4.952680  7.319831e-07
cincome:educ    0.01239790  0.002033034   6.098224  1.072537e-09
```

Then we can calculate the 95% confidence intervals and combine with our bootstrapped results (dropping the fourth column labeling the type of the result).

```
> coef.res <- cbind(boot.res2[1:6, -4],
+               NormalLL = coef.tab[, 1] + qnorm(.025) * coef.tab[, 2],
+               NormalUL = coef.tab[, 1] + qnorm(.975) * coef.tab[, 2])
```

```
> coef.res
                Estimate           LL           UL       NormalLL      NormalUL
(Intercept):1  0.96472914  0.065709812  1.888282581   0.022285994  1.907172279
(Intercept):2 -1.18874068 -2.096506820 -0.262608836  -2.132012714 -0.245468639
Agec           0.16925731  0.124358398  0.212613375   0.126549646  0.211964972
cincome       -0.06112373 -0.112977921 -0.007421777  -0.115246998 -0.007000457
educ          -0.18290044 -0.254102950 -0.111955065  -0.255281108 -0.110519774
cincome:educ   0.01239790  0.008504279  0.016193052   0.008413223  0.016382571
```

While there are some differences, in this particular case, they appear quite small. These results might encourage us to believe that these data are "well-behaved" and the parametric assumptions we made are fairly reasonable. In other cases, results may differ more and we would have to try to understand why and decide which results we trusted.

So far we have seen how bootstrapping can be applied in many situations; in some of those situations confidence intervals are not well-defined (like the median) and in other cases we may use bootstrapping as a sort of sensitivity analysis or a check that our results are robust. Before we conclude our discussion of bootstrapping, we will look at one more example that shows how flexible bootstrapping can be.

Suppose we wanted test whether the difference in the probability of being financially satisfied between an 18-year-old and an 89-year-old, who both had 16 years of education and an average income bin, was exactly canceling each other out (i.e., the same magnitude but opposite sign differences):

$$\Delta Satisfied = P(satisfied \mid age = 89) - P(satisfied \mid age = 18)$$

$$\Delta \, Not \, Satisfied = P(not \, satisfied \mid age = 89) - P(not \, satisfied \mid age = 18)$$

$$\Delta \, Satisfied + \Delta \, Not \, Satisfied \overset{?}{=} 0$$

```
> subset(finaldat, Agec %in% c(0, 7.1) & educ == 16 & Type != "More/Less Satisfied")
       Estimate        LL        UL          Type Agec  cincome educ
51    0.4068473 0.3678249 0.4481580 Not Satisfied  0.0 17.04056   16
100   0.1709739 0.1440701 0.2042896 Not Satisfied  7.1 17.04056   16
513   0.1447413 0.1241949 0.1686146     Satisified  0.0 17.04056   16
1002  0.3601464 0.3127528 0.4066795     Satisified  7.1 17.04056   16
```

From here, we can see that we want the 51st and 100th for the first and third outcome level. We can make an index variable to grab these and check that it works.

```
> index <- c(51, 100, 51 + 300, 100 + 300)
> finaldat[index, ]
       Estimate        LL        UL          Type Agec  cincome educ
51    0.4068473 0.3678249 0.4481580 Not Satisfied  0.0 17.04056   16
100   0.1709739 0.1440701 0.2042896 Not Satisfied  7.1 17.04056   16
513   0.1447413 0.1241949 0.1686146     Satisified  0.0 17.04056   16
1002  0.3601464 0.3127528 0.4066795     Satisified  7.1 17.04056   16
```

Now we can go to the bootstrapping results, noting that since the first six bootstrap statistics are for coefficients, we need to add 6 to our index variable, recalling that t0 has the actual estimates in the real data and t has the bootstrapped distribution.

```
> tmp.bootres <- boot.res$t0[index + 6]
> btmp.bootres <- boot.res$t[, index + 6]
```

Now we can calculate the differences and test them. We show the resulting histogram in Figure 16-12.

```
> deltaSatisfied <- tmp.bootres[4] - tmp.bootres[3]
> deltaNotSatisfied <- tmp.bootres[2] - tmp.bootres[1]

> bdeltaSatisfied <- btmp.bootres[, 4] - btmp.bootres[, 3]
> bdeltaNotSatisfied <- btmp.bootres[, 2] - btmp.bootres[, 1]

> test <- deltaSatisfied + deltaNotSatisfied
> btest <- bdeltaSatisfied + bdeltaNotSatisfied

> hist(btest, breaks = 50)
> abline(v = test, col = "blue", lwd = 5)
> abline(v = quantile(btest, probs = .025), col = "yellow", lwd = 5)
> abline(v = quantile(btest, probs = .975), col = "yellow", lwd = 5)
```

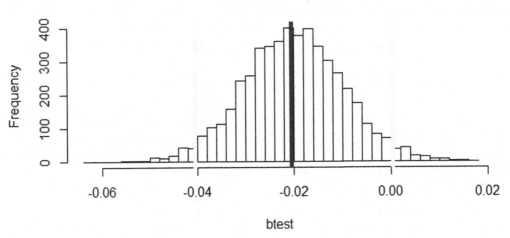

Figure 16-12. *Histogram of btest*

The 95% confidence interval just includes zero, suggesting that we cannot reject the hypothesis that

$$\Delta\, Satisfied + \Delta\, Not\, Satisfied = 0$$

and practically speaking, suggesting that indeed the difference between young and old in probability of being financially satisfied is about the same magnitude as the difference in probability of being not financially satisfied. This same approach would work, even if we had a more complex hypothesis and various nonlinear transformations. While those are challenges for deriving standard errors, they are comparatively straightforward in regard to bootstrapping.

16.4 Final Thought

For centuries, statistics has been concerned with taking sample data and using them along with clever models to determine, within some level of confidence, how the population data are behaving. Generally, this has required making various assumptions about how the population data might be expected to behave. Through nonparametric models, we are able to relax or even remove some assumptions or preconditions on our data, while still having actionable models. With bootstrapping, we are even able to cope with data that may well have very few known characteristics. However, these come with a price. A nonparametric model may well not be as "tight" a confidence interval as a similar parametric model. This, of course, may be solved with collecting more data, yet even that comes with a computation load cost. And, as we saw for bootstrapping, that computational load may well be comparatively high. Nevertheless, computers are very helpful, and to explore and understand data without them would be perhaps foolish. We turn now to a look at data visualization with the rich graphics of the medium, before we spend some time discovering just how to exploit as much computational efficiency in a machine as possible.

References

Canty, A., & Ripley, B. boot: Bootstrap R (S-Plus) Functions. R package version 1.3-17, 2015.

Carpenter, J., & Bithell, J. "Bootstrap confidence intervals: when, which, what? A practical guide for medical statisticians." *Statistics in Medicine, 19*(9), 1141–1164 (2000).

Hollander, M., & Wolfe, D. A. *Nonparametric Statistical Methods.* New York: John Wiley & Sons, 1973.

Hothorn, T., Hornik, K., van de Wiel, M. A., & Zeileis, A. (A Lego system for conditional inference. *The American Statistician, 60*(3), 257–263 (2006).

R Core Team. R: A language and environment for statistical computing. Vienna, Austria: R Foundation for Statistical Computing, 2015. www.R-project.org/.

Schloerke, B., Crowley, J., Cook, D., Hofmann, H., Wickham, H., Briatte, F., Marbach, M., & and Thoen, E. GGally: Extension to ggplot2. R package version 0.5.0, 2014. http://CRAN.R-project.org/package=GGally.

Wickham, H. "Reshaping data with the reshape package. *Journal of Statistical Software, 21*(12), 1-20 (2007). www.jstatsoft.org/v21/i12/.

Wickham., H. *ggplot2: Elegant Graphics for Data Analysis.* New York: Springer, 2009.

Wickham, H. scales: Scale Functions for Visualization. R package version 0.2.5, 2015. http://CRAN.R-project.org/package=scales.

■ ■ ■

CHAPTER 17

Data Visualization Cookbook

Throughout the book we used quite a few graphs to help you visualize and understand data, but we never went through them systematically. In this *cookbook* chapter, we will show you how to make a number of different kinds of common graphs in R (most of which you have not seen yet, though for completeness we duplicate one or two).

17.1 Required Packages

First, we will load some packages. Be sure to use `install.packages("packageName")` for any packages that are not yet installed on your computer. In the section "References," we cite all these packages, and our reader(s) will note that many are actually quite new (or at least newly updated).

```
install.packages(c("gridExtra", "plot3D", "cowplot", "Hmisc"))
library(grid)
library(gridExtra)
library(ggplot2)
library(GGally)
library(RColorBrewer)
library(plot3D)
library(scatterplot3d)
library(scales)
library(hexbin)
library(cowplot)
library(boot)
library(Hmisc)
```

17.2 Univariate Plots

We will start off with plots of a single variable. For continuous variables, we might want to know what the distribution of the variable is. Histograms and density plots are commonly used to visualize the distribution of continuous variables, and they work fairly well for small and for very large datasets. We see the results in Figure 17-1 and Figure 17-2.

```
p1 <- ggplot(mtcars, aes(mpg))
p1 + geom_histogram() + ggtitle("Histogram")
p1 + geom_density() + ggtitle("Density Plot")
```

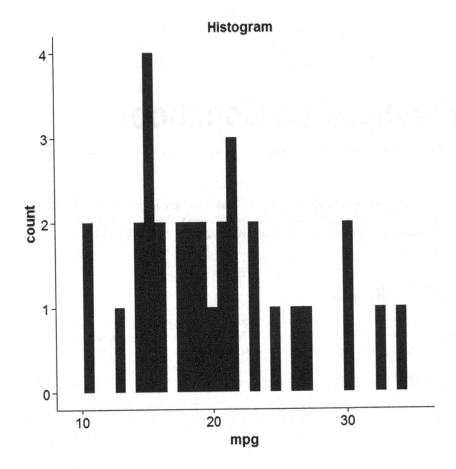

Figure 17-1. Histogram

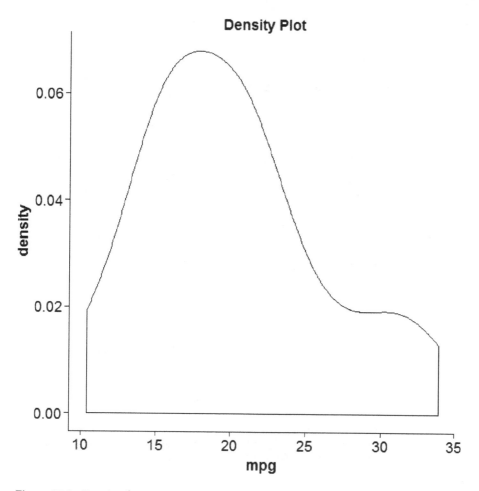

Figure 17-2. *Density plot*

We could overlay the density plot on the histogram (see Figure 17-3) if we wished, but for that we need to make the y axes the same for both, which we can do by making the histogram plot densities rather than counts. We also change the fill color to make the density line easier to see (black on dark gray is not easy), and make each bin of the histogram wider to smooth it a bit more, like the density plot, which is quite smooth.

```
p1 + geom_histogram(aes(y = ..density..), binwidth = 3, fill = "grey50") +
  geom_density(size = 1) +
  ggtitle("Histogram with Density Overlay")
```

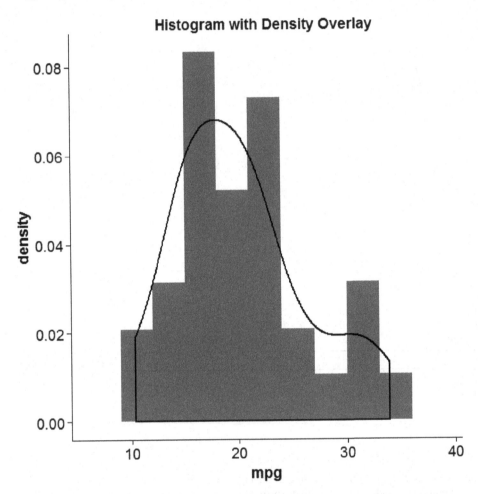

Figure 17-3. *Adjusting scales and altering colors are common data visualization techniques*

As we mentioned, this also works well for large datasets, such as the diamonds data, which has 53,940 rows. Notice the rather small density measurements in Figure 17-4.

```
ggplot(diamonds, aes(price)) +
  geom_histogram(aes(y = ..density..), fill = "grey50") +
  geom_density(size = 1) +
  ggtitle("Histogram with Density Overlay")
```

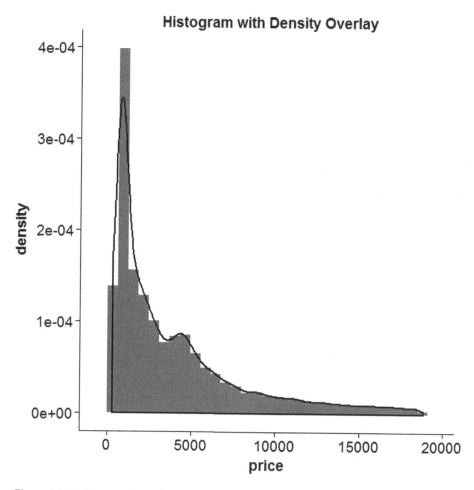

Figure 17-4. *Even very large datasets are readily graphed*

For small datasets, a dotplot (Figure 17-5) provides a natural representation of the raw data, although it does not work well for a large dataset, even with just a few hundred or a few thousand dots they become confusing and overly 'busy'.

```
p1 + geom_dotplot() + ggtitle("Dotplot")
```

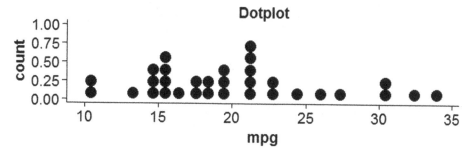

Figure 17-5. *Dotplot is best to pictorially show smaller datasets in full*

It can also be helpful to show summary statistics about a distribution—for example, where the mean or median is perhaps with a confidence interval (CI). We can get the mean and 95% CI from a *t*-test and then use the values for plotting. The result is subtle but highlights the central tendency and our uncertainty about the mtcars data shown in Figure 17-6.

```
sumstats <- t.test(mtcars$mpg)

p1 +
  geom_histogram(aes(y = ..density..), binwidth = 3, fill = "grey50") +
  geom_point(aes(x = sumstats$estimate, y = -.001), ) +
  geom_segment(aes(x = sumstats$conf.int[1], xend = sumstats$conf.int[2], y = -.001, yend =
-.001)) +
  ggtitle("Histogram with Mean and 95% CI")
```

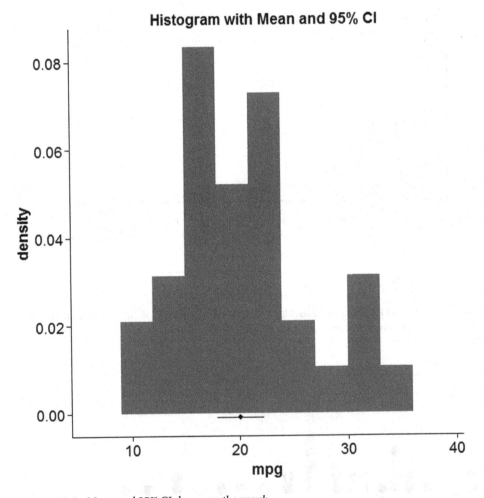

Figure 17-6. Mean and 95% CI shown on the graph

Finally, a boxplot or a box-and-whisker plot (Figure 17-7) can be a helpful summary of a continuous variables distribution. The bar in the middle is the median, and the box is the lower and upper quartiles, with the whiskers extending the range of the data or until the point of outliers (represented as dots).

```
ggplot(mtcars, aes("MPG", mpg)) + geom_boxplot()
```

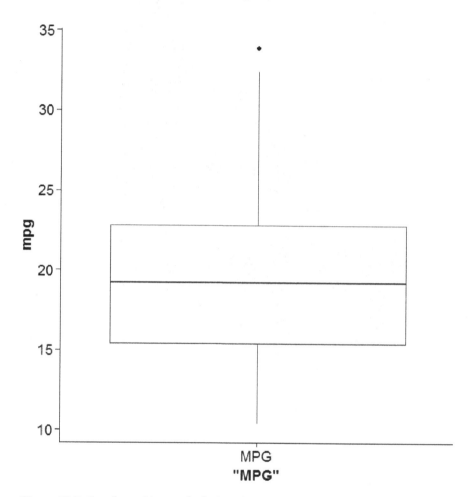

Figure 17-7. *Boxplot and box-and-whisker plot with outlier, bold median line, and 25th and 75th percentile hinges*

For discrete, univariate data, we can visualize the distribution using a barplot of the frequencies in Figure 17-8.

```
ggplot(diamonds, aes(cut)) +
  geom_bar()
```

221

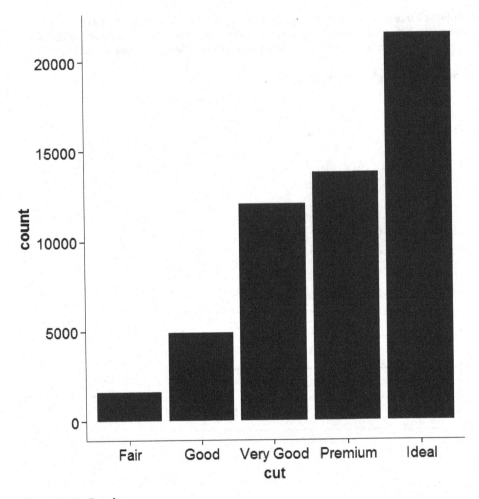

Figure 17-8. *Barplot*

We can also make a stacked barplot as graphed in Figure 17-9.

```
ggplot(diamonds, aes("Cut", fill = cut)) +
  geom_bar()
```

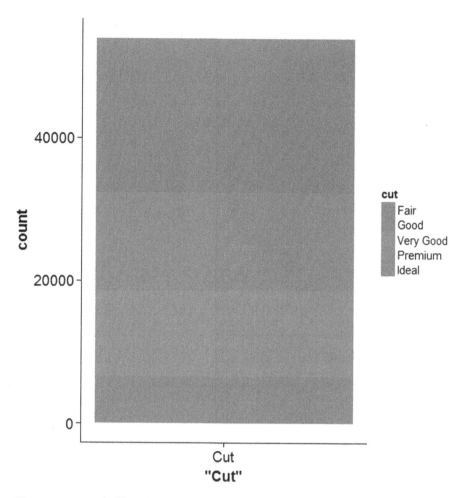

Figure 17-9. *Stacked barplots serve dual roles as both barplots and rectangular pie charts*

If we make a stacked barplot but use polar coordinates, we have a pie chart (Figure 17-10).

```
ggplot(diamonds, aes("Cut", fill = cut)) +
  geom_bar(width = 1) +
  coord_polar(theta = "y")
```

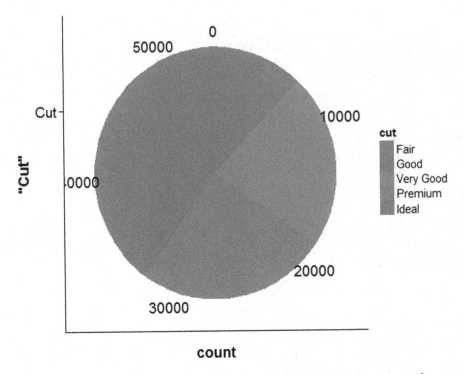

Figure 17-10. *Polar coordinates are quite useful, and pie charts are just one example*

To make the numbers proportions, we can divide by the total, and Figure 17-11 looks more like a traditional pie chart.

```
ggplot(diamonds, aes("Cut", fill = cut)) +
  geom_bar(aes(y = ..count.. / sum(..count..)), width = 1) +
  coord_polar(theta = "y")
```

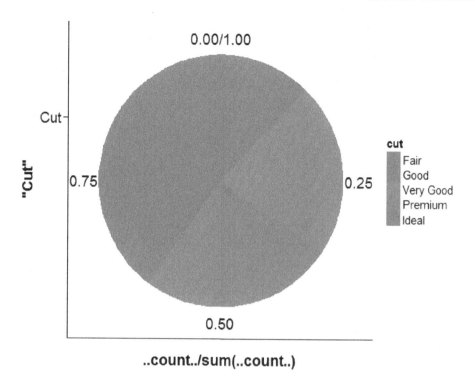

Figure 17-11. *Traditional pie chart with percents*

We are not limited to using barplots either. Points work equally well to convey the proportion of diamonds with each cut. Although bars are more traditional, most of the space filled by the bars is not informative; all that really matters is the height of each bar, which can be shown more succinctly with a point. Figure 17-12 would also have little room for either misinterpretation or introducing any bias

```
ggplot(diamonds, aes(cut)) +
  geom_point(aes(y = ..count.. / sum(..count..)),
            stat = "bin", size = 4)
```

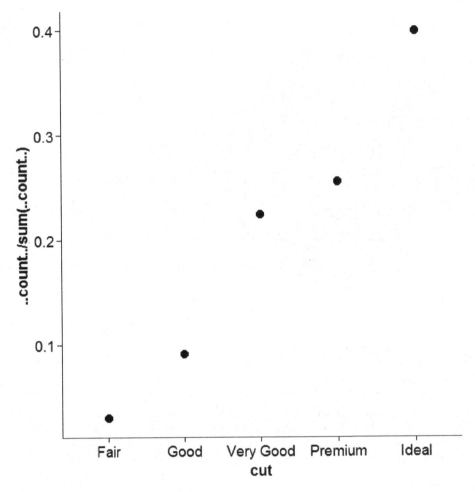

Figure 17-12. *A very honest graph*

17.3 Customizing and Polishing Plots

One of the most challenging tasks with graphics is often not making the initial graph but customizing it to get it ready for presentation or publication. In this section, we will continue with some of the distribution graphs we showed earlier but focus on examples of how to customize each piece. As a starting point, we can adjust the axis labels as we did in Figure 17-13.

```
p1 + geom_histogram(binwidth = 3) +
  xlab("Miles per gallon (MPG)") +
  ylab("Number of Cars") +
  ggtitle("Histogram showing the distribution of miles per gallon")
```

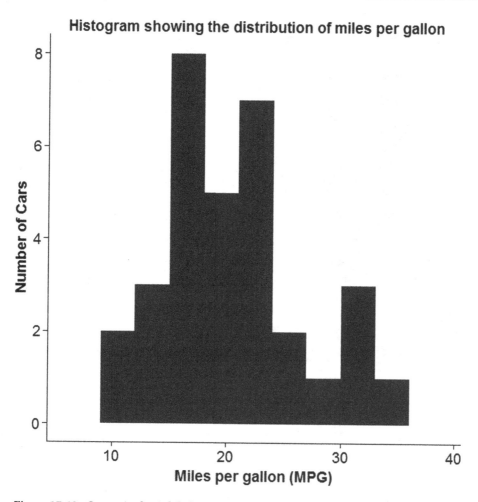

Figure 17-13. *Customized axis labels*

It is also possible to adjust the font type, color, and size of the text, as well as use math symbols (Figure 17-14).

```
p1 + geom_histogram(binwidth = 3) +
  xlab(expression(frac("Miles", "Gallon"))) +
  ylab("Number of Cars") +
  ggtitle(expression("Math Example: Histogram showing the distribution of "~frac("Miles",
"Gallon")))
```

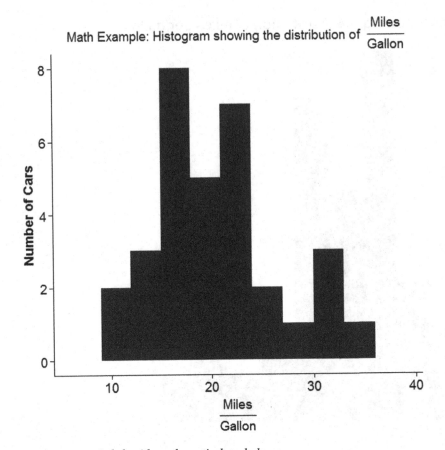

Figure 17-14. *Labels with mathematical symbols*

If we wanted to adjust the fonts, we could create a custom theme object. In Figure 17-15, we change the family for the axis text (the numbers), the axis titles (the labels), and the overall plot title. We can also adjust the size of the fonts and color, inside the element_text() function.

```
font.sans <- theme(
    axis.text = element_text(family = "serif", size = 12, color = "grey40"),
    axis.title = element_text(family = "serif", size = 12, color = "grey40"),
    plot.title = element_text(family = "serif", size = 16))

p1 + geom_histogram(binwidth = 3) +
    xlab("Miles per Gallon") +
    ylab("Number of Cars") +
    ggtitle("Size and Font Example: Histogram showing the distribution of MPG") +
    font.sans
```

Size and Font Example: Histogram showing the distribution of MPG

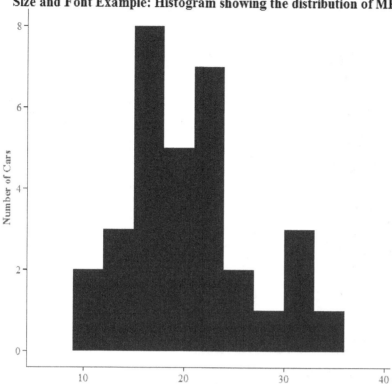

Figure 17-15. *Size and font example*

We can manually create our own themes, but for a "minimalist" theme, theme_classic() is a nice option. We can also adjust the axis limits so there is less blank space using coord_cartesian(). This trims the viewing area of the plot, but not the range of values accepted. For example, if there were an outlier in the data, that would still be used for plotting, but coord_cartesian() would just adjust what is actually shown, which is different from adjusting limits using the scale_*() functions. We do this with the following code and show it in Figure 17-16:

```
p1 + geom_histogram(binwidth = 3) +
  theme_classic() +
  coord_cartesian(xlim = c(8, 38), ylim = c(0, 8)) +
  xlab("Miles per gallon (MPG)") +
  ylab("Number of cars") +
  ggtitle("Histogram showing the distribution of miles per gallon")
```

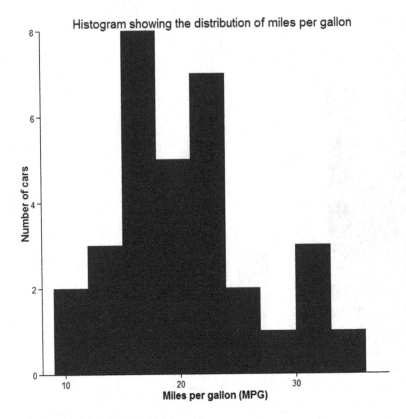

Figure 17-16. *Controlled viewing area*

We can also use less ink by outlining the histogram bars with black and filling them with white. In general, in ggplot2, "color" refers to the color used on the edge, and fill refers to the color used to fill the shape up. These options apply in many cases beyond just histograms. Figure 17-17 shows an example.

```
p1 + geom_histogram(color = "black", fill = "white", binwidth = 3) +
    theme_classic() +
    coord_cartesian(xlim = c(8, 38), ylim = c(0, 8)) +
    xlab("Miles per gallon (MPG)") +
    ylab("Number of cars") +
    ggtitle("Histogram showing the distribution of miles per gallon")
```

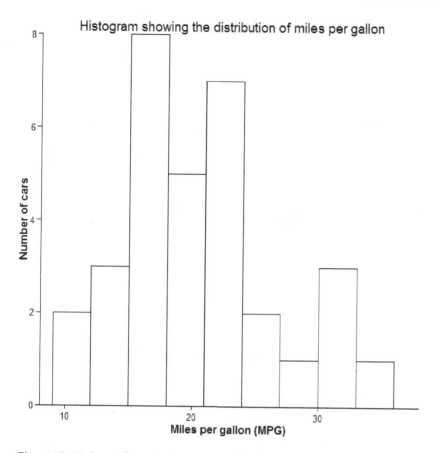

Figure 17-17. *Low-ink graphs demonstrating the use of color and fill*

Even if we have numerical/quantitative data, we could add labels, if that would make it more informative, as shown in Figure 17-18.

```
p1 + geom_histogram(color = "black", fill = "white", binwidth = 3) +
  scale_x_continuous(breaks = c(10, 20, 30), labels = c("Terrible", "Okay", "Good")) +
  theme_classic() +
  coord_cartesian(xlim = c(8, 38), ylim = c(0, 8)) +
  xlab("Miles per gallon (MPG)") +
  ylab("Number of cars") +
  ggtitle("Histogram showing the distribution of miles per gallon")
```

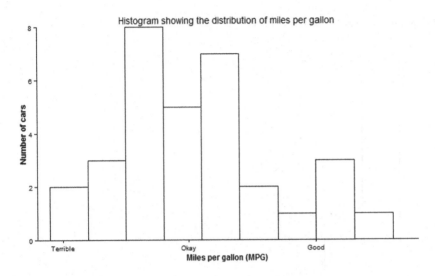

Figure 17-18. *Qualitative labels for quantitative data*

With longer labels, sometimes the orientation needs to be adjusted (Figure 17-19). The angle can be set using element_text(), as can the horizontal and vertical adjustments, which range from 0 to 1.

```
p1 + geom_histogram(color = "black", fill = "white", binwidth = 3) +
  scale_x_continuous(breaks = c(10, 20, 30), labels = c("Terrible", "Okay", "Good")) +
  theme_classic() +
  theme(axis.text.x = element_text(angle = 45, hjust = 1, vjust = 1)) +
  coord_cartesian(xlim = c(8, 38), ylim = c(0, 8)) +
  xlab("Miles per gallon (MPG)") +
  ylab("Number of cars") +
  ggtitle("Histogram showing the distribution of miles per gallon")
```

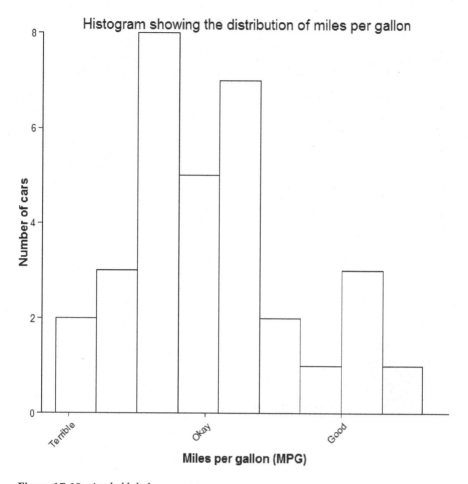

Figure 17-19. Angled labels

For some data, linear scales are not the best to visualize the data. For example, the price of diamonds is a rather skewed distribution, making it hard to see (Figure 17-20).

```
ggplot(diamonds, aes(price)) +
  geom_histogram()
```

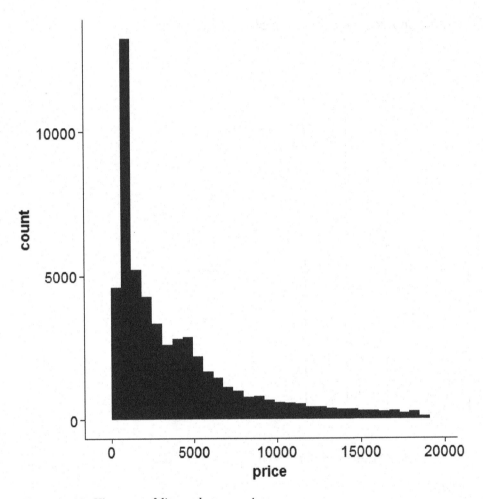

Figure 17-20. *Histogram of diamonds versus price*

We can use a square root or log scale instead. In this example, we also use grid.arrange() from the gridExtra package to put two plots together as in Figure 17-21.

```
grid.arrange(
  ggplot(diamonds, aes(price)) +
    geom_histogram() +
    scale_x_sqrt() +
    ggtitle("Square root x scale"),
  ggplot(diamonds, aes(price)) +
    geom_histogram() +
    scale_x_log10() +
    ggtitle("log base 10 x scale"))
```

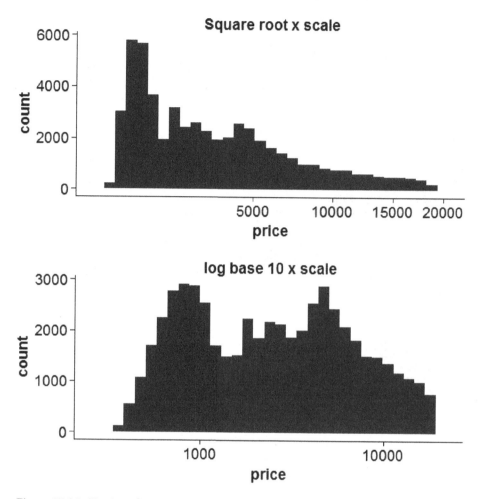

Figure 17-21. *X axis under various scales*

Instead of changing the actual scale of the data, we could also just change the coordinate system. First, though, we need to adjust the scale of the data, because with zero and some negative values included, not in the data but on the scale of the plot, square roots and logarithms will not work. So first we use scale_x_continuous() to adjust the scale to be exactly the range of the diamond prices, with no expansion, and then we can transform the coordinates. We show this in Figure 17-22.

```
grid.arrange(
  ggplot(diamonds, aes(price)) +
    geom_histogram() +
    scale_x_continuous(limits = range(diamonds$price), expand = c(0, 0)) +
    coord_trans(x = "sqrt") +
    ggtitle("Square root coordinate system"),
  ggplot(diamonds, aes(price)) +
    geom_histogram() +
```

```
    scale_x_continuous(limits = range(diamonds$price), expand = c(0, 0)) +
    coord_trans(x = "log10") +
    ggtitle("Log base 10 coordinate system"))
```

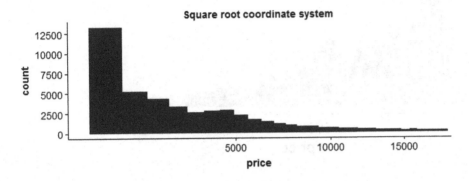

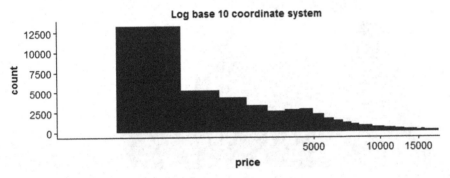

Figure 17-22. *Change coordinate system*

A final aspect of graphs that often needs adjustment is colors, shapes, and legends. Using the diamonds data, we can look at a density plot colored by cut of the diamond in Figure 17-23.

```
ggplot(diamonds, aes(price, color = cut)) +
  geom_density(size = 1) +
  scale_x_log10() +
  ggtitle("Density plots colored by cut")
```

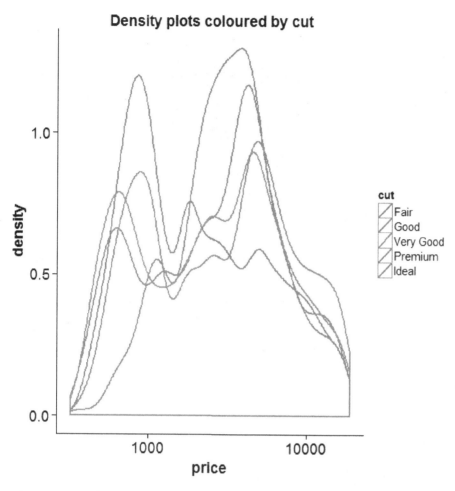

Figure 17-23. *Adjusting color by cut*

The ggplot2 package has a default color palette, but we can also examine others. The RColorBrewer package has a number of color palettes available. We can view the different color palettes for five levels, using the function display.brewer.all(). Using an option, we can pick colors that are colorblind friendly, so that the widest possible audience will be able to easily read our graphs. The type specifies whether we want a sequential palette ("seq", nice for gradients or ordered data) or a qualitative ("qual", for unordered discrete data), or a divergent color palette ("div", emphasizing extremes). We used "all" to indicate we want to see all palettes. Please run the code that follows or view the electronic version of this text to see Figure 17-24 in full color.

```
display.brewer.all(n = 5, type = "all", colorblindFriendly=TRUE)
```

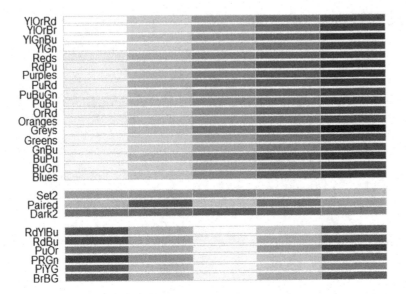

Figure 17-24. *The full color palette*

From here, perhaps we like the "Set2" palette, in which case we can use scale_color_brewer() or, if we wanted to use color as a fill, scale_fill_brewer() to pick the palette. We will also move the legend down to the bottom (or remove it altogether using legend.position = "none") in Figure 17-25.

```
ggplot(diamonds, aes(price, color = cut)) +
  geom_density(size = 1) +
  scale_color_brewer(palette = "Set2") +
  scale_x_log10() +
  ggtitle("Density plots colored by cut") +
  theme(legend.position = "bottom")
```

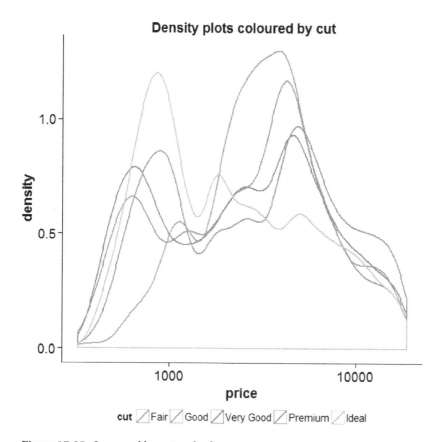

Figure 17-25. *Improved layout and color*

We can change the legend orientation, using the legend.direction argument, and by using the scale names that create the legend (in this case, only color, but it could also be color and shape, or color and linetype, or any other combination) we can also adjust the legend title. If we wanted, we could use math notation here as well, just as we showed for the title and axis legends. We show our code and then Figure 17-26:

```
ggplot(diamonds, aes(price, color = cut)) +
  geom_density(size = 1) +
  scale_color_brewer(palette = "Set2") +
  scale_x_log10() +
  scale_color_discrete("Diamond Cut") +
  ggtitle("Density plots colored by cut") +
  theme(legend.position = "bottom", legend.direction = "vertical")
```

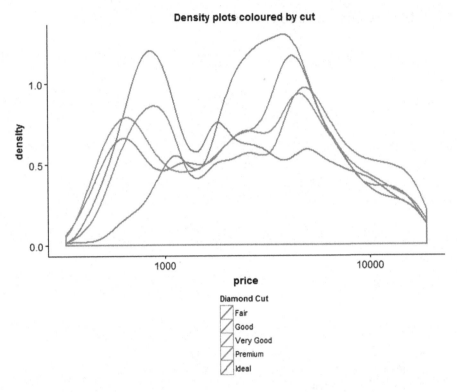

Figure 17-26. *Vertical legend*

We can also move the legend into the graph, by specifying the position as two numerical numbers, one for the x, y coordinates and also by specifying the justification of the legend with respect to the position coordinates (Figure 17-27).

```
ggplot(diamonds, aes(price, color = cut)) +
  geom_density(size = 1) +
  scale_color_discrete("Diamond Cut") +
  ggtitle("Density plots colored by cut") +
  theme(legend.position = c(1, 1), legend.justification = c(1, 1))
```

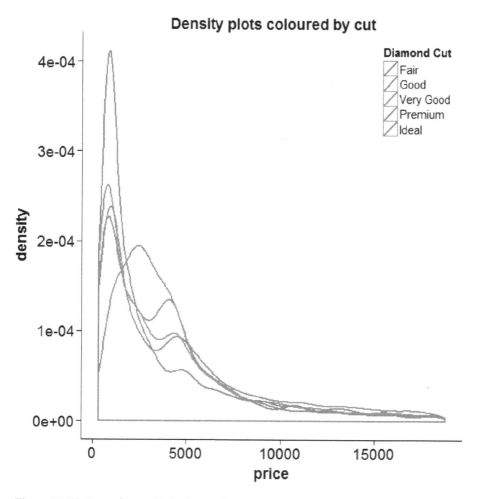

Figure 17-27. *Legend moved into the graph*

With the scales package loaded (which we did at the start), there are a number of special formats available for axis text, such as percent or dollar. We have price data on the x axis so will use the dollar labels for Figure 17-28. We can also use element_blank() to remove almost any aspect of the plot we want—in this case removing all the y axis information, as density is not a very informative number beyond what we can visually see—thus simplifying the graph.

```
ggplot(diamonds, aes(price, color = cut)) +
  geom_density(size = 1) +
  scale_color_discrete("Diamond Cut") +
  scale_x_continuous(labels = dollar) +
  ggtitle("Density plot of diamond price by cut") +
  theme_classic() +
  theme(legend.position = c(1, 1),
        legend.justification = c(1, 1),
        axis.line.x = element_blank(),
        axis.line.y = element_blank(),
```

```
        axis.ticks.y = element_blank(),
        axis.text.y = element_blank(),
        axis.title = element_blank()) +
coord_cartesian(xlim = c(0, max(diamonds$price)), ylim = c(0, 4.2e-04))
```

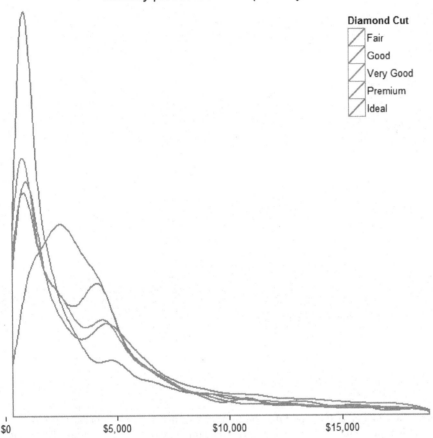

Figure 17-28. *Adjusting axis scales*

We can also flip the axes. This can be helpful sometimes with long labels or to make it easier to read some of the labels. Figure 17-29, with boxplots, demonstrates.

```
grid.arrange(
ggplot(diamonds, aes(cut, price)) +
  geom_boxplot() +
  ggtitle("Boxplots of diamond price by cut") +
  theme_classic(),
ggplot(diamonds, aes(cut, price)) +
  geom_boxplot() +
```

```
ggtitle("Boxplots of diamond price by cut - flipped") +
theme_classic() +
coord_flip())
```

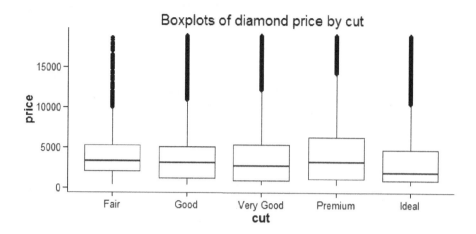

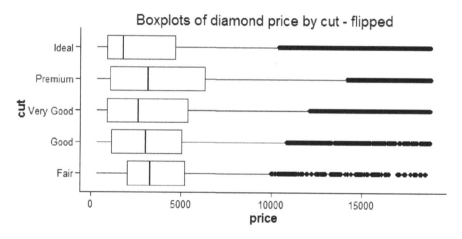

Figure 17-29. *Boxplots with flipped axis*

17.4 Multivariate Plots

In this section we will show how to make a wide variety of multivariate plots. To start, we will examine a bivariate scatterplot. Scatterplots (Figure 17-30) are great for showing the relationship between two continuous variables.

```
ggplot(mtcars, aes(mpg, hp)) +
  geom_point(size = 3)
```

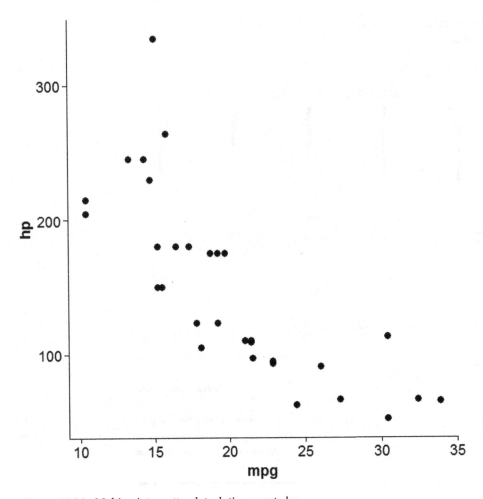

Figure 17-30. *Multivariate scatterplot relating mpg to hp*

For smaller datasets, rather than plotting points, we can plot the text labels to help understand which cases may stand out (here, for example, the Maserati). As we see in Figure 17-31, such labels are not always perfectly clear (depending on point location), and for larger datasets the text would be unreadable. Although not shown, plotting labels and points can be combined by adding both points and text.

```
ggplot(mtcars, aes(mpg, hp)) +
  geom_text(aes(label = rownames(mtcars)), size = 2.5)
```

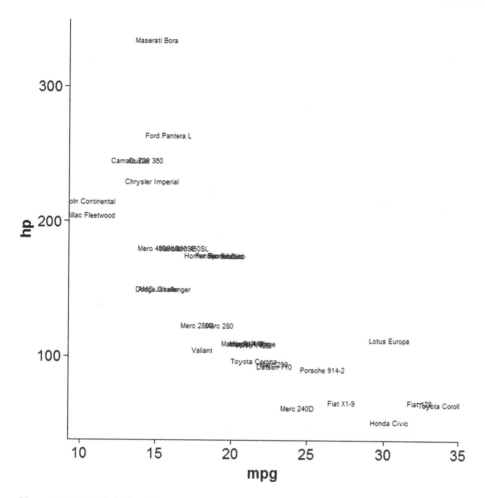

Figure 17-31. *Labeled points*

We can add another layer of information to scatterplots by coloring the points by a third variable. If the variable is discrete, we can convert it to a factor to get a discrete color palette (Figure 17-32).

```
ggplot(mtcars, aes(mpg, hp, color = factor(cyl))) +
  geom_point(size = 3)
```

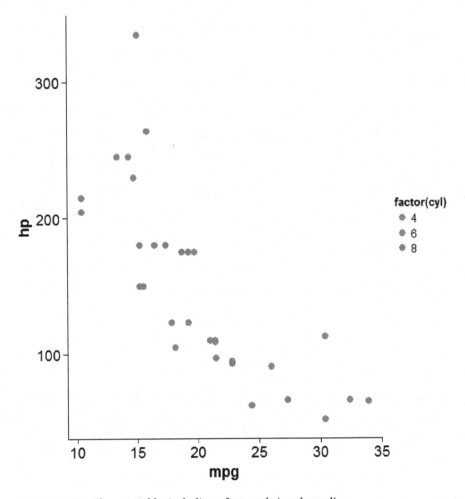

Figure 17-32. *Three variables including a factor cyl via color coding*

If the coloring variable is continuous, a gradient may be used instead as shown in Figure 17-33.

```
ggplot(mtcars, aes(mpg, hp, color = disp)) +
  geom_point(size=3)
```

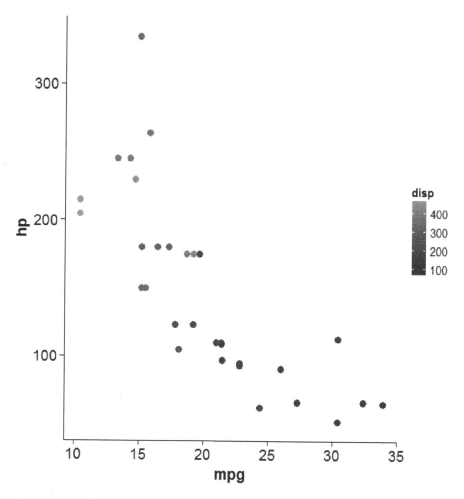

Figure 17-33. *Continuous third variable colored with a gradient rather than factoring*

We can push this even farther by changing the shapes. Putting all this together, we can visually see quite a bit of overlap, where cars with the highest horsepower tend to have higher displacement and eight cylinders, and cars with the highest miles per gallon tend to have only four cylinders and lower displacement. Figure 17-34 shows four variables.

```
ggplot(mtcars, aes(mpg, hp, color = disp, shape = factor(cyl))) +
  geom_point(size=3)
```

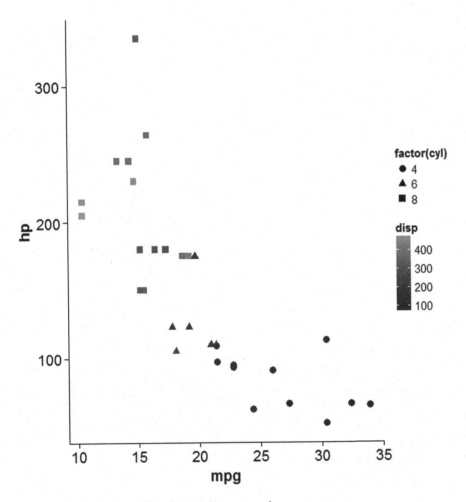

Figure 17-34. *Four variables displayed in one graph*

Adding a regression or smooth line to scatterplots can help highlight the trend in the data (Figure 17-35). By default for small datasets, ggplot2 will use a loess smoother, which is very flexible, to fit the data.

```
ggplot(mtcars, aes(mpg, hp)) +
  geom_point(size=3) +
  stat_smooth()
```

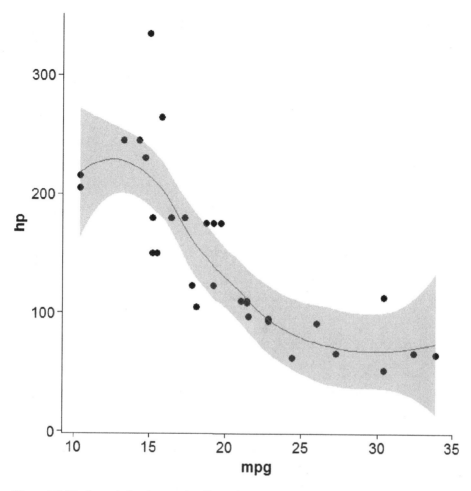

Figure 17-35. *Smooth fitted regression line to highlight trend*

We could get a linear line of best fit by setting the method on stat_smooth() directly (Figure 17-36).

```
ggplot(mtcars, aes(mpg, hp)) +
  geom_point(size=3) +
  stat_smooth(method = "lm")
```

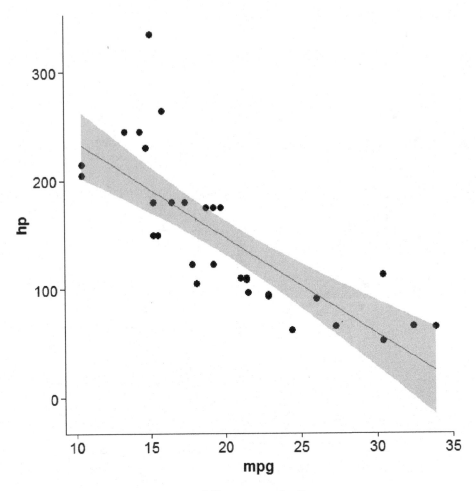

Figure 17-36. *Our familiar linear model linear regression line*

A nice feature is that if we drill down by coloring the data, the smooth line also drills down. The command se = FALSE turns off the shaded region indicating the confidence interval. Figure 17-37 shows rather well how different cylinders influence miles per gallon and horsepower.

```
ggplot(mtcars, aes(mpg, hp, color = factor(cyl))) +
  geom_point(size=3) +
  stat_smooth(method = "lm", se = FALSE, size = 2)
```

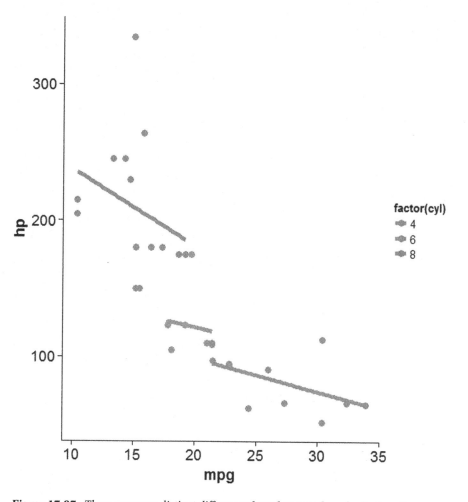

Figure 17-37. *There are some distinct differences based on number of cylinders, it seems*

If we wanted to color the points but have one overall summary line, we could override the color for stat_smooth() specifically (Figure 17-38).

```
ggplot(mtcars, aes(mpg, hp, color = factor(cyl))) +
  geom_point(size=3) +
  stat_smooth(aes(color = NULL), se = FALSE, size = 2)
```

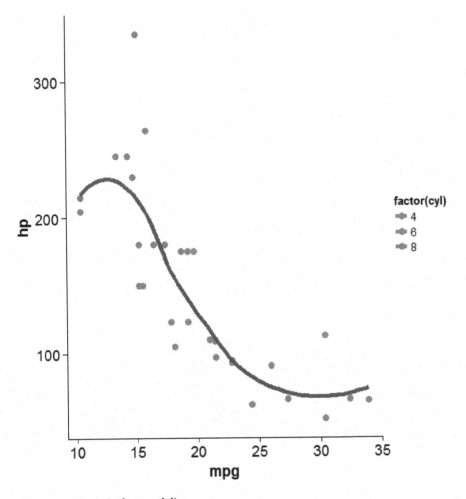

Figure 17-38. *A single smooth line*

In general in ggplot2, most geometric objects can have different colors, fill colors, shapes, or linetypes applied to them, resulting in a finer-grained view of the data if there are summary functions like smooth lines, density plots, histograms, and so on.

For larger datasets, scatterplots can be hard to read. Two approaches to make it easier to see high-density regions are to make points smaller and semitransparent. We show an example in Figure 17-39.

```
ggplot(diamonds, aes(price, carat)) +
  geom_point(size = 1, alpha = .25)
```

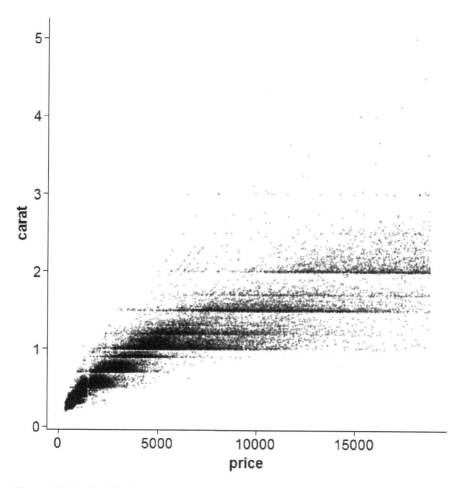

Figure 17-39. Smaller dots

Another approach is to bin them and color them by how many points fall within a bin. This is somewhat similar to what happens with histograms for a single variable. Dots within a certain area are grouped together as one, and then color is used to indicate how many observations a particular dot represents. This helps to see the "core" high-density area. We show this in Figure 17-40.

```
ggplot(diamonds, aes(price, carat)) +
  geom_hex(bins = 75)
```

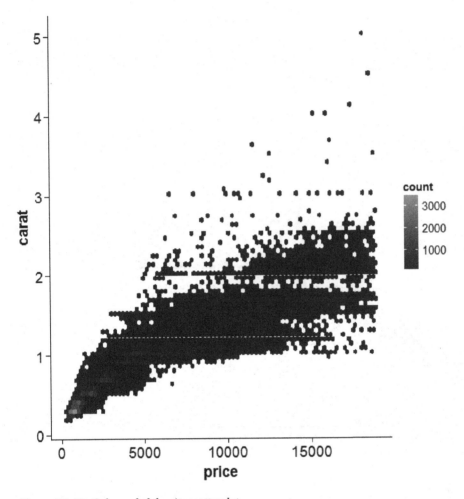

Figure 17-40. *Color-coded density scatterplot*

Another approach is to bin the data (Figure 17-41), which we can do using the cut() function to make ten bins each containing about 10% of the sample. Then we can use a boxplot of the carats for each price decile to see the relationship. The automatic labels from the cut() function help to show what price values are included.

```
diamonds <- within(diamonds, {
  pricecat <- cut(price, breaks = quantile(price, probs = seq(0, 1, length.out = 11)),
include.lowest = TRUE)
})

ggplot(diamonds, aes(pricecat, carat)) +
  geom_boxplot() +
  theme(axis.text.x = element_text(angle = 45, hjust = 1, vjust = 1))
```

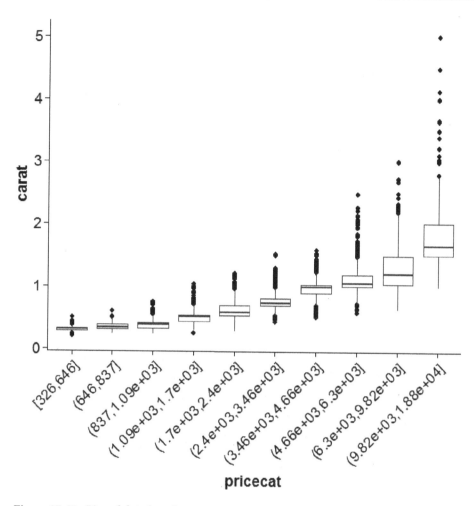

Figure 17-41. *Binned data boxplots*

To get even more detailed distributional data, we could use a violin plot, which is essentially a series of density plots on their side, and putting carats on a log base 10 scale can help us to more clearly see in Figure 17-42.

```
ggplot(diamonds, aes(pricecat, carat)) +
  geom_violin() +
  scale_y_log10() +
  theme(axis.text.x = element_text(angle = 45, hjust = 1, vjust = 1))
```

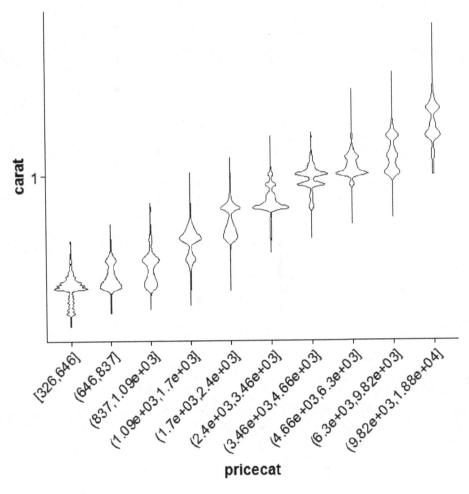

Figure 17-42. *Binned violin plots*

Next we use the Indometh data, which records drug concentration in six subjects over time after administration to assess how quickly the drug is processed. Figure 17-43 shows the use of a line plot to visualize these data. We use the group argument to make individual lines for each of the subjects.

```
ggplot(Indometh, aes(time, conc, group = Subject)) +
  geom_line()
```

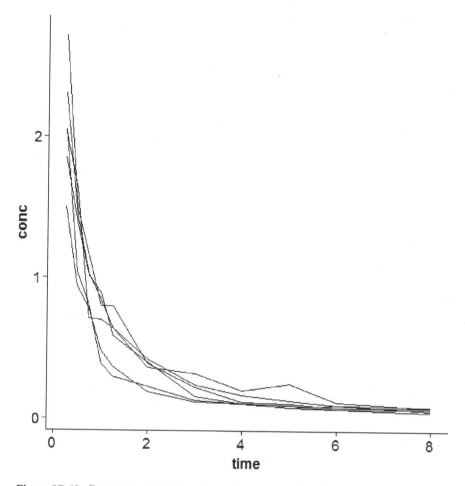

Figure 17-43. *Drug concentration vs. time with grouping by subject*

We could add points to Figure 17-44 as well if we wanted to, although that is not terribly helpful in this case.

```
ggplot(Indometh, aes(time, conc, group = Subject)) +
  geom_line() +
  geom_point()
```

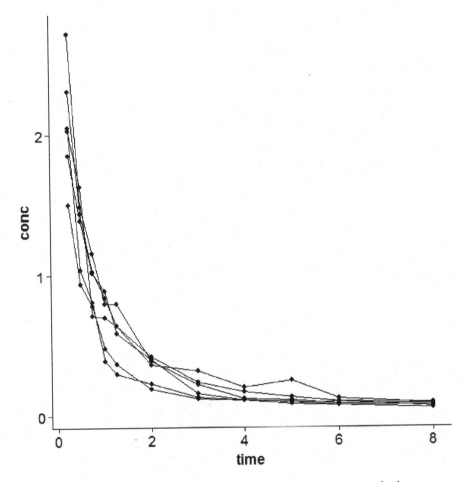

Figure 17-44. *Specific points added to show precise concentration at certain times*

With so few subjects, a boxplot at each time point would not make a great summary, but perhaps the mean or median would. The stat_summary() function is a powerful function to calculate summaries of the data. Note that because we want to summarize across subjects, we turn off grouping for the summary in Figure 17-45 (although it is used for the lines).

```
ggplot(Indometh, aes(time, conc, group = Subject)) +
  geom_line() +
  stat_summary(aes(group = NULL), fun.y = mean, geom = "line", color = "blue", size = 2)
```

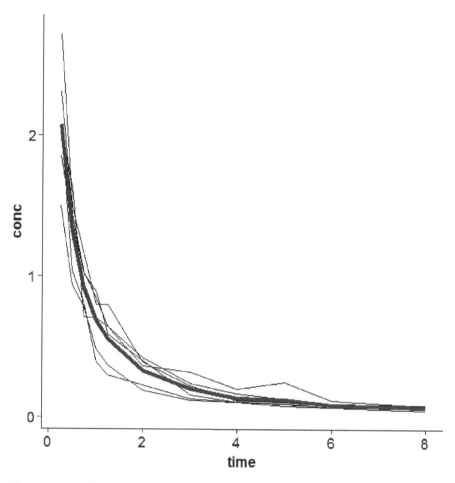

Figure 17-45. *Shows how various aspects may be set on or to null*

Using the `stat_summary()` we could also get the mean and CI at each time point, and plot using a point for the mean and a line for the 95% CI. Figure 17-46 shows estimates for each time.

```
ggplot(Indometh, aes(time, conc)) +
  stat_summary(fun.data = mean_cl_normal, geom = "pointrange")
```

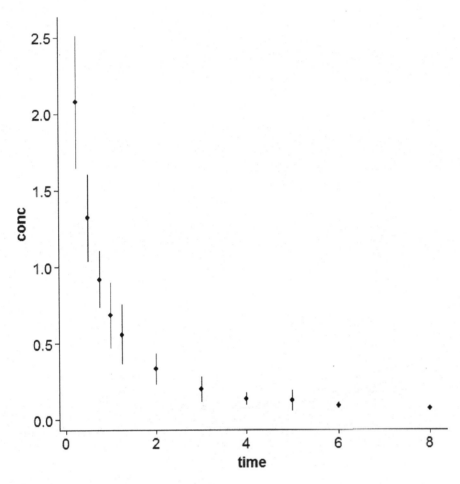

Figure 17-46. *95% CIs for each specified time*

When one variable is discrete and another is continuous, a barplot of the means of the continuous variable by the discrete variable is popular. We go back to the diamonds data and look at the price of the diamond by the cut in Figure 17-47.

```
ggplot(diamonds, aes(cut, price)) +
  stat_summary(fun.y = mean, geom = "bar", fill = "white", color = "black")
```

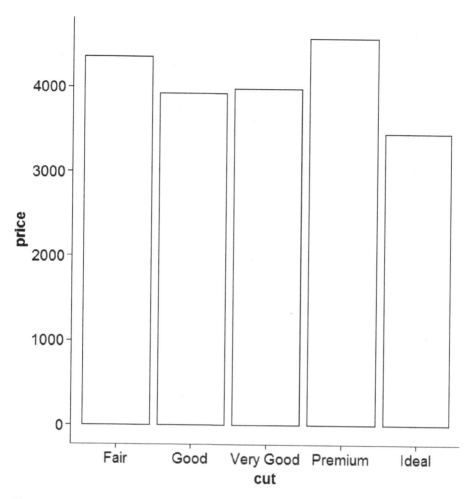

Figure 17-47. *Price by grade of cut*

It is also common to use the bars to show the mean, and add error bars to show the CI around the mean, which we do in Figure 17-48. The width option adjusts how wide (from left to right) the error bars are in Figure 17-48.

```
ggplot(diamonds, aes(cut, price)) +
  stat_summary(fun.y = mean, geom = "bar", fill = "white", color = "black") +
  stat_summary(fun.data = mean_cl_normal, geom = "errorbar", width = .2)
```

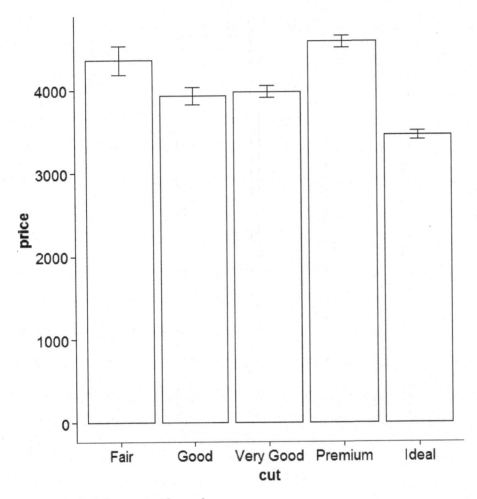

Figure 17-48. *Price vs. cut with error bars*

Because we know the price data are not normal, we may be concerned about using the mean and thus prefer to use the median. To get a CI for the medians, we can write our own median bootstrap function. As output, it must return a data frame with columns for y, ymin, and ymax. This function builds on several things we have done so far in this book. In this case, we use the function is.null() call to see if we want to default to 1,000 bootstraps. Otherwise, we may call our function with a specific value other than 1,000.

```
median_cl_boot <- function(x, ...) {
  require(boot)
  args <- list(...)
  # if missing, default to 1000 bootstraps
  if (is.null(args$R)) {
    args$R <- 1000
  }
  result <- boot(x, function(x, i) {median(x[i])}, R = args$R)
  cis <- boot.ci(result, type = "perc")
```

```
data.frame(y = result$t0,
           ymin = cis$percent[1, 4],
           ymax = cis$percent[1, 5])
}
```

Now we can make our plot as before, but passing our newly written function to fun.data. Not surprisingly given that the price data were highly skewed, the median price is considerably lower than the average. Figure 17-49 shows the difference the median makes.

```
ggplot(diamonds, aes(cut, price)) +
  stat_summary(fun.y = median, geom = "bar", fill = "white", color = "black") +
  stat_summary(fun.data = median_cl_boot, geom = "errorbar", width = .2)
```

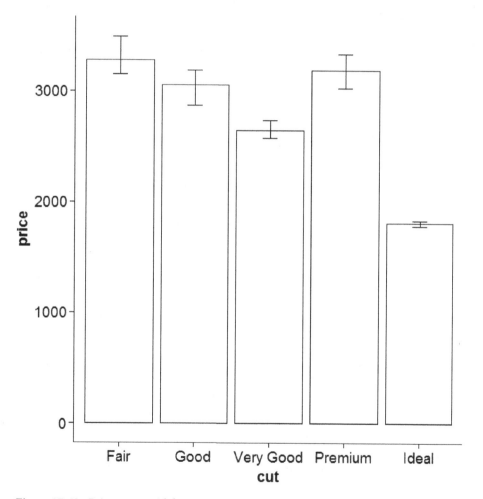

Figure 17-49. *Price vs. cut with bootstrapped median error bars*

Another type of plot used in business is a waterfall plot (Figure 17-52). Suppose we had the following data for net income each month for a company. We could have R make a nice visual table (Figure 17-50) of the data using the grid.table() function from the gridExtra package.

```
company <- data.frame(
  Month = months(as.Date(paste0("2015-", 1:12, "-01"))),
  NetIncome = c(-6, 7, -5, 5, 13, -3, -4, -1, 11, 4, -10, 8))
grid.newpage()
grid.table(company)
```

	Month	NetIncome
1	January	-6
2	February	7
3	March	-5
4	April	5
5	May	13
6	June	-3
7	July	-4
8	August	-1
9	September	11
10	October	4
11	November	-10
12	December	8

Figure 17-50. A table showing month and net income

Next we need to do a bit of data manipulation to create the cumulative position over time, and then we use Figure 17-51 to look at the results.

```
company <- within(company, {
  MonthC <- as.numeric(factor(Month, levels = Month))
  MonthEnd <- c(head(cumsum(NetIncome), -1), 0)
  MonthStart <- c(0, head(MonthEnd, -1))
  GainLoss <- factor(as.integer(NetIncome > 0), levels = 0:1, labels = c("Loss", "Gain"))
})
grid.newpage()
grid.table(company)
```

	Month	NetIncome	GainLoss	MonthStart	MonthEnd	MonthC
1	January	-6	Loss	0	-6	1
2	February	7	Gain	-6	1	2
3	March	-5	Loss	1	-4	3
4	April	5	Gain	-4	1	4
5	May	13	Gain	1	14	5
6	June	-3	Loss	14	11	6
7	July	-4	Loss	11	7	7
8	August	-1	Loss	7	6	8
9	September	11	Gain	6	17	9
10	October	4	Gain	17	21	10
11	November	-10	Loss	21	11	11
12	December	8	Gain	11	0	12

Figure 17-51. *Cumulative position over time*

Now we are ready to make a waterfall plot in R (see Figure 17-52). Although these are basically bars, we do not use geom_bar() but rather geom_rect(), because barplots typically never go under zero, while waterfall plots may. We also add a horizontal line at zero, and make it dashed using linetype = 2. We use a manual fill scale to specify exactly the colors we want for losses and gains, relabel the numeric 1 to 12 months to use their natural names. We label the y axis in dollars, and then adjust the axis labels, put the legend in the upper right corner, and remove the legend title using element_blank().

```
ggplot(company, aes(MonthC, fill = GainLoss)) +
  geom_rect(aes(xmin = MonthC - .5, xmax = MonthC + .5,
                ymin = MonthEnd, ymax = MonthStart)) +
  geom_hline(yintercept = 0, size = 2, linetype = 2) +
  scale_fill_manual(values = c("Loss" = "orange", "Gain" = "blue")) +
  scale_x_continuous(breaks = company$MonthC, labels = company$Month) +
  xlab("") +
  scale_y_continuous(labels = dollar) +
  ylab("Net Income in Thousands") +
  theme_classic() +
  theme(axis.text.x = element_text(angle = 45, hjust = 1, vjust = 1),
        legend.position = c(0, 1),
        legend.justification = c(0, 1),
        legend.title = element_blank())
```

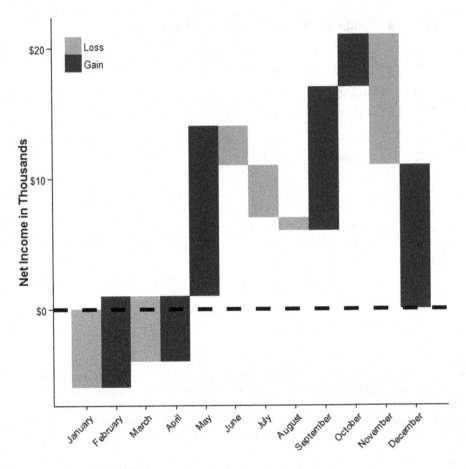

Figure 17-52. *Waterfall plot*

17.5 Multiple Plots

Often it can be helpful to separate data and have multiple plots. For example, in the diamonds data, suppose we wanted to look at the relationship again between carat and price, but we wanted to explore the impact of cut, clarity, and color of the diamond. That would be too much to fit into one single plot, but it could be shown as a panel of plots. We can do this by using the facet_grid() function, which facets plots by row (the left-hand side) and column (the right-hand side). Figure 17-53 shows the resulting graph.

```
ggplot(diamonds, aes(carat, price, color = color)) +
  geom_point() +
  stat_smooth(method = "loess", se = FALSE, color = "black") +
  facet_grid(clarity ~ cut) +
  theme_bw() +
  theme(legend.position = "bottom",
        legend.title = element_blank())
```

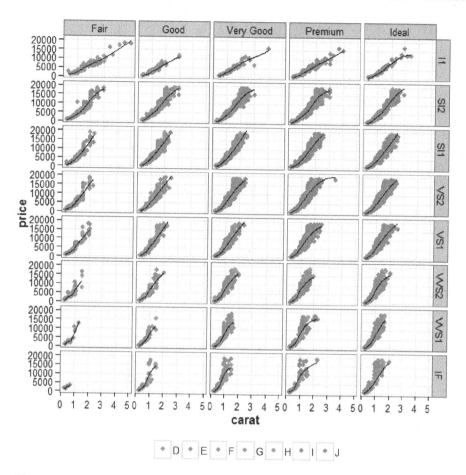

Figure 17-53. *Price vs. carat as well as cut, clarity, and color*

If we do not want a grid, we can just wrap a series of plots together. By default, the individual plots all use the same axis limits, but if the range of the data is very different, to help see each plot clearly, we may want to free the scales (which can also be done in the same way in the facet_grid() function used previously). A downside of freeing the scales, as shown in Figure 17-54, is that for each plot, comparison across plots becomes more difficult.

```
ggplot(diamonds, aes(carat, color = cut)) +
  geom_density() +
  facet_wrap(~clarity, scales = "free") +
  theme_bw() +
  theme(legend.position = "bottom",
        legend.title = element_blank())
```

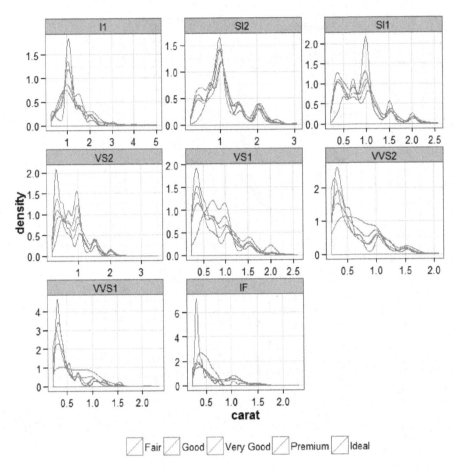

Figure 17-54. *Freeing the scales does give more freedom; with great power comes great responsibility*

When working with a dataset, it can be helpful to get a general overview of the relations among a number of variables. A scatterplot matrix such as the one in Figure 17-55 is one way to do this, and it is conveniently implemented in the GGally package. The lower diagonal shows the bivariate scatterplots, the diagonal has density plots for each individual variable, and the upper diagonal has the Pearson correlation coefficients.

```
ggscatmat(mtcars[, c("mpg", "disp", "hp", "drat", "wt", "qsec")])
```

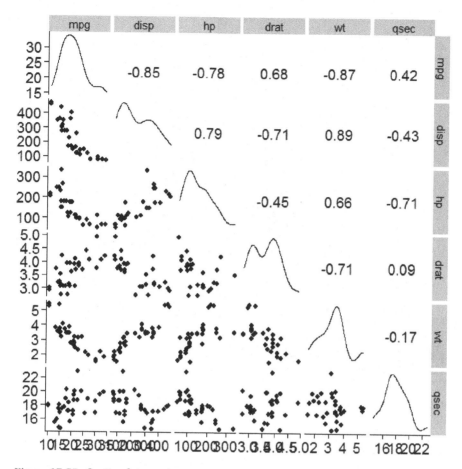

Figure 17-55. *Scatterplot matrix*

To get a simple visual summary of the magnitudes of correlations, we could also use the ggcorr() function, which creates the heatmap in Figure 17-56 based on the correlation size.

```
ggcorr(mtcars[, c("mpg", "disp", "hp", "drat", "wt", "qsec")])
```

269

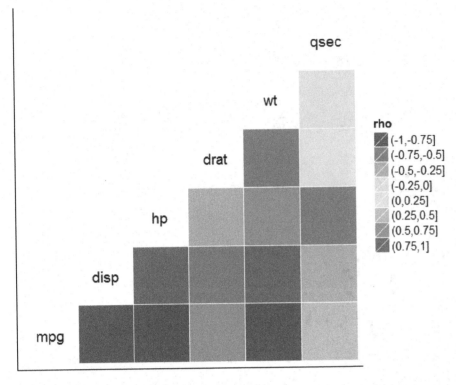

Figure 17-56. A heatmap

The approaches for creating multiple plots we've examined so far work well when the data are all together and we are making essentially the same plot repeatedly, but sometimes we want to make a panel of plots that are each quite different. For example, in the code that follows we make three plots to go into a panel of graphs, and store them in R objects:

```
plota <- ggplot(mtcars, aes(mpg, hp)) +
  geom_point(size = 3) +
  stat_smooth(se = FALSE)
plotb <- ggplot(mtcars, aes(mpg)) +
  geom_density() +
  theme(axis.text.y = element_blank(),
        axis.ticks.y = element_blank(),
        axis.title.y = element_blank(),
        axis.line.y = element_blank())
plotc <- ggplot(mtcars, aes(hp)) +
  geom_density() +
  theme(axis.text.y = element_blank(),
        axis.ticks.y = element_blank(),
        axis.title.y = element_blank(),
        axis.line.y = element_blank())
```

Now we plot them all together in Figure 17-57 using functions from the cowplot package. Each plot is drawn, and the x and y coordinates are given, along with its width and its height. We can also add labels to indicate which panel is which (A, B, and C, in this case).

```
ggdraw() +
  draw_plot(plota, 0, 0, 2/3, 1) +
  draw_plot(plotb, 2/3, .5, 1/3, .5) +
  draw_plot(plotc, 2/3, 0, 1/3, .5) +
  draw_plot_label(c("A", "B", "C"), c(0, 2/3, 2/3), c(1, 1, .5), size = 15)
```

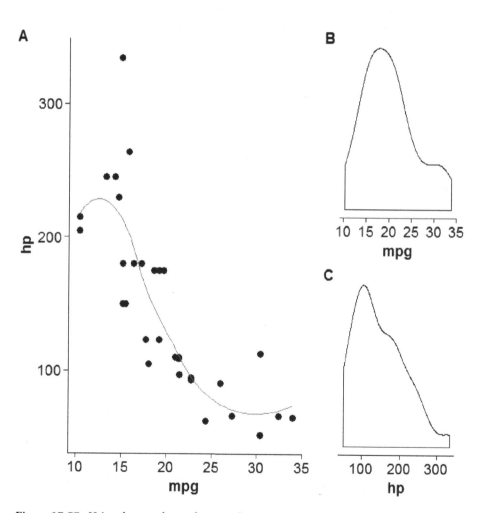

Figure 17-57. *Using the cowplot package to plot many graphs together*

17.6 Three-Dimensional Graphs

In closing, we are going to examine a few less common but nonetheless helpful ways of visualizing data. We begin by looking at some ways to visualize three-dimensional data. First is the contour plot. Contour plots show two variables on the x and y axis, and the third variable (dimension) using lines. A line always has the same value on the third dimension. To show how this works, we can set up a linear model with some interactions and quadratic terms with carat and x predicting the price of diamonds, and then use the model on some new data to get the predicted prices.

```
m <- lm(price ~ (carat + I(carat^2)) * (x + I(x^2)), data = diamonds)

newdat <- expand.grid(carat = seq(min(diamonds$carat), max(diamonds$carat), length.out =
100),
                      x = seq(min(diamonds$x), max(diamonds$x), length.out = 100))

newdat$price <- predict(m, newdata = newdat)
```

Now we can easily graph the data in Figure 17-58 using geom_contour(). We color each line by the log of the level (here price). Examining the bottom line, we can see that the model predicts the same price for the diamond that is just over 1 carat and 0 x as it does for nearly 10 x and close to 0 carats. Again each line indicates a single price value, so the line shows you how different combinations of the predictors, sometimes nonlinearly, can result in the same predicted price value.

```
ggplot(newdat, aes(x = x, y = carat, z = price)) +
  geom_contour(aes(color = log(..level..)), bins = 30, size = 1)
```

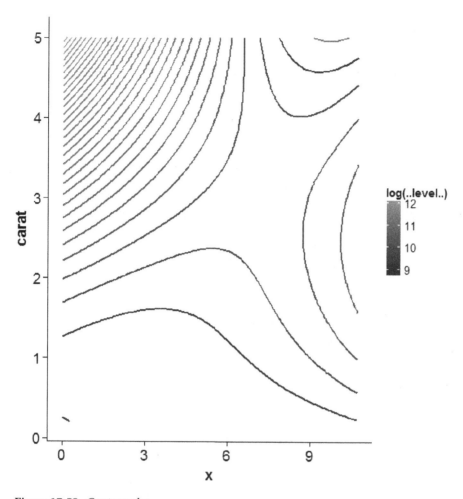

Figure 17-58. *Contour plot*

When making contour plots from predicted values, it is important to consider whether the values are extrapolations or not. For example, even though we made our predicted values of carat and x within the range of the real data, a quick examination of the relationship between carat and x (Figure 17-59) shows that not all carat sizes occur at all possible values of x, so many of the lines in our contour plot are extrapolations from the data to the scenario, "what if there were a __ carat diamonds with __ x?" rather than being grounded in reality.

```
ggplot(diamonds, aes(carat, x)) +
  geom_point(alpha = .25, size = 1)
```

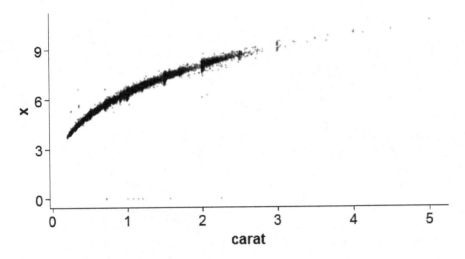

Figure 17-59. *A quick look at carat and x*

Another way we can plot three-dimensional data is using a three-dimensional plot projected into two dimensions. The ggplot2 package does not do this, so we will use functions from the plot3D packages. To start with, we can examine a three-dimensional scatterplot in Figure 17-60.

```
with(mtcars, scatter3D(hp, wt, mpg, pch = 16, type = "h", colvar = NULL))
```

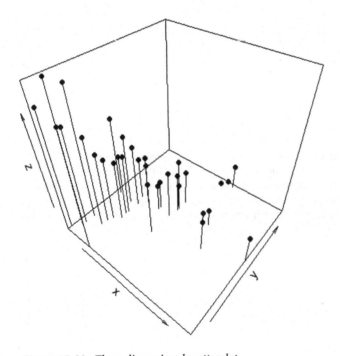

Figure 17-60. *Three-dimensional scatterplot*

As before, we can color the points and add titles, although the arguments to do this differ from ggplot2 as this is a different package. Another challenge with three-dimensional plots is choosing the angle from which to view it. The best angle (or perhaps a few) depends on the data and what features you want to highlight, so it often involves trial and error to find a nice set. To put more than one graph together, we use the par() function, and then simply plot two graphs, also showing how to add color and detailed labels in Figure 17-61.

```
par(mfrow = c(2, 1))

with(mtcars, scatter3D(hp, wt, mpg,
  colvar = cyl, col = c("blue", "orange", "black"),
  colkey = FALSE,
  pch = 16, type = "h",
  theta = 0, phi = 30,
  ticktype = "detailed",
  main = "Three-dimensional colored scatterplot"))

with(mtcars, scatter3D(hp, wt, mpg,
  colvar = cyl, col = c("blue", "orange", "black"),
  colkey = FALSE,
  pch = 16, type = "h",
  theta = 220, phi = 10,
  ticktype = "detailed",
  xlab = "Horsepower", ylab = "Weight", zlab = "Miles per Gallon",
  main = "Three-dimensional colored scatterplot"))
```

Three-dimensional colored scatterplot

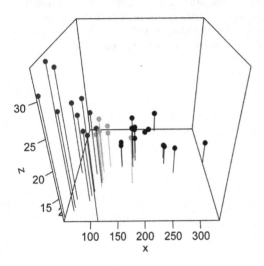

Three-dimensional colored scatterplot

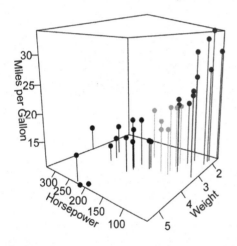

Figure 17-61. Different angles and colors and labels of the same 3D scatterplot

We hope this cookbook chapter has been helpful. The graphs are ones we have used ourselves over the years, and sometimes, when looking at some data, one of the most helpful things to do (especially when attempting to explain to fellow team members what the data indicate) is to reference graphs and charts. One of the authors regularly hoards snippets of code for graphs that either look visually appealing or present well certain types of data. Then, when he encounters data in the wild that might benefit from such a graph, he has the code to make that happen readily available. We turn our attention in the next chapter to exploiting some advantages of modern hardware configurations.

References

Auguie, B. gridExtra: Miscellaneous Functions for "Grid" Graphics. R package version 2.0.0, 2015. http://CRAN.R-project.org/package=gridExtra.

Canty, A., & Ripley, B. boot: Bootstrap R (S-Plus) Functions. R package version 1.3-17, 2015.

Carr, D., ported by Nicholas Lewin-Koh, Martin Maechler and contains copies of lattice function written by Deepayan Sarkar. hexbin: Hexagonal Binning Routines. R package version 1.27.0, 2014. http://CRAN.R-project.org/package=hexbin.

Davison, A. C., & Hinkley, D. V. *Bootstrap Methods and Their Applications.* Cambridge, MA: Cambridge University Press, 1997.

Harrell, F. E. Jr., with contributions from Charles Dupont and many others. Hmisc: Harrell Miscellaneous. R package version 3.16-0, 2015. http://CRAN.R-project.org/package=Hmisc.

Ligges, U., & Mächler, M. "Scatterplot3d—an R package for visualizing multivariate data." *Journal of Statistical Software, 8*(11), 1-20 (2003).

Neuwirth, E. RColorBrewer: ColorBrewer Palettes. R package version 1.1-2, 2014. http://CRAN.R-project.org/package=RColorBrewer.

R Core Team. R: A language and environment for statistical computing. R Foundation for Statistical Computing, Vienna, Austria, 2015. www.R-project.org/.

Schloerke, B., Crowley, J., Cook, D., Hofmann, H., Wickham, H., Briatte, F., Marbach, M., & and Thoen, E. GGally: Extension to ggplot2. R package version 0.5.0, 2014. http://CRAN.R-project.org/package=GGally.

Soetaert, K. plot3D: Plotting multi-dimensional data. R package version 1.0-2, 2014. http://CRAN.R-project.org/package=plot3D.

Wickham, H. *ggplot2: Elegant graphics for data analysis.* New York: Springer, 2009.

Wickham, H. scales: Scale Functions for Visualization. R package version 0.2.5, 2015. http://CRAN.R-project.org/package=scales.

Wilke, C. O. cowplot: Streamlined Plot Theme and Plot Annotations for 'ggplot2'. R package version 0.5.0, 2015. http://CRAN.R-project.org/package=cowplot.

CHAPTER 18

■ ■ ■

High-Performance Computing

In this chapter, we introduce high-performance computing. Broadly, computing may be slow because we have larger datasets and/or because we are doing more computations. We will talk a little about ways to deal with both in R. When people say *high-performance computing* or *big data* they can mean very different things. In this chapter we will not discuss processing terabytes of data or analyses that require large clusters. Instead, we only assume a fairly standard desktop or laptop that has **at least two cores**. Note that some of the code examples in this chapter may take some time to run. That is deliberate so it is both more realistic and starts to convey the "feel" of larger data. Making a typo can be more painful when it takes minutes or hours to get your result and you find out it is wrong and you have to run it again!

18.1 Data

First, we will discuss working with larger datasets. The R package nycflights13 (Wickham, 2014) has some datasets with a few hundred thousand observations.

```
> install.packages("nycflights13")
> install.packages("iterators")
> library(nycflights13)
> library(iterators)
> head(flights)
  year month day dep_time dep_delay arr_time arr_delay carrier tailnum flight
1 2013     1   1      517         2      830        11      UA  N14228   1545
2 2013     1   1      533         4      850        20      UA  N24211   1714
3 2013     1   1      542         2      923        33      AA  N619AA   1141
4 2013     1   1      544        -1     1004       -18      B6  N804JB    725
5 2013     1   1      554        -6      812       -25      DL  N668DN    461
6 2013     1   1      554        -4      740        12      UA  N39463   1696
  origin dest air_time distance hour minute
1    EWR  IAH      227     1400    5     17
2    LGA  IAH      227     1416    5     33
3    JFK  MIA      160     1089    5     42
4    JFK  BQN      183     1576    5     44
5    LGA  ATL      116      762    5     54
6    EWR  ORD      150      719    5     54
```

Now suppose that we wanted to create a new variable in the data that was the standard deviation of arrival time delays by destination airport. We could use the ave() function. It performs an operation (such as calculating the standard deviation) by an index. For example, suppose we had some data from three different groups.

Group 1	Group 2	Group 3
1	4	7
2	5	8
3	6	9

If these data were shaped in "long" form, they would look like as shown in the table that follows, where all the values are in one column, and another column indicates which group each value belongs to

Value	Group
1	1
2	1
3	1
4	2
5	2
6	2
7	3
8	3
9	3

Now, what if we wanted to calculate something by each group? For example, we could calculate the means per group, which are 2, 5, and 8 for groups 1, 2, and 3, respectively. However, if we want the mean per group to be a new variable in the dataset, we need to fill in the mean of group 1 for every row belonging to group 1, and the mean of group 2 for every row belonging to group 2. In other words, the mean (or whatever we calculate) needs to be repeated as many times as the data from which it came. That is exactly what ave() does and following is a simple example of ave() in action. The first argument is the data to use for calculation. The second argument is the index variable (in our previous example, group), and the third argument is the function to be used for calculation. You can see in the output that the means, 2, 5, and 8, have each been repeated the same number of times as the index variable

```
> ave(1:9, c(1, 1, 1, 2, 2, 2, 3, 3, 3), FUN = mean)
[1] 2 2 2 5 5 5 8 8 8
```

Following is one way we may try to accomplish our goal in the flights data. We will make use of the system.time() function throughout this chapter to examine how long it takes to run different pieces of code, noting that these results are not intended to indicate how long it will take on your machine or your data but to compare different coding approaches. The results are in seconds, and we will focus on the elapsed time.

```
system.time(
+ flights <- within(flights, {
+   ArrDelaySD <- ave(arr_delay, dest, FUN = function(x) sd(x, na.rm = TRUE))
+ })
+ )
   user  system elapsed
   0.05    0.01    0.06
```

What about just finding the mean arrival delay for flights departing in the first half of the year?

```
system.time(
+   mean(subset(flights, month < 7)$arr_delay)
+ )
   user  system elapsed
   0.22    0.00    0.22
```

It does not take long in this case, but it is starting to be noticeable and we are still dealing with small data. Often, great performance improvements can be had just by using optimized code. The data.table package provides an alternative to data frames that makes fewer copies and can be much faster. We are using version 1.9.5 data.table package for this chapter, as there have been some recent advances. As of the writing of this book, 1.9.5 is the development version, which is only available from GitHub, but thanks to the devtools package, which has a function install_github(), it is easy to install the latest development versions of any R package hosted on GitHub. Although generally it is perhaps safer to use packages on CRAN as they are more stable, as you start to push the limits of R and come closer to the cutting edge, it is helpful to be able to install from GitHub, where many R package developers choose to host the development source code of their packages. If you are on Windows or Mac and have not already, now is good time to get the development tools. For Windows, you can download them from https://cran.r-project.org/bin/windows/Rtools/. For Mac, all you need to do is install Xcode.

```
> install.packages("devtools")
> library(devtools)
> install_github("Rdatatable/data.table")
Downloading github repo Rdatatable/data.table@master
Installing data.table
## Much more output here about the package being compiled
mv data.table.dll datatable.dll
installing to c:/usr/R/R-3.2.2/library/data.table/libs/x64
** R
** inst
** tests
** byte-compile and prepare package for lazy loading
** help
*** installing help indices
** building package indices
** installing vignettes
** testing if installed package can be loaded
* DONE (data.table)
```

Now, we can load the data.table package and convert the flights data into a data.table object, and then try out the same calculations listed previously.

```
> library(data.table)
data.table 1.9.5  For help type: ?data.table
*** NB: by=.EACHI is now explicit. See README to restore previous behaviour.

> flights2 <- as.data.table(flights)

> system.time(
+ flights2[, ArrDelaySD := sd(arr_delay, na.rm = TRUE), by = dest]
+ )
   user  system elapsed
   0.01    0.00    0.02
> all.equal(flights2$ArrDelaySD, flights$ArrDelaySD)
[1] TRUE

> system.time(
+ mean(flights2[month < 7]$arr_delay)
+ )
   user  system elapsed
   0.03    0.02    0.04
```

Using data.table gives identical results and the code is much faster. Although the data.table package does not use multiple cores, it is highly optimized for speed and also tries to reduce memory usage. In regular R data frames, many common operations result in copies being made. In data.table, objects are often modified in place meaning where needed, and data are changed in place in memory rather than making a whole new copy. The end result is that basic data manipulation operations may work several times faster using data.table than using a regular data frame in R. Next, we will explore how to use data.table in more detail, as its syntax differs from those of data frames in some important ways.

To start, we can see what happens if we just type the data.table object in R.

```
> flights2
        year month day dep_time dep_delay arr_time arr_delay carrier tailnum
     1: 2013     1   1      517         2      830        11      UA  N14228
     2: 2013     1   1      533         4      850        20      UA  N24211
     3: 2013     1   1      542         2      923        33      AA  N619AA
     4: 2013     1   1      544        -1     1004       -18      B6  N804JB
     5: 2013     1   1      554        -6      812       -25      DL  N668DN
   ---
336772: 2013     9  30       NA        NA       NA        NA      9E
336773: 2013     9  30       NA        NA       NA        NA      9E
336774: 2013     9  30       NA        NA       NA        NA      MQ  N535MQ
336775: 2013     9  30       NA        NA       NA        NA      MQ  N511MQ
336776: 2013     9  30       NA        NA       NA        NA      MQ  N839MQ
        flight origin dest air_time distance hour minute ArrDelaySD
     1:   1545    EWR  IAH      227     1400    5     17   41.00647
     2:   1714    LGA  IAH      227     1416    5     33   41.00647
     3:   1141    JFK  MIA      160     1089    5     42   41.29391
     4:    725    JFK  BQN      183     1576    5     44   34.45790
     5:    461    LGA  ATL      116      762    5     54   46.96864
   ---
```

```
336772:   3393   JFK   DCA      NA   213   NA   NA   39.91506
336773:   3525   LGA   SYR      NA   198   NA   NA   41.84991
336774:   3461   LGA   BNA      NA   764   NA   NA   48.34005
336775:   3572   LGA   CLE      NA   419   NA   NA   45.83643
336776:   3531   LGA   RDU      NA   431   NA   NA   42.26542
```

The data.table object has printing methods that automatically print the first few and last few rows, rather than returning everything. In data.table any object within the brackets tends to be assumed to be a variable in the dataset. This often means that you do not need to explicitly reference the dataset or use quotes. For example, to select all rows of the data where the carrier was Delta, we type the following:

```
> flights2[carrier == "DL"]
## output omitted
```

This is compared with how we would do the same thing in base R:

```
> head(flights[flights$carrier == "DL", ])
> head(subset(flights, carrier == "DL"))
## output omitted
```

We can select columns in a similar way. For example, to tabulate the destinations of Delta flights, we can type the following:

```
> table(flights2[carrier == "DL", dest])
```

```
  ATL    AUS    BNA    BOS    BUF    CVG    DCA    DEN    DTW    EYW    FLL    IND    JAC
10571    357      1    972      3      4      2   1043   3875     17   2903      2      2
  JAX    LAS    LAX    MCI    MCO    MEM    MIA    MSP    MSY    OMA    PBI    PDX    PHL
    1   1673   2501     82   3663    432   2929   2864   1129      1   1466    458      2
  PHX    PIT    PWM    RSW    SAN    SAT    SEA    SFO    SJU    SLC    SRQ    STL    STT
  469    250    235    426    575    303   1213   1858   1301   2102    265      1     30
  TPA
 2129
```

To create a new variable, we can use the := syntax. For example, we can create a new variable encoding the difference between departing and arrival delays (a similar approach could be used to create other scores, such as the sum of correct answers on a test).

```
> flights2[, NewVariable := dep_delay - arr_delay]
> colnames(flights2)
 [1] "year"       "month"      "day"        "dep_time"   "dep_delay"
 [6] "arr_time"   "arr_delay"  "carrier"    "tailnum"    "flight"
[11] "origin"     "dest"       "air_time"   "distance"   "hour"
[16] "minute"     "ArrDelaySD" "NewVariable"
```

We can also make a new variable by recoding an existing variable. Here we will overwrite NewVariable. Suppose we consider delays greater than two hours to be true delays and otherwise just a variation around normal (i.e., no delay). We can overwrite the variable using ifelse() to encode delays greater than 120 minutes as "Delayed" and everything else as "No Delay". We can then count the number of delays and no delays using .N which returns the number of the last row in data.table, and doing this by NewVariable, which effectively works to count, much like table().

```
> flights2[, NewVariable := ifelse(arr_delay > 120, "Delayed", "No Delay")]
> flights2[, .N, by = NewVariable]
   NewVariable      N
1:    No Delay 317312
2:     Delayed  10034
3:          NA   9430
```

Here we can see that data.table also listed the number of missing values. Another useful way to use .N is as an index. This can be particularly powerful combined with order(). For example, suppose we wanted to see the least and most delayed flight arrivals by whether they meet our definition of delayed (> 120 minutes) or not. The example that follows orders by our NewVariable and then by arrival delay, and then gets the first two and last two rows for arrival delay by NewVariable. Note that 1:0 expands into c(1, 0), which is helpful as we could also have written 5:0 if we wanted the last five, making it easy to get however many first or last values we want.

```
> flights2[order(NewVariable, arr_delay), arr_delay[c(1:2, .N - 1:0)], by = NewVariable]
    NewVariable   V1
1:     Delayed   121
2:     Delayed   121
3:     Delayed  1127
4:     Delayed  1272
5:    No Delay   -86
6:    No Delay   -79
7:    No Delay   120
8:    No Delay   120
9:          NA    NA
10:         NA    NA
11:         NA    NA
12:         NA    NA
```

Another common operation is dropping a variable. To remove a variable, simply set it to NULL. In data.table this is a very fast operation as no copy of the dataset is made, unlike in base R where the data are essentially copied without that variable.

```
> flights2[, NewVariable := NULL]
> colnames(flights2)
 [1] "year"      "month"     "day"       "dep_time"  "dep_delay"
 [6] "arr_time"  "arr_delay" "carrier"   "tailnum"   "flight"
[11] "origin"    "dest"      "air_time"  "distance"  "hour"
[16] "minute"    "ArrDelaySD"
```

If only certain rows of the data are selected when a variable is created, the rest will be missing.

```
> flights2[carrier == "DL", NewVariable := "Test"]
> table(is.na(flights2[carrier == "DL", NewVariable]))

FALSE
48110
> table(is.na(flights2[carrier != "DL", NewVariable]))
```

```
   TRUE
288666
> flights2[, NewVariable := NULL]
```

data.table also has a very powerful and flexible way of performing operations by a variable in the dataset (e.g., getting the mean delay by month of the year).

```
> flights2[, mean(arr_delay, na.rm=TRUE), by = month]
     month          V1
 1:      1   6.1299720
 2:     10  -0.1670627
 3:     11   0.4613474
 4:     12  14.8703553
 5:      2   5.6130194
 6:      3   5.8075765
 7:      4  11.1760630
 8:      5   3.5215088
 9:      6  16.4813296
10:      7  16.7113067
11:      8   6.0406524
12:      9  -4.0183636
```

It is even easy to make multiple summary variables by another variable.

```
> flights2[, .(M = mean(arr_delay, na.rm=TRUE),
+             SD = sd(arr_delay, na.rm=TRUE)),
+          by = month]
     month          M       SD
 1:      1   6.1299720 40.42390
 2:     10  -0.1670627 32.64986
 3:     11   0.4613474 31.38741
 4:     12  14.8703553 46.13311
 5:      2   5.6130194 39.52862
 6:      3   5.8075765 44.11919
 7:      4  11.1760630 47.49115
 8:      5   3.5215088 44.23761
 9:      6  16.4813296 56.13087
10:      7  16.7113067 57.11709
11:      8   6.0406524 42.59514
12:      9  -4.0183636 39.71031
```

Or to do so by multiple variables, such as by month and by destination.

```
> flights2[, .(M = mean(arr_delay, na.rm=TRUE),
+             SD = sd(arr_delay, na.rm=TRUE)),
+          by = .(month, dest)]
```

```
      month dest          M        SD
   1:     1 IAH    4.1627907 33.74079
   2:     1 MIA   -2.1506148 32.42194
   3:     1 BQN    2.6451613 30.01545
   4:     1 ATL    4.1520468 34.17429
   5:     1 ORD    7.2876936 47.88168
 ---
1109:     9 TYS  -14.0425532 30.62605
1110:     9 BHM   -0.2727273 49.71172
1111:     9 ALB  -11.3684211 17.26657
1112:     9 CHO   10.2105263 40.62098
1113:     9 ILM   -7.9000000 26.79140
```

Notice that data.table also automatically includes the grouping by variables (here month and dest) in the results so we know what each mean and standard deviation apply to. Sometimes, how we want to group data by is not always a variable in the dataset directly. For example, we could compare mean flight delays between Fall and Spring vs. Spring to Fall months. Operations can be done directly within the by statement.

```
> flights2[, .(M = mean(arr_delay, na.rm=TRUE),
+              SD = sd(arr_delay, na.rm=TRUE)),
+          by = .(Winter = month %in% c(9:12, 1:3))]
   Winter        M       SD
1:   TRUE  4.038362 39.83271
2:  FALSE 10.727385 50.10366
```

To include our summary variables in the original dataset rather than a new summarized dataset, we use the := operator again. Here we also show how to create multiple new variables at once, rather than having to create one new variable at a time. Note that the values will be recycled to fill as many rows as the dataset (in the code that follows we can see the mean for all rows for month 1 are the same).

```
> flights2[, c("MonthDelayM", "MonthDelaySD") := .(
+   mean(arr_delay, na.rm=TRUE),
+   sd(arr_delay, na.rm=TRUE)), by = month]
> ## view results
> flights2[, .(month, MonthDelayM, MonthDelaySD)]
        month MonthDelayM MonthDelaySD
   1:       1    6.129972     40.42390
   2:       1    6.129972     40.42390
   3:       1    6.129972     40.42390
   4:       1    6.129972     40.42390
   5:       1    6.129972     40.42390
 ---
336772:       9   -4.018364     39.71031
336773:       9   -4.018364     39.71031
336774:       9   -4.018364     39.71031
336775:       9   -4.018364     39.71031
336776:       9   -4.018364     39.71031
```

If there is a key, such as an ID or some other variable we will often be summarizing others by, we can use the setkey() function which sorts and indexes the data, making operations involving the key variable much faster. For example, we can set month as the key.

```
> setkey(flights2, month)
```

Once the key is set, we can refer to it using the J() operator. For example, to get months 3 to 7, we can type the following:

```
> system.time(flights2[J(3:7)])
   user  system elapsed
   0.01    0.00    0.01
```

which is much faster than the equivalent in base R.

```
> system.time(subset(flights, month %in% 3:7))
   user  system elapsed
   0.16    0.05    0.20
```

Here we can see that data.table has a tremendous speed advantage (admittedly, it takes a bit of time to set the key in the first place, but for repeated use, that is a one-time cost). It might seem difficult to use a whole new type of data structure, but because data.table inherits from data frame, most functions that work on a data frame will work on a data.table object. If they are designed for it, they may be much faster. If not, at least they will still work as well as for a regular data frame. For example, in a regular linear regression:

```
> summary(lm(arr_delay ~ dep_time, data = flights2))

Call:
lm(formula = arr_delay ~ dep_time, data = flights2)

Residuals:
    Min      1Q  Median      3Q     Max
-100.67  -23.21   -8.76    9.07 1280.13

Coefficients:
              Estimate Std. Error t value Pr(>|t|)
(Intercept) -2.174e+01  2.229e-01  -97.55   <2e-16 ***
dep_time     2.123e-02  1.554e-04  136.65   <2e-16 ***
---
Signif. codes:  0 '***' 0.001 '**' 0.01 '*' 0.05 '.' 0.1 ' ' 1

Residual standard error: 43.41 on 327344 degrees of freedom
  (9430 observations deleted due to missingness)
Multiple R-squared:  0.05397,   Adjusted R-squared:  0.05396
F-statistic: 1.867e+04 on 1 and 327344 DF,  p-value: < 2.2e-16
```

Operations can also be paired with subsetting. For example, earlier we saw how to use the .N convenience function. Now we count how many flights in each month were delayed by more than 12 hours. Here there are only ten rows because some months had zero flights delayed by more than 12 hours. April and June appear to have been particularly bad months.

```
> flights2[arr_delay > 60*12, .N, by = month]
    month N
1:      1 3
2:      2 4
```

```
 3:      3 2
 4:      4 5
 5:      5 2
 6:      6 5
 7:      7 2
 8:      9 1
 9:     11 1
10:     12 4
```

Another dataset, airlines, has the full names of each carrier. We can merge it with the flights dataset to have detailed carrier names (first converting the airlines data into a data.table object). This merging (or join) is fast because the data are already ordered by the key following the call to setkey(). Note that it is also possible to do nested joins (e.g., Dataset1[Dataset2[Dataset3]]), as long as the datasets all use the same keys they will be evaluated from the innermost outward. For joins, the nomatch argument controls what happens if no match can be found, either filling it with missing values (NA) or the default, or dropping those rows if nomatch = 0 is specified. The documentation for ?data.table has more details.

```
> airlines2 <- as.data.table(airlines)
> setkey(airlines2, carrier)
> setkey(flights2, carrier)

> ## join the data.tables by their key
> flights3 <- flights2[airlines2]

> ## view just three variables
> flights3[, .(year, carrier, name)]
        year carrier               name
     1: 2013      9E  Endeavor Air Inc.
     2: 2013      9E  Endeavor Air Inc.
     3: 2013      9E  Endeavor Air Inc.
     4: 2013      9E  Endeavor Air Inc.
     5: 2013      9E  Endeavor Air Inc.
    ---
336772: 2013      YV  Mesa Airlines Inc.
336773: 2013      YV  Mesa Airlines Inc.
336774: 2013      YV  Mesa Airlines Inc.
336775: 2013      YV  Mesa Airlines Inc.
336776: 2013      YV  Mesa Airlines Inc.
```

Joinings can also be done by multiple keys. For example, another dataset has weather data by month, day, and airport. To join this with the flights data, we would set month, day, and origin airport as keys. Of course we have to convert the weather data frame to a data.table object first.

```
> weather2 <- as.data.table(weather)
> weather2
     origin year month day hour  temp  dewp humid wind_dir wind_speed
  1:    EWR 2013    NA  NA   NA 44.96 17.96 33.55       20    3.45234
  2:    EWR 2013     1   1    0 37.04 21.92 53.97      230   10.35702
  3:    EWR 2013     1   1    1 37.04 21.92 53.97      230   13.80936
  4:    EWR 2013     1   1    2 37.94 21.92 52.09      230   12.65858
  5:    EWR 2013     1   1    3 37.94 23.00 54.51      230   13.80936
    ---
```

```
8715:    EWR 2013    12  30   19 37.04 21.02 51.95      320   17.26170
8716:    EWR 2013    12  30   20 35.06 17.96 49.30      340   17.26170
8717:    EWR 2013    12  30   21 33.08 15.98 48.98      320   14.96014
8718:    EWR 2013    12  30   22 30.92 12.92 46.74      340   16.11092
8719:    EWR 2013    12  30   23 28.94 12.02 48.69      330   14.96014
         wind_gust precip pressure visib
   1:   3.972884      0   1025.9     10
   2:  11.918651      0   1013.9     10
   3:  15.891535      0   1013.0     10
   4:  14.567241      0   1012.6     10
   5:  15.891535      0   1012.7     10
  ---
8715:  19.864419      0   1017.6     10
8716:  19.864419      0   1019.1     10
8717:  17.215830      0   1019.8     10
8718:  18.540125      0   1020.5     10
8719:  17.215830      0   1021.1     10
```

```
> setkey(flights2, month, day, origin)
> setkey(weather2, month, day, origin)
```

Because the weather data have hourly data, before we can join, we need to collapse the data somehow. We will take the mean. One way to do this is just by writing out each column we care about.

```
> weather2b <- weather2[, .(temp = mean(temp, na.rm=TRUE),
+                           precip = mean(precip, na.rm=TRUE),
+                           visib = mean(visib, na.rm=TRUE)),
+                          by = .(month, day, origin)]
> weather2b
     month day origin    temp      precip      visib
   1:   NA  NA    EWR 44.9600 0.00000000 10.000000
   2:    1   1    EWR 38.4800 0.00000000 10.000000
   3:    1   2    EWR 28.8350 0.00000000 10.000000
   4:    1   3    EWR 29.4575 0.00000000 10.000000
   5:    1   4    EWR 33.4775 0.00000000 10.000000
  ---
 369:   12  26    EWR 31.0475 0.00000000  9.541667
 370:   12  27    EWR 34.2425 0.00000000 10.000000
 371:   12  28    EWR 39.1550 0.00000000 10.000000
 372:   12  29    EWR 43.0475 0.03291667  7.947917
 373:   12  30    EWR 38.9000 0.00000000 10.000000
```

However, writing each column or variable name becomes time-consuming when there are many columns. Fortunately, there is a way around this. There is another special way to refer to the columns in a data.table object, .SD. We can use this to get the mean of all columns except the ones we are grouping by.

```
> weather2c <- weather2[, lapply(.SD, mean, na.rm=TRUE),
+                          by = .(month, day, origin)]
> weather2c
     month day origin year     hour    temp      dewp    humid wind_dir
  1:    NA  NA    EWR 2013      NaN 44.9600 17.96000 33.55000  20.0000
  2:     1   1    EWR 2013 11.78261 38.4800 25.05043 58.38609 263.0435
  3:     1   2    EWR 2013 11.50000 28.8350 11.38250 47.78625 307.9167
  4:     1   3    EWR 2013 11.50000 29.4575 14.78000 54.39583 276.9565
  5:     1   4    EWR 2013 11.50000 33.4775 19.20500 55.88042 242.9167
 ---
369:    12  26    EWR 2013 11.50000 31.0475 19.04750 60.90417 153.7500
370:    12  27    EWR 2013 11.50000 34.2425 19.87250 56.68750 253.7500
371:    12  28    EWR 2013 11.50000 39.1550 23.00750 54.89750 222.9167
372:    12  29    EWR 2013 11.50000 43.0475 32.33000 67.60208 166.5217
373:    12  30    EWR 2013 11.50000 38.9000 30.71750 73.83875 280.8333
     wind_speed wind_gust     precip pressure     visib
  1:   3.452340  3.972884 0.00000000 1025.900 10.000000
  2:  12.758648 14.682397 0.00000000 1012.443 10.000000
  3:  12.514732 14.401704 0.00000000 1017.337 10.000000
  4:   7.863663  9.049346 0.00000000 1021.058 10.000000
  5:  13.857309 15.946714 0.00000000 1017.533 10.000000
 ---
369:   5.801849  6.676652 0.00000000 1027.129  9.541667
370:   8.343155  9.601136 0.00000000 1026.475 10.000000
371:   8.822647 10.152925 0.00000000 1023.117 10.000000
372:   8.103409  9.325241 0.03291667 1014.595  7.947917
373:  12.035241 13.849914 0.00000000 1012.541 10.000000
```

Now we are ready to join the datasets. We can see that we end up with the same number of rows but have now added additional columns for the weather data.

```
> flights4 <- weather2c[flights2]

> dim(flights2)
[1] 336776     17
> dim(flights4)
[1] 336776     28
```

Finally, in data.table, almost any operation can be done within the middle argument, even functions that are called for their side effects, not what they return. In the code that follows we calculate the regression of arrival delay on visibility and we do this by carrier (airline).

```
> flights4[, as.list(coef(lm(arr_delay ~ visib))), by = carrier]
    carrier (Intercept)      visib
 1:      AA    46.58181  -4.859830
 2:      AS    51.46830  -6.645643
 3:      B6    54.26659  -4.758500
 4:      DL    49.36366  -4.505132
 5:      EV    78.28173  -6.600792
 6:      MQ    52.29302  -3.868518
 7:      UA    35.47410  -3.463089
 8:      US    38.34697  -4.007031
 9:      WN    65.21767  -5.847156
10:      9E    45.61693  -4.690411
11:      HA   -29.45361   2.268041
12:      VX    25.30893  -2.789938
13:      F9    12.50000         NA
14:      FL    97.11111         NA
15:      YV     4.00000         NA
16:      OO   -88.79863  11.939863
```

We can even make plots. To catch multiple plots, we use the par() function. Of course, as we saw in Chapter 17, it would be easy to do this in ggplot2; this is just an example of the different operations you can do in a data.table object and by other variables. Because the plot() function creates a plot but returns no data, we end up with an empty data.table object.

```
> par(mfrow = c(4, 3))
> flights4[, plot(density(na.omit(arr_delay)), main = "Arival Delay", xlab = "", ylab =
"Density"), by = month]
Empty data.table (0 rows) of 1 col: month
```

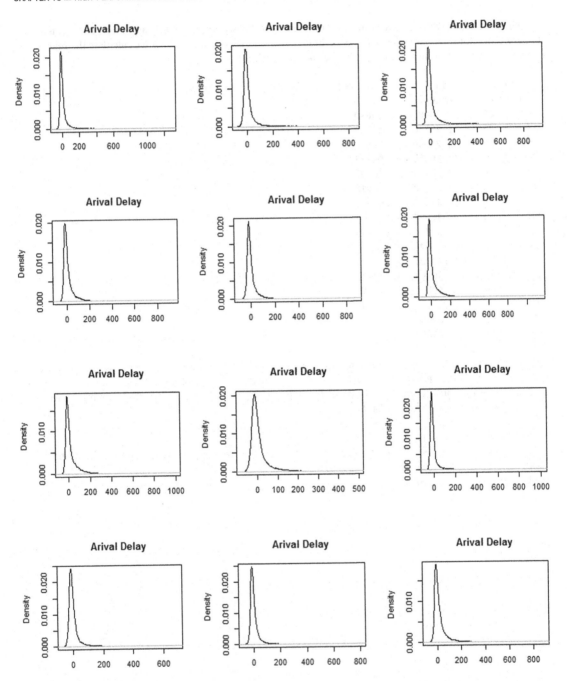

So far we have just explored the data.table package in R, which allows for faster and somewhat more memory-efficient data management in R. However, it still requires the data to be loaded into memory. Many larger datasets will be too big for memory. For data that cannot be loaded into memory, there are a few options. The ff package uses flat files stored on disk and links them to R. The dplyr package also supports linking to databases, including SQLite, MySQL, Postgresql, and Bigquery. Although, ultimately, the data often have to be read into R, you rarely need all the data at once. For example, from a large database, you may only need to select certain observations, and read in two variables to examine their relationship. Even if the full dataset cannot fit in memory, by linking to a database and only pulling in what you need when you need it, you can use the memory available to go a lot farther. The package homepage for dplyr (https://cran.r-project.org/web/packages/dplyr/) has many introductions to these topics.

18.2 Parallel Processing

The other easy way to increase performance for some operations is through parallel processing. Again we are going to restrict ourselves to using multiple cores just on one machine, not distributed computing. To see many of the packages available to help with this, a good place to start is the High-Performance Computing CRAN task view (https://cran.r-project.org/web/views/HighPerformanceComputing.html). One thing worth noting is that many of the parallel processing functions work better or only work on Linux or Mac (built on Linux). In order to make this chapter more general, we will focus on methods that apply across operating systems.

The parallel package is built into R now and provides a few facilities for parallel processing. A little later, we'll examine other options. To start, we load the package. For Linux machines, there are some multicore functions we could use straight away, but to make this generic, we will create a local cluster that takes advantage of multiple cores and works on Linux, Mac, and Windows. We will make one assuming four cores are available. If you have two cores, you would just change the 4 to a 2. If you have more cores, you could increase the number. If you don't know what your computer has, you can use the detectCores() function, which should tell you (note that this does not distinguish physical and logical cores, so, for example, two physical cores with hyperthreading will count as four).

```
> library(parallel)
> cl <- makeCluster(4)
```

Because there is some overhead in sending commands to and getting results back from the cluster, for trivial operations, like addition, it may actually be slower to use the parallel version. We have used lapply() function before to loop through some index and perform operations. Here we will use parLapply() which is a parallel version, and the main workhorse.

```
> system.time(lapply(1:1000, function(i) i + 1))
   user  system elapsed
      0       0       0
> system.time(parLapply(cl, 1:1000, function(i) i + 1))
   user  system elapsed
      0       0       0
```

We can notice the real-time difference as the task becomes more computationally demanding.

```
> time1 <- system.time(lapply(1:1000, function(i) mean(rnorm(4e4))))
> time2 <- system.time(parLapply(cl, 1:1000, function(i) mean(rnorm(4e4))))
```

The nonparallel version here took about four times as long (the code that follows shows how to get the ratio of elapsed time), which is what we would expect for this sort of easily parallelized example (easy because no data need to be transferred, results are simple, each task is about equally computationally demanding, and no operations depend on a previous operation).

```
> time1["elapsed"] / time2["elapsed"]
 elapsed
4.063063
```

To give a practical example of the benefits of parallelization, we can go back to our bootstrapping example from Chapter 16.

```
> library(boot)
> library(VGAM)
> library(foreign)

> gss2012 <- read.spss("GSS2012merged_R5.sav", to.data.frame = TRUE)
> gssr <- gss2012[, c("age", "sex", "marital", "educ", "income06", "satfin", "happy",
"health")]
> gssr <- na.omit(gssr)
> gssr <- within(gssr, {
+    age <- as.numeric(age)
+    Agec <- (gssr$age - 18) / 10
+    educ <- as.numeric(educ)
+    # recode income categories to numeric
+    cincome <- as.numeric(income06)
+    satfin <- factor(satfin,
+                  levels = c("NOT AT ALL SAT", "MORE OR LESS", "SATISFIED"),
+                  ordered = TRUE)
+ })

> m <- vglm(satfin ~ Agec + cincome * educ,
+           family = cumulative(link = "logit", parallel = TRUE, reverse = TRUE),
+           data = gssr)

> ## write function to pass to boot()
> model_coef_predictions <- function(d, i) {
+
+    m.tmp <- vglm(satfin ~ Agec + cincome * educ,
+               family = cumulative(link = "logit", parallel = TRUE, reverse = TRUE),
+               data = d[i, ])
+    newdat <- expand.grid(
+      Agec = seq(from = 0, to = (89 - 18)/10, length.out = 50),
+      cincome = mean(d$cincom),
+      educ = c(12, 16, 20))
+    bs <- coef(m.tmp)
+    predicted.probs <- predict(m.tmp, newdata = newdat,
+                          type = "response")
+    out <- c(bs, predicted.probs[, 1], predicted.probs[, 2], predicted.probs[, 3])
+    return(out)
+ }
```

In order to use the bootstrap on the cluster, we need the cluster to have everything set up. For example, we need to load the relevant packages on the cluster. The boot() function is rather unique in R, in that it is designed to be parallelized and accepts arguments for a cluster to use. As we will see, most functions are not like that and rely on us being able to somehow break the task down into smaller chunks and distribute them to the cluster ourselves. We can evaluate commands on the cluster using the clusterEvalQ() function, which returns results from each of the nodes (here four).

```
> clusterEvalQ(cl, {
+   library(VGAM)
+ })
[[1]]
 [1] "VGAM"      "splines"  "stats4"    "methods" "stats"    "graphics"
 [7] "grDevices" "utils"    "datasets"  "base"


[[2]]
 [1] "VGAM"      "splines"  "stats4"    "methods" "stats"    "graphics"
 [7] "grDevices" "utils"    "datasets"  "base"


[[3]]
 [1] "VGAM"      "splines"  "stats4"    "methods" "stats"    "graphics"
 [7] "grDevices" "utils"    "datasets"  "base"


[[4]]
 [1] "VGAM"      "splines"  "stats4"    "methods" "stats"    "graphics"
 [7] "grDevices" "utils"    "datasets"  "base"

> clusterSetRNGStream(cl, iseed = 1234)
> boot.res <- boot(
+   data = gssr,
+   statistic = model_coef_predictions,
+   R = 5000,
+   parallel = "snow",
+   ncpus = 4,
+   cl = cl)
```

Next we calculate the 95% bias-corrected and accelerated bootstrap confidence intervals. The function call boot.ci() is not designed to be parallel, so we can use the parLapply() function again. Now because we are calling a boot.ci() function within the cluster, we need to load the book package on the cluster (before we called boot() which then had the cluster do operations, but boot() was called in our current R instance, not on the cluster; hence we did not need to load the boot package on the cluster before). We will also find that although our local R instance has the boot.res object, the cluster does not. We need to export the data from our local R instance to the cluster. Note that if we were using Linux, we could use mclapply() which is a multicore version and relies on forking which allows processes to share memory, reducing the need to export data explicitly as for the local cluster we created. However, the cluster approach works across operating systems, while the mclapply() approach does not.

```
> clusterEvalQ(cl, {
>   library(boot)
> })
> ## output omitted
> clusterExport(cl, varlist = "boot.res")
```

```
> boot.res2 <- parLapply(cl, 1:6, function(i) {
+   cis <- boot.ci(boot.res, index = i, type = "bca")
+   data.frame(Estimate = boot.res$t0[i],
+              LL = cis$bca[1, 4],
+              UL = cis$bca[1, 5])
+ })
```

Even parallelized, this code takes quite a bit of time to run. Here we just show it for the six coefficients, rather than all the predicted probabilities. We could easily change this by indexing over all of boot.res$t0 rather than only 1:6. It is substantially faster than the naive single-core version, and the actual code required to make it parallel is fairly easy.

```
> ## combine row-wise
> boot.res2 <- do.call(rbind, boot.res2)
> round(boot.res2, 3)
                Estimate     LL     UL
(Intercept):1      0.965  0.008  1.834
(Intercept):2     -1.189 -2.128 -0.300
Agec               0.169  0.128  0.215
cincome           -0.061 -0.112 -0.007
educ              -0.183 -0.251 -0.108
cincome:educ       0.012  0.008  0.016
```

18.2.1 Other Parallel Processing Approaches

Another approach to parallel processing is using the foreach package. The foreach package is really just a consistent front end to parallelize for loops. What is nice about it is that it can use a variety of parallel back ends, including multiple cores and clusters. This means that the appropriate back end for a specific system can be chosen and registered, and then the rest of the code will work the same. For this example, we will continue using the cluster we created, but first we will install the necessary packages. So in addition to loading the foreach package, we need to load the doSNOW package and then register the cluster we created. On Linux or Mac, we could load the doMC library instead and use the registerDoMC() specifying the number of cores to achieve a similar result but using forking instead of a local cluster.

```
> install.packages("foreach")
> install.packages("doSNOW")

> library(foreach)
> library(doSNOW)
> registerDoSNOW(cl)
```

From here, we can use the foreach() function to iterate over a variable and do something, here just taking the mean of some random data as we examined before using parLapply(). To make foreach() parallel, we use %dopar% instead of %do%. Another nice feature is that if no parallel back end is registered, %dopar% will still work, but it will run sequentially instead of in parallel. However, it will still run, which can be helpful for ensuring that code works (even if slowly) on many different machines and configurations. Finally, notice that we specify the function used to combine results. Since, for each run, we will get a single numeric mean, we can combine these into a vector using the c() function. For more complex examples, we could use different functions to combine the results. In the code that follows we show both approaches, along with timing and the histograms (Figure 18-1) to show that the results are comparable (differences are due to random variation).

```
> system.time(
+   res1 <- foreach(i = 1:1000, .combine = 'c') %do% mean(rnorm(4e4))
+ )
   user  system elapsed
   5.24    0.00    5.23
> system.time(
+   res2 <- foreach(i = 1:1000, .combine = 'c') %dopar% mean(rnorm(4e4))
+ )
   user  system elapsed
   0.53    0.02    1.94
> par(mfrow = c(1, 2))
> hist(res1)
> hist(res2)
```

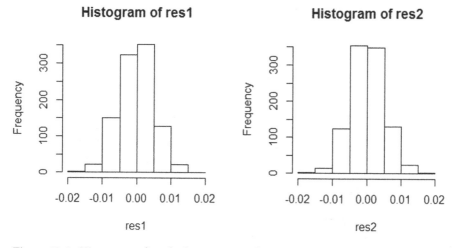

Figure 18-1. *Histograms of results from sequential and parallel processing*

The foreach package also makes use of the iterators package, which has some special iterators to make life easier. For example, suppose we wanted to calculate the coefficient of variation (the ratio of the mean to the variance) for each variable in a dataset. We can do this using the iter() function on the mtcars dataset, and specifying we want to iterate over the dataset by columns, and the variable that is passed should be called "x." Here we choose to combine the results using rbind() to put them into a one-column matrix.

```
> foreach(x=iter(mtcars, by='col'), .combine = rbind) %dopar% (mean(x) / var(x))
                 [,1]
result.1   0.55309350
result.2   1.93994943
result.3   0.01502017
result.4   0.03120435
result.5  12.58061252
```

```
result.6    3.36047700
result.7    5.58967159
result.8    1.72222222
result.9    1.63157895
result.10   6.77407407
result.11   1.07805255
```

Now let's consider a more advanced example. Suppose we wanted to regress every continuous variable in the diamonds dataset on cut, color, and clarity. More generally, it is not uncommon to have a fixed set of predictors and a variety of outcomes or the reverse—a fixed outcome but a variety of potential predictors. To test which sets of predictors or outcomes are related, we may want to iterate over the predictors (or outcomes) via running multiple independent regressions. To have nice results, we might write a short function to show the estimate and 95% confidence interval. We can then use the foreach() function to iterate over the continuous variables in the diamonds data, and use cbind() to combine the results column-wise.

```
> prettyout <- function(object) {
+   cis <- confint(object)
+   bs <- coef(object)
+   out <- sprintf("%0.2f [%0.2f, %0.2f]", bs, cis[, 1], cis[, 2])
+   names(out) <- names(bs)
+   return(out)
+ }

> continuous.vars <- sapply(diamonds, is.numeric)
> results <- foreach(dv=iter(diamonds[, continuous.vars], by='col'), .combine = cbind)
%dopar%
+   prettyout(lm(dv ~ cut + color + clarity, data = diamonds))
```

Now we can print the results. To remove all the quotation marks, we explicitly call print() and use the quote = FALSE argument. To avoid too much output, we only examine the first two columns.

```
> print(results[, 1:2], quote = FALSE)
            result.1                result.2
(Intercept) 0.85 [0.85, 0.86]      62.24 [62.22, 62.27]
cut.L       -0.09 [-0.10, -0.07]   -1.77 [-1.81, -1.72]
cut.Q       0.01 [-0.00, 0.02]     1.11 [1.07, 1.15]
cut.C       -0.08 [-0.09, -0.07]   -0.01 [-0.05, 0.02]
cut^4       -0.02 [-0.03, -0.01]   0.26 [0.24, 0.29]
color.L     0.45 [0.44, 0.46]      0.19 [0.15, 0.23]
color.Q     0.07 [0.06, 0.08]      -0.01 [-0.04, 0.03]
color.C     -0.01 [-0.02, 0.00]    -0.07 [-0.10, -0.03]
color^4     0.01 [-0.00, 0.02]     0.03 [0.00, 0.06]
color^5     -0.02 [-0.03, -0.01]   0.02 [-0.01, 0.05]
color^6     0.01 [-0.00, 0.01]     -0.02 [-0.04, 0.01]
clarity.L   -0.64 [-0.66, -0.62]   -0.41 [-0.47, -0.34]
clarity.Q   0.14 [0.12, 0.16]      0.10 [0.04, 0.17]
clarity.C   -0.03 [-0.04, -0.01]   -0.16 [-0.22, -0.10]
clarity^4   0.01 [-0.00, 0.03]     0.08 [0.03, 0.12]
clarity^5   0.07 [0.06, 0.08]      -0.14 [-0.17, -0.10]
clarity^6   -0.02 [-0.03, -0.01]   0.07 [0.04, 0.10]
clarity^7   0.01 [0.00, 0.02]      -0.01 [-0.03, 0.02]
```

Next we examine another case where parallel processing can be helpful. Cross-validation is a commonly used technique in machine learning and other exploratory modeling. The idea is that models will tend to overfit the data, even if only slightly, and so evaluating the performance of a model on sample predictions will be overly optimistic. Instead, it is better to evaluate the performance of a model on out-of-sample predictions (i.e., on data not used in the model). K-fold cross-validation separates the data into k groups, and then systematically leaves one out, trains the model on the remaining k - 1 group, and then predicts from the model on the hold-out data, and iterates through until all parts of the data have been used for training and as the hold-out testing data. A common number for k is 10, which requires ten identical models to be run on different subsets of the data—a perfect case that is easy to parallelize.

First we will create a list of row indices to be dropped from a given training model and used as the hold-out test data, and then use foreach to iterate through. In the example code that follows, we want to calculate a cross-validated R^2, then combine the results into a vector, and finally calculate the mean. We can specify all of that in the call to foreach(). Then the results are compared to a linear regression model on the full data.

```
> ## cross validated R squared
> drop.index <- tapply(1:nrow(gssr),
+    rep(1:10, each = ceiling(nrow(gssr)/10))[1:nrow(gssr)],
+    function(x) x)

> CV <- foreach(i = drop.index, .combine = 'c', .final = mean) %dopar% {
+    m <- lm(cincome ~ educ, data = gssr[-i, ])
+    cor(gssr[i, "cincome"], predict(m, newdata = gssr[i, ]))^2
+ }

> summary(lm(cincome ~ educ, data = gssr))

Call:
lm(formula = cincome ~ educ, data = gssr)

Residuals:
     Min      1Q  Median      3Q     Max
-21.2006  -2.8900  0.9035  3.6270  14.0418

Coefficients:
             Estimate Std. Error t value Pr(>|t|)
(Intercept)  5.64760    0.45438   12.43   <2e-16 ***
educ         0.82765    0.03224   25.67   <2e-16 ***
---
Signif. codes:  0 '***' 0.001 '**' 0.01 '*' 0.05 '.' 0.1 ' ' 1

Residual standard error: 5.183 on 2833 degrees of freedom
Multiple R-squared:  0.1887,    Adjusted R-squared:  0.1884
F-statistic: 658.9 on 1 and 2833 DF,  p-value: < 2.2e-16

> CV
[1] 0.1829171
```

Although the results here are not too different, it illustrates how cross-validation can be performed, in parallel, to obtain more realistic estimates of model performance. Of course in this case, we have the adjusted R^2, but for performance statistics where we do not know how to adjust them, cross-validation provides a computationally intense but conceptually straightforward approach.

The foreach package can also handle nested parallel loops. For example, we could use cross-validation combined with screening a number of predictor variables to identify which predictors explained the largest amount of variance in income bins in the GSS data. This can be done by chaining foreach() calls together using the %:% operator. The result looks like this and at the end we add the column names back and show the variance accounted for across all ten cross-validations

```
> CV2 <-
+   foreach(x = iter(gssr[, 1:4], by = "col"), .combine = "cbind") %:%
+     foreach(i = drop.index, .combine = 'rbind') %dopar% {
+       x2 <- x[-i]
+       m <- lm(gssr$cincome[-i] ~ x2)
+       cor(gssr$cincome[i], predict(m, newdata = data.frame(x2 = x[i])))^2
+ }

> colnames(CV2) <- colnames(gssr)[1:4]
> round(CV2, 2)
           age  sex marital educ
result.1  0.00 0.02    0.19 0.19
result.2  0.00 0.00    0.19 0.23
result.3  0.01 0.01    0.27 0.19
result.4  0.01 0.01    0.18 0.15
result.5  0.01 0.02    0.22 0.23
result.6  0.01 0.02    0.22 0.13
result.7  0.04 0.00    0.14 0.16
result.8  0.00 0.02    0.19 0.24
result.9  0.00 0.06    0.27 0.21
result.10 0.00 0.00    0.25 0.09
```

We will close this section by showing how to do conditional evaluation. Recall that in our first experiment with the iterators, we iterated over the numeric columns of the diamonds dataset. Using the same operator we used for nested loops, %:%, we can add when statements, so that the functions are only executed when certain conditions are meant. For example, we could use a when statement to only include numeric variables, rather than preselecting only columns we knew were numeric. This can also be useful for resampling statistics like the bootstrap. For example, if one of the predictors was a rare event, it is possible that in a particular bootstrap sample, none of the sampled cases would have the event, in which case the predictor would have no variability. We might prefer to not evaluate these rather than get results with missing or infinite coefficients.

```
> results <- foreach(dv=iter(diamonds, by='col'), .combine = cbind) %:%
+   when(is.numeric(dv)) %dopar%
+   prettyout(lm(dv ~ cut + color + clarity, data = diamonds))

> print(results[, 1:2], quote = FALSE)
              result.1               result.2
(Intercept) 0.85 [0.85, 0.86]    62.24 [62.22, 62.27]
cut.L       -0.09 [-0.10, -0.07] -1.77 [-1.81, -1.72]
cut.Q       0.01 [-0.00, 0.02]    1.11 [1.07, 1.15]
cut.C       -0.08 [-0.09, -0.07] -0.01 [-0.05, 0.02]
cut^4       -0.02 [-0.03, -0.01] 0.26 [0.24, 0.29]
color.L     0.45 [0.44, 0.46]     0.19 [0.15, 0.23]
color.Q     0.07 [0.06, 0.08]    -0.01 [-0.04, 0.03]
color.C     -0.01 [-0.02, 0.00]  -0.07 [-0.10, -0.03]
```

```
color^4      0.01 [-0.00, 0.02]   0.03 [0.00, 0.06]
color^5     -0.02 [-0.03, -0.01] 0.02 [-0.01, 0.05]
color^6      0.01 [-0.00, 0.01]  -0.02 [-0.04, 0.01]
clarity.L   -0.64 [-0.66, -0.62] -0.41 [-0.47, -0.34]
clarity.Q    0.14 [0.12, 0.16]    0.10 [0.04, 0.17]
clarity.C   -0.03 [-0.04, -0.01] -0.16 [-0.22, -0.10]
clarity^4    0.01 [-0.00, 0.03]   0.08 [0.03, 0.12]
clarity^5    0.07 [0.06, 0.08]   -0.14 [-0.17, -0.10]
clarity^6   -0.02 [-0.03, -0.01] 0.07 [0.04, 0.10]
clarity^7    0.01 [0.00, 0.02]   -0.01 [-0.03, 0.02]
```

Finally, once we are done using a cluster, we need to shut it down, which can be done using the stopCluster() command. Otherwise, even if we no longer use the cluster or workers, they will sit there and use system resources like memory.

```
> stopCluster(cl)
```

In closing, we have seen how using data management packages designed for large data and speed can have a dramatic impact in the time it takes to do data manipulation and management on larger datasets, although still requiring that they fit within memory. We have also seen how, for some problems, it is easy to gain great speed advantages through parallel processing when multiple cores are available. All the parallel processing examples in this chapter were explicit parallelization. That is, we processed variables or for loops in parallel. None of these approaches would help if you had a single regression model that was very slow to complete or matrix multiplication or decomposition that took a long time. Currently, there are not many R functions designed with implicit parallelization. One way such implicit parallelization can be achieved is by linking R to parallel linear algebra systems such as ATLAS or GoToBlas2, although this is a decidedly nonbeginning topic and outside the scope of this book. One easy way to get going with this is to use a modified version of R provided by Revolution Analytics (www.revolutionanalytics.com/revolution-r-open) which uses Intel Math Kernel Library for parallel processing of a variety of math operations, speeding up tasks such as matrix multiplication and principal component analysis.

References

Revolution Analytics. iterators: Iterator construct for R. R package version 1.0.7, 2014. http://CRAN.R-project.org/package=iterators.

Wickham, H. nycflights13: Data about flights departing NYC in 2013. R package version 0.1, 2014. http://CRAN.R-project.org/package=nycflights13.

CHAPTER 19

■ ■ ■

Text Mining

Our final topic is *text mining* or text data mining. It is really only something that can be done with access to comparatively decent computing power (at least historically speaking). The concept is simple enough. Read text data into R that can then be quantitatively analyzed. The benefits are easier to imagine than the mechanics. Put simply, imagine if one could determine the most common words in a chapter, or a textbook. What if the common words in one text could be compared to the common words in other texts? What might those comparisons teach us? Perhaps different authors have a set of go-to words they more frequently use. Perhaps there is a way to discover who wrote a historical text (or at least provide some likely suspects). Perhaps a model may be trained to sort "good" essays from "bad" essays (or to sort spam and ham in e-mail files). Full disclaimer: this is a beginning R text. There are many more things that would be brilliant to do to text data than what we will do in this chapter.

So what will we do in this chapter? For starters, we will discuss how to import text into R and get it ready for analysis. Text can come in many formats these days, and depending on the size and scope of your project, some ways may be more or less feasible. We will discuss some implementations that (currently) allow for importing a collection of common file(s). We'll also discuss pulling in some regularly updating files from the Internet.

Along the way, we will do some exploratory data analysis (EDA) with word clouds. Not only will this EDA let us confirm that we have successfully imported a document, but it will let us get to know what is in the text. An imported text file (e.g., .txt, .pdf, or .docx) is called a *corpus*. We'll discuss various transformations that are possible on the corpus, and we'll visualize just what those changes do.

From there, we will start to perform more in-depth inspections and analytics of a corpus: counting word frequency, finding correlations, visualizing correlations, topic models, and even some clever uses of our familiar glm() function to do some sorting.

Importing information from random file types can be difficult. UTF-8 *.txt files are quite universal and thus are often comparatively easy. These days, most of the Microsoft Word files are XML files, and R tends to play well with XML files once you remove the wrappers that make them *.docx files. Older Word formats (such as .doc pre-2006 or so) require more esoteric methods to use primarily just R. If you routinely deal in many different file types, we recommend learning a language other than R that is designed to process many formats into a consistent one to prepare a corpus of documents for analysis.

As you may well already know, but if not you will certainly discover, dealing with data usually requires data munging. For simplicity's sake, we will start off with basic .txt files, and build on additional formats from there as space allows. First, though, we need to install the right software.

19.1 Installing Needed Packages and Software

Several pieces of software are needed to run many of these examples. It may seem tedious to get them all working, and for that we do apologize. Text mining is fairly new, and the way we understand what may be done is changing very quickly. As with any effort that requires such an array of software to work, error messages or odd results may be more the norm than the exception. The web links we provide may prove to be inaccurate (although we have done our best to select more stable links). Our advice is to approach getting text mining functional as a series of steps in an adventure, after generous quantities of sleep, patience, and caffeine. As always with R, Google will prove a loyal friend. The R community is a clever bunch (although message board civility on occasion merits a "needs improvement" rating).

19.1.1 Java

It is important that you install Java on your computer. It is also important that you have installed the correct version(s) of R, RStudio, and Java. In this chapter we will provide some guidance for Windows users, as they make up a sizable cohort of users. For Windows 7, click the start button, right-click My Computer, and click properties. Next to system type it should say 64 bit, although it may say 32 bit. More detailed instructions may be found at http://windows.microsoft.com/en-us/windows7/find-out-32-or-64-bit for XP, Vista, or 7. Visit https://support.microsoft.com/en-us/kb/827218 for Windows 8 or 10 or use the search option to find "Settings" and then select system. From there, select "about" and see next to system type that it says 64 bit, although it may say 32 bit. It is possible to try your luck with Sys.info() in the R command line. Ideally, under the machine output, you'd want to see something with a "64." This command returns information about the current system.

Once you've (ideally) confirmed you're on a 64-bit system, you may use the R.Version() command to see what version and type of R you installed. The information that follows is about the platform on which R was *built*, not the one on which it is running. There is quite a bit of output, but following are just a few key pieces to see the version of R you have and also whether it is 32 or 64 bit.

```
> R.Version()

$arch
[1] "x86_64"

$language
[1] "R"

$version.string
[1] "R version 3.2.1 (2015-06-18)"

$nickname
[1] "World-Famous Astronaut"
```

Provided your 64 bits (or 32 bits as the case may be) are all lined up, then all that remains is to make sure that you have the correct version of Java installed. Visit www.java.com/en/download/manual.jsp and select the 64-bit (or 32-bit) version to install. A restart or two of your system would be wise, and from there it should work seamlessly. Those are famous last words, and if they prove untrue, a quick Google of the error message(s) should prove helpful.

19.1.2 PDF Software

To allow for PDF files to be used, we need to have the Xpdf suite of tools available. It is perhaps simplest to download the zip file from www.foolabs.com/xpdf/download.html. To make the Xpdf suite work properly, we need to add it to the windows PATH variable so that it can be found from the command line and R. From the foregoing web site, download the .zip file. Extract the zip files to a convenient directory (e.g., C:\usr\xpdfbin-win-3.04). Right-click the Windows start menu, select "system," select "Advanced system settings," and in the system properties window that opens, select the "Advanced" tab. Then select the "Environment Variables," in the lower "System variables" box, scroll down until you see the "Path" line, select it to highlight, and click "Edit." Click the "Variable value:" box, being sure to only unhighlight the text. Go to the end (you can hit "End" on your keyboard to do this), and type ;C:\usr\xpdfbin-win-3.04\bin64 and then select "OK." If you unzipped the files to another location, change the path appropriately. Also if you are using a 32-bit system and R, you should choose the 32-bit Xpdf suite by using the other directory. This will make it easier for R to find the correct file. Please be careful when doing this—it is not beyond the realm of possibility to cause heartache and grief.

19.1.3 R Packages

We also need a few R packages.

```
> install.packages("tm")
> install.packages("wordcloud")
> install.packages("tm.plugin.webmining")
> install.packages("topicmodels")
> install.packages("SnowballC")
>library(tm)
Loading required package: NLP
> library(wordcloud)
Loading required package: RColorBrewer
> library(tm.plugin.webmining)

Attaching package: 'tm.plugin.webmining'

The following object is masked from 'package:base':

    parse

> library(topicmodels)
> library(SnowballC)
```

19.1.4 Some Needed Files

Finally, we turn our attention to having some local files for R to read into a *corpus*. First of all, in your working directory (really only for convenience and you may check with getwd()), please create a folder named ch19 as shown in Figure 19-1.

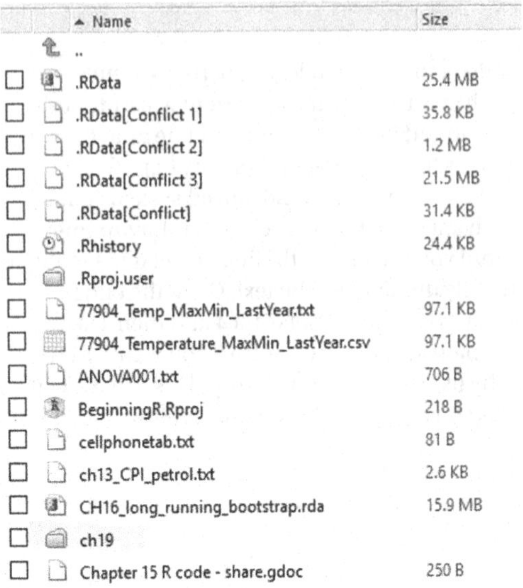

▲ Name	Size
🔼 ..	
☐ 📊 .RData	25.4 MB
☐ 📄 .RData[Conflict 1]	35.8 KB
☐ 📄 .RData[Conflict 2]	1.2 MB
☐ 📄 .RData[Conflict 3]	21.5 MB
☐ 📄 .RData[Conflict]	31.4 KB
☐ 📄 .Rhistory	24.4 KB
☐ 📁 .Rproj.user	
☐ 📄 77904_Temp_MaxMin_LastYear.txt	97.1 KB
☐ 📊 77904_Temperature_MaxMin_LastYear.csv	97.1 KB
☐ 📄 ANOVA001.txt	706 B
☐ 📄 BeginningR.Rproj	218 B
☐ 📄 cellphonetab.txt	81 B
☐ 📄 ch13_CPI_petrol.txt	2.6 KB
☐ 📊 CH16_long_running_bootstrap.rda	15.9 MB
☐ 📁 ch19	
☐ 📄 Chapter 15 R code - share.gdoc	250 B

Figure 19-1. *Screenshot of folder in working directory*

From there, please visit www.gutenberg.org/ebooks/author/68 and download the text files for *Pride and Prejudice, Emma, Sense and Sensibility,* and *Mansfield Park.* Also download the PDF for *Pride and Prejudice.*

▲ Name	Size
🔼 ..	
☐ 📄 1342-pdf.pdf	1.5 MB
☐ 📄 1342_doc.doc	952 KB
☐ 📄 pg1342.txt	700.8 KB
☐ 📄 pg141.txt	896.8 KB
☐ 📄 pg158.txt	897.4 KB
☐ 📄 pg161.txt	689.6 KB

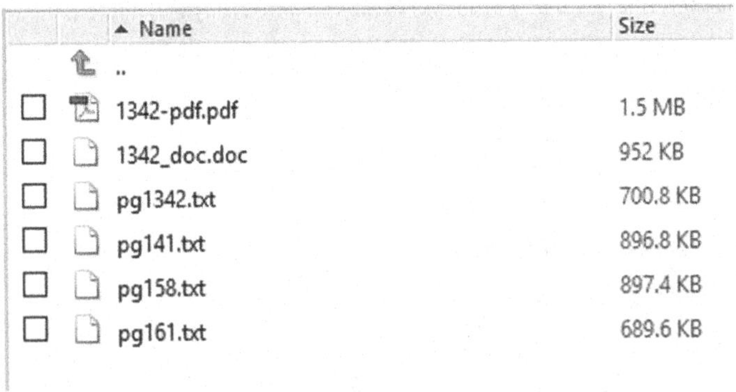

Figure 19-2. *Screenshot of ch19 folder contents*

You are now ready to learn to do some text mining!

19.2 Text Mining

UTF-8 text files are the most common file type and the most readily managed in R. The first step is to get the textual information into R and in a format that our tm package can manipulate. There are several new function calls and arguments to discuss. We want to create a Corpus() and the self-titled function does just that. This command first takes an object (for us it will usually be a file), can take a type of "reader" if needed (e.g., to read PDF files), and can be given a language argument (the default is "en" for English). Our files are in a folder in our working directory called ch19. We use DirSource(directory = ".", pattern = NULL, recursive = FALSE, ignore.case = FALSE, mode = "text") to get files into R. A note on this function call is that the directory (which defaults to our working directory) can be given paths to folders outside the getwd(). The pattern and ignore.case variables may be used to set filename patterns so that only the files you wish are read into R. The recursive argument could be used to go deeper into the directory that you named. We show our first example that selects the *Pride and Prejudice* text file pg1342.txt as the sole source.

```
> austen <- Corpus (DirSource("ch19/", pattern="pg1342"))
> inspect(austen)
<<VCorpus>>
Metadata:  corpus specific: 0, document level (indexed): 0
Content:   documents: 1

[[1]]
<<PlainTextDocument>>
Metadata:  7
Content:   chars: 690723

> summary(austen)
             Length Class               Mode
pg1342.txt 2        PlainTextDocument   list
```

As you can see, we have some information that indicates a successful read-in of our file. Another success indicator is that the global environment is now updated. If you're using RStudio, it would look like Figure 19-3.

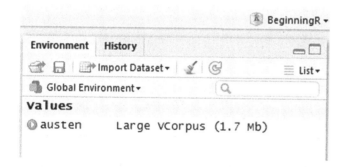

Figure 19-3. Screenshot of Pride and Prejudice VCorpus

19.2.1 Word Clouds and Transformations

Let's attempt to obtain a visual idea of what this corpus actually holds. In its raw form, the text file (and we recommend at least a quick glance through the raw text file to see what it contains) has many words. In real life, there would be some advantage to removing the "header" information and table of contents style information. We have not done that here. To get a sense of what is in our corpus, we turn to a *word cloud*. The wordcloud package has a function call named wordcloud(words,freq,scale=c(4,.5),min.freq=3,max.words=Inf, random.order=TRUE, random.color=FALSE, rot.per=.1, colors="black",ordered.colors=FALSE,use.r.layout=FALSE, fixed.asp=TRUE, ...) which takes several inputs. The first term, *words*, takes in a corpus. The scale argument assigns the range of word sizes (more common words are larger). The variable max.words sets the maximum number of words that show up in the cloud. Remember, there are many words in this corpus. Depending on screen real estate, you may well find efforts to show more words throw an error, thus our compromise of the top 100. The 0.35 of rot. per limits the vertical words to 35% of the total. Looking at the code that follows (which creates the output seen in Figure 19-4), we can see several of these arguments in action. Note, if you are getting warnings and a square output, then adjusting your viewing area to be larger may help. In R, this can be done simply by resizing the graphics window. In RStudio, this can be done by going full screen and using your mouse to increase the viewing area for the plots tab.

```
> wordcloud(austen, scale=c(5,0.5), max.words=100, random.order=FALSE,
+ rot.per=0.35, use.r.layout=FALSE, colors=brewer.pal(8, "Dark2"))
```

Figure 19-4. *Word cloud of unprocessed corpus text*

Notice that not only are there several words that are quite boring, but the word *elizabeth* shows up at least twice. Generally, we find it convenient to perform some transformations to the corpus to get the sorts of words we would expect from a text file. The function call tm_map() takes a corpus as its first input and then a function call to a transformation to apply to that corpus. We do not discuss the specifics of the various transformations simply because they are well named as shown in the following code. Note that removeWords can also take a custom word list. Of note, stop words are words to be removed prior to analysis. Canonically these are words such as "the" or "and," which do not add any real substance and simply serve to connect other words. It can be helpful when performing analytics on technical writing to remove words that may not be of interest (e.g., if analyzing R code, you may want to remove the assignment operator, <-). Figure 19-5 shows our new word cloud after transformations and removing punctuation, whitespace, and stop words.

```
> austen <- tm_map(austen, content_transformer(tolower))
> austen <- tm_map(austen, removePunctuation)
> austen <- tm_map(austen, removeWords, stopwords("english"))
> austen <- tm_map(austen, content_transformer(stripWhitespace))

> wordcloud(austen, scale=c(5,0.5), max.words=100, random.order=FALSE,
+ rot.per=0.35, use.r.layout=FALSE, colors=brewer.pal(8, "Dark2"))
```

Figure 19-5. *Word cloud with several transformations performed*

This might be a fairly basic and common set of transformations. Notice that the words *sister* and *sisters* show up. We might not care about such repeats, and if that were the case, we'd be interested in finding only word stems. The SnowballC package can help with such stems. We run our code one last time and see the result in Figure 19-6. This transformation will take words such as *lady, ladies,* and *ladies'* and write it as a common stem *ladi*.

```
austen <- tm_map(austen, stemDocument)
```

```
> wordcloud(austen, scale=c(5,0.5), max.words=100, random.order=FALSE,
+ rot.per=0.35, use.r.layout=FALSE, colors=brewer.pal(8, "Dark2"))
```

Figure 19-6. *Word cloud with word stemming. Notice the ladi three words below elizabeth*

Word clouds are essentially EDA for text mining. Our readers will note that Ms Elizabeth seems to be the principal word and focus of *Pride and Prejudice*. Before we turn our attention to some other aspects of text mining, let us take our text transformation operations and package them into a single function. We have commented out a few additional possibilities, and leave it to the reader to use or not use pieces of this function as seems best for a particular document or set of documents.

```
> txttrans = function(text){
+    text = tm_map(text, content_transformer(tolower))
+    text = tm_map(text, removePunctuation)
+    ##text = tm_map(text, content_transformer(removeNumbers))
+    text = tm_map(text, removeWords, stopwords("english"))
+    text = tm_map(text, content_transformer(stripWhitespace))
+    ##text = tm_map(text, stemDocument)
+    text
+ }
```

While the word cloud creates a nice visual, it is not readily used to run additional code or analysis. Generally, we prefer to use TermDocumentMatrix() or DocumentTermMatrix() function calls. They create essentially the same structure (e.g., a matrix), and the difference is entirely whether the rows are terms or documents. Of course, for this specific example, we only have one document.

```
> austen = TermDocumentMatrix(austen)
> austen
<<TermDocumentMatrix (terms: 4365, documents: 1)>>
Non-/sparse entries: 4365/0
Sparsity           : 0%
Maximal term length: 26
Weighting          : term frequency (tf)
```

It can also be helpful not only to see a word cloud, where there is simply the top 100 words, but to see all the words above (or below for that matter) a certain frequency. The function call findFreqTerms(x, lowfreq = 0, highfreq = Inf) does just that on a Term Document or Document Term Matrix. Output is sorted alphabetically for all terms in *Pride and Prejudice* that show up at least 100 times. Notice these words have been stemmed, so words like *marry*, *marries*, and *married* would all be just *marri* as seen in row [49].

```
> findFreqTerms(austen, low = 100)

[1]  "alway"    "answer"    "appear"    "attent"    "away"     "believ"
[7]  "bennet"   "bingley"   "can"       "catherin"  "certain"  "collin"
[13] "come"     "darci"     "daughter"  "day"       "dear"     "elizabeth"
[19] "enough"   "even"      "ever"      "everi"     "expect"   "famili"
[25] "father"   "feel"      "felt"      "first"     "friend"   "gardin"
[31] "give"     "good"      "great"     "happi"     "hope"     "hous"
[37] "howev"    "jane"      "know"      "ladi"      "last"     "letter"
[43] "like"     "littl"     "long"      "look"      "love"     "lydia"
[49] "made"     "make"      "man"       "mani"      "manner"   "marri"
[55] "may"      "mean"      "might"     "miss"      "mother"   "mrs"
[61] "much"     "must"      "never"     "noth"      "now"      "one"
[67] "quit"     "receiv"    "repli"     "return"    "room"     "said"
[73] "saw"      "say"       "see"       "seem"      "shall"    "sister"
[79] "soon"     "speak"     "sure"      "take"      "talk"     "think"
[85] "though"   "thought"   "time"      "two"       "walk"     "way"
[91] "well"     "wickham"   "will"      "wish"      "without"  "work"
[97] "young"
```

So far we have accomplished a fair bit. Text has been input into a corpus, and we begin to have a sense of what makes that particular set of words perhaps unique. Still, that isn't the real power of what this was designed to do. We need more words. While we could simply get more text files (and indeed we have already), not all words come from text files. So first, we take a brief detour to the Portable Document Format (PDF).

19.2.2 PDF Text Input

We have our function, txttrans(), which can quickly process a corpus into something that may be readily analyzed. We have the correct software for PDFs, and our path is ready to help. With all that legwork done, it is quite simple to input a PDF file (or a few hundred). We do so with a PDF version of *Pride and Prejudice*, primarily to see that it is in fact equivalent to text. Note that if other PDF files were in this same directory, they would also be read in, so you may want to either specify the particular file or make sure the directory only has PDFs in it that you wish to read into R. To quickly demonstrate this, we show another word cloud in Figure 19-7. Note that for this to work, it is important that the pdftotext program discussed earlier (in the section "PDF Software") can be executed directly from the command line. On Windows, this means ensuring it is correctly added to the PATH variable. On Linux or Mac, the program will need to be where the system usually searches for applications.

```
> austen2<-Corpus(DirSource("ch19/", pattern="pdf"), readerControl = list(reader=readPDF))
> austen2 <- txttrans(austen2)
```

```
> summary(austen2)
          Length Class             Mode
1342-pdf.pdf 2     PlainTextDocument list

> wordcloud(austen2, scale=c(5,0.5), max.words=100, random.order=FALSE,
+ rot.per=0.35, use.r.layout=FALSE, colors=brewer.pal(8, "Dark2"))
```

Figure 19-7. *Word cloud of Pride and Prejudice from a PDF version*

Once the information is in a corpus, it doesn't really matter from what type of file it came. Analytics may be readily performed on it. However, what is currently limiting us is that we only have a single document in these corpora. So, let's get 100 documents online in a relatively painless way.

19.2.3 Google News Input

Because we are getting these online, please be aware that your output may not match ours perfectly. The world of news involving Jane Austen is a happening place! The first thing to notice is that we have quite a few more documents than we had before. Still, all the same, we have what should now be a familiar process. Figure 19-8 is not quite the same as our prior word clouds. Regardless, it seems clear our search was successful.

```
> austen4 = WebCorpus(GoogleNewsSource("Jane Austen"))
> austen4
<<WebCorpus>>
Metadata:  corpus specific: 3, document level (indexed): 0
Content:   documents: 100

> austen4 = txttrans(austen4)
> wordcloud(austen4, scale=c(5,0.5), max.words=100, random.order=FALSE,
+ rot.per=0.35, use.r.layout=FALSE, colors=brewer.pal(8, "Dark2"))
```

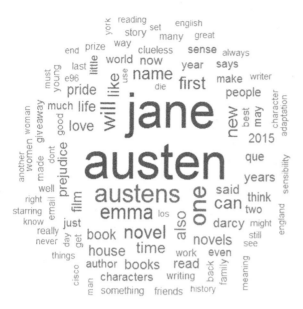

Figure 19-8. *Google News word cloud on "jane austen" search term*

The `tm.plugin.webmining` package has quite a few functions that are similar to `GoogleNewsSource()`. A brief look at the help file shows options for *Reuters*, *NYT*, financial news, and *Yahoo*. These are prepackaged and work well. There are other functions that may require a bit more processing afterward, yet they will allow reading in various types of web-based files. To keep our and your outputs looking the same, we return to the world of Jane Austen, and input several of her novels.

19.2.4 Topic Models

The `topicmodels` package allows a corpus to be readily parsed into a topic model. First, let's run our now very familiar code, and see the resulting word cloud in Figure 19-9 for a single corpus that holds four of Ms Austen's novels.

```
> austen_pesm <- Corpus(DirSource("ch19/", pattern="pg"))

> summary(austen_pesm)
          Length Class             Mode
pg1342.txt 2      PlainTextDocument list
pg141.txt  2      PlainTextDocument list
pg158.txt  2      PlainTextDocument list
pg161.txt  2      PlainTextDocument list

> austen_pesm = txttrans(austen_pesm)

> wordcloud(austen_pesm, scale=c(5,0.5), max.words=100, random.order=FALSE,
+ rot.per=0.35, use.r.layout=FALSE, colors=brewer.pal(8, "Dark2"))
```

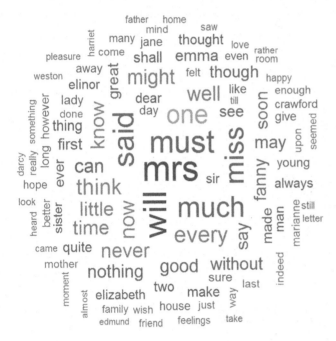

Figure 19-9. *Word cloud of Pride and Prejudice, Emma, Mansfield Park, and Sense and Sensibility*

Notice the difference in the word cloud. Across many novels, *mrs* becomes a much more common word. We begin to see that while in a single novel there may be an intense focus on Ms Elizabeth or Ms Woodhouse, there are certain recurring themes across the collection of novels. We could contrast this word cloud with one created by the works of Shakespeare and perhaps notice some defining differences. If you cared about spam vs. ham in electronic mail, you might do similar sorts of checks on e-mails to see if they looked more like the word cloud for spam or more like the word cloud for ham. You might even begin to perform some of the more familiar analytics we've already done to see if one could train some sort of model on ham or spam, and then assign a probability to a new message as to whether it should go into one folder or another.

That sort of activity quickly gets beyond the scope of this book, however. We shall delve into topic models, now that we have enough words and documents to make something sensible. First, while we have the word cloud, let us take a close look at the most frequent words. Since we have four novels instead of one, let's quadruple our low count to 400.

```
> austen_pesm_DTM = DocumentTermMatrix(austen_pesm)

> findFreqTerms(austen_pesm_DTM, low = 400)
 [1] "always"    "away"      "better"    "can"       "come"      "crawford"
 [7] "day"       "dear"      "done"      "elinor"    "elizabeth" "emma"
[13] "enough"    "even"      "ever"      "every"     "family"    "fanny"
[19] "feelings"  "felt"      "first"     "friend"    "give"      "good"
[25] "great"     "happy"     "hope"      "house"     "however"   "indeed"
[31] "jane"      "just"      "know"      "lady"      "last"      "like"
[37] "little"    "long"      "love"      "made"      "make"      "man"
[43] "many"      "marianne"  "may"       "might"     "mind"      "miss"
[49] "mother"    "mrs"       "much"      "must"      "never"     "nothing"
[55] "now"       "one"       "quite"     "really"    "room"      "said"
```

[61]	"saw"	"say"	"see"	"seemed"	"shall"	"sir"
[67]	"sister"	"soon"	"still"	"sure"	"thing"	"think"
[73]	"though"	"thought"	"time"	"two"	"upon"	"way"
[79]	"well"	"will"	"wish"	"without"	"young"	

Since *elizabeth, emma,* and *miss* are frequent words, let's go ahead and see what sorts of associations can be made to those words that are both common and perhaps of interest. Before we do that, go back and rerun our text processing function, this time allowing stemming to occur.

```
> txttrans = function(text){
+    text = tm_map(text, content_transformer(tolower))
+    text = tm_map(text, removePunctuation)
+    text = tm_map(text, content_transformer(removeNumbers))
+    text = tm_map(text, removeWords, stopwords("english"))
+    text = tm_map(text, content_transformer(stripWhitespace))
+    text = tm_map(text, stemDocument)
+    text
+ }

> austen_pesm = txttrans(austen_pesm)
> austen_a = findAssocs(austen_pesm_DTM, terms = c("elizabeth", "emma", "miss"),
+ corlim =  c(0.85, 0.90, 0.95))
```

Even with such a high set of correlations requested for each of these terms (and notice one can ask for different levels for different terms), the list is fairly long. For brevity's sake, we only show the correlations with *miss*. Even still, we only show some of the words in that one alone—there are many words. Perhaps more important, Jane Austen appears quite liberal in her use of that word. Notice these are sorted by correlation, and alphabetically inside a particular correlation.

```
austen_a$miss
          agreed         appears          barely            bear        chances
            1.00            1.00            1.00            1.00           1.00
  communications          degree           equal         exactly           five
            1.00            1.00            1.00            1.00           1.00
         flutter           never          occupy             pay      peculiarly
            1.00            1.00            1.00            1.00           1.00
      pleasantly         putting          talked      understand        warmest
            1.00            1.00            1.00            1.00           1.00
      absolutely        anywhere         arrange         article        blessed
            0.99            0.99            0.99            0.99           0.99
            blue            came             can       certainly      cheerfully
            0.99            0.99            0.99            0.99           0.99
          clever      concurrence        decisive      encumbrance       excepting
            0.99            0.99            0.99            0.99           0.99
           fault         feature           feels   fourandtwenty       frightened
            0.99            0.99            0.99            0.99           0.99
          health            hear           hurry        included           irish
            0.99            0.99            0.99            0.99           0.99
          little            need        occupied           older         penance
            0.99            0.99            0.99            0.99           0.99
      prosperous           quite             sad        sanction          seized
```

0.99	0.99	0.99	0.99	0.99
shake	sort	south	spoken	substance
0.99	0.99	0.99	0.99	0.99
talents	visiting	will	worst	young
0.99	0.99	0.99	0.99	0.99
absenting	advise	agree	airy	amuses
0.98	0.98	0.98	0.98	0.98
apart	appealed	appropriated	approval	approved
0.98	0.98	0.98	0.98	0.98
arrangement	associates	augur	augusta	averted
0.98	0.98	0.98	0.98	0.98
basin	begin	biscuits	blended	blindness
0.98	0.98	0.98	0.98	0.98
breathe	commit	complains	conceived	conduce
0.98	0.98	0.98	0.98	0.98
convictions	council	dancer	dangers	dealings
0.98	0.98	0.98	0.98	0.98
decidedly	delighted	deplore	deserve	discipline
0.98	0.98	0.98	0.98	0.98
doubly	elegancies	english	enlivened	escorted
0.98	0.98	0.98	0.98	0.98
fasten	favouring	feasible	felicities	friendly
0.98	0.98	0.98	0.98	0.98
wainscot	watercolours	well	wholesome	writingdesk
0.98	0.98	0.98	0.98	0.98

Rather than look at such a chart, it might be better to connect each word to any related words above a certain threshold. Figure 19-10 shows the first attempt at such a graph. However, first note that to make this plot, you will need the Rgraphviz package available. This is not on CRAN, but instead is on another package repository, Bioconductor. We can install it relatively painlessly using the code that follows, and then make our graph.

```
> source("http://bioconductor.org/biocLite.R")
> biocLite("Rgraphviz")

> plot(austen_pesm_DTM, terms = findFreqTerms(austen_pesm_DTM, lowfreq = 400),
+ corThreshold = 0.65)
```

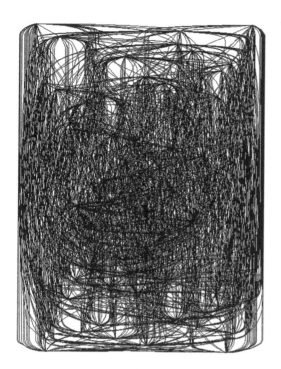

Figure 19-10. *A first attempt at a plot of frequently associated terms*

Clearly this is fairly useless. Well, that's not an entirely fair statement. What one sees is that there is a great deal of similarity between all these documents. Austen writes on fairly common theme(s), perhaps. We're going to have to be much more selective in our choice of both word frequency and correlation cut-off in order to have something readable. We take a second pass next and see that Figure 19-11 is more legible. All the same, it is not quite there yet.

```
> plot(austen_pesm_DTM, terms = findFreqTerms(austen_pesm_DTM, lowfreq = 800),
+ corThreshold = 0.65)
```

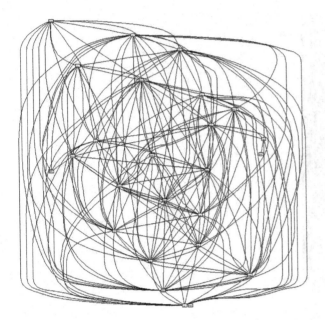

Figure 19-11. *We've combed the hairball, and it gets tamer*

One last pass, and we see that words actually live in the miniature boxes in Figure 19-12.

```
> plot(austen_pesm_DTM, terms = findFreqTerms(austen_pesm_DTM, lowfreq = 850),
+ corThreshold = 0.95)
```

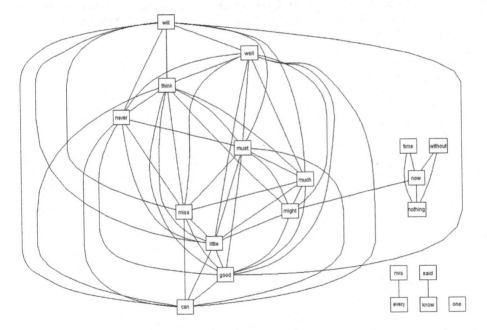

Figure 19-12. *We can see words that are related in a nice graph*

Our last bit of code is the actual topic model. Again, you may experiment with and on this to see what sorts of topics you may uncover. Also, again, there is a great deal more that you may do to determine how many topics might exist in a corpus under stable conditions. That is, it seems sensible that there are likely a certain number of distinct topics in any collection of texts. There ought to be a mathematical way to identify what the correct number of topics might be. One such way is using Latent Dirichlet Allocation (LDA, performed by the function with the same name).

Although we will not go into them in depth, there are many options to control these models and to assess quality. A common issue is that during optimization when R tries to figure out the "best" answer, the results you get may depend on where it started searching! One way around this is to have the model repeat itself many times from different random starts. In the example that follows, we use 100 different starting points, and R will pick the results that are most likely. You may get different results than we do based on a different random start set. If these were real analyses, we might keep adjusting the control parameters until we could get consistent results and be confident we had truly found the "best" solution.

To see all the options, you can (unintuitively) go to the documentation for the class of the object that the function expects to be used, which can be found by typing `?TopicModelcontrol-class` in the R console. This is where you can find out the names to use in the list to control how to estimate the LDA model, and how we knew to use the `alpha` and `nstart` in arguments. For now, we will simply note that even with 100 starting points, the model can take some time to finish running.

```
> austen_pesm_DTM
<<DocumentTermMatrix (documents: 4, terms: 16861)>>
Non-/sparse entries: 32951/34493
Sparsity           : 51%
Maximal term length: 32
Weighting          : term frequency (tf)

> rowTotals <- apply(austen_pesm_DTM, 1, sum)
> austen_pesm_DTM <- austen_pesm_DTM[rowTotals>0,]

> k <- 2
> austen_pesm_lda <- LDA(austen_pesm_DTM, control = list(alpha=0.2, nstart = 100), k)

> topics(austen_pesm_lda)
pg1342.txt  pg141.txt  pg158.txt  pg161.txt
         1          2          2          1

> terms(austen_pesm_lda, 5)
     Topic 1  Topic 2
[1,] "mrs"    "must"
[2,] "said"   "mrs"
[3,] "will"   "will"
[4,] "much"   "miss"
[5,] "elinor" "much"
```

In the foregoing code, k may be adjusted to various numbers, although from our plot, 2 or 3 looked about correct. With that, we are done with our brief introduction to text mining.

19.3 Final Thoughts

For text mining, our final thought is that this is a very exciting and really quite new field of research and study. Everything from movie reviews to research participant transcripts may be pulled into various corpora, and from there, you may perform many sorts of analytics. The generalized linear models we met in earlier chapters are helpful here, as are k nearest-neighbor cross-validation methods. One of the authors recalls reading an article, not too many years ago, that showed how various historical documents of unknown authorship could be fairly reliably matched (via comparison with known writings) to precise authors. More recently, anti-plagiarism methods can be similarly constructed from these sorts of inputs—or, as we mentioned, sorting spam and ham.

In the last few decades alone, the world of data analytics has undergone enormous changes. The way we think about data problems is changing. Nonparametric methods, bootstrapping, and text mining methods were not feasible in the past. Now, even for the large lakes of data we have access to, all of these methods are suddenly possible. It's a brave new world. Thank you for exploring it with us.

References

Annau, M. tm.plugin.webmining: Retrieve Structured, Textual Data from Various Web Sources. R package version 1.3, 2015. `http://CRAN.R-project.org/package=tm.plugin.webmining`.

Bouchet-Valat, M. SnowballC: Snowball stemmers based on the C libstemmer UTF-8 library. R package version 0.5.1, 2014. `http://CRAN.R-project.org/package=SnowballC`.

Feinerer, I., & Hornik, K. tm: Text Mining Package. R package version 0.6-2, 2015. `http://CRAN.R-project.org/package=tm`.

Fellows, I. wordcloud: Word Clouds. R package version 2.5, 2014. `http://CRAN.R-project.org/package=wordcloud`.

Gruen, B., & Hornik, K. "topicmodels: An R Package for Fitting Topic Models." Journal of Statistical Software, *40*(13), 1-30 (2011).

Index

Get the eBook for only $5!

Why limit yourself?

Now you can take the weightless companion with you wherever you go and access your content on your PC, phone, tablet, or reader.

Since you've purchased this print book, we're happy to offer you the eBook in all 3 formats for just $5.

Convenient and fully searchable, the PDF version enables you to easily find and copy code—or perform examples by quickly toggling between instructions and applications. The MOBI format is ideal for your Kindle, while the ePUB can be utilized on a variety of mobile devices.

To learn more, go to www.apress.com/companion or contact support@apress.com.

Apress®
THE EXPERT'S VOICE™

Printed in the United States
By Bookmasters